EVANGELICALS
IN THE PUBLIC
SQUARE

EVANGELICALS
IN THE PUBLIC
SQUARE

Four Formative Voices on Political Thought and Action

J. Budziszewski

WITH RESPONSES BY
David L. Weeks
John Bolt
William Edgar
Ashley Woodiwiss

INTRODUCTION BY Michael Cromartie
AFTERWORD BY Jean Bethke Elshtain

Baker Academic
Grand Rapids, Michigan

© 2006 by J. Budziszewski

Published by Baker Academic
a division of Baker Publishing Group
P.O. Box 6287, Grand Rapids, MI 49516-6287
www.bakeracademic.com

Printed in the United States of America

Library of Congress Cataloging-in-Publication Data
Budziszewski, J., 1952–
    Evangelicals in the public square : four formative voices on political
    thought and action / J. Budziszewski ; with responses by David L.
    Weeks . . . [et al.].
        p.   cm.
    Includes bibliographical references and index.
    ISBN 10: 0-8010-3156-7 (pbk.)
    ISBN 978-0-8010-3156-4 (pbk.)
    1. Christianity and politics. 2. Evangelicalism. I. Weeks, David L.
    II. Title.
BR115.P7B72 2006
261.70973—dc22   2005034691

In memory of Carl F. H. Henry
1913–2003
Pioneer

Contents

Introduction

Michael Cromartie

Ten years ago, in a cover story in the influential literary magazine the *Atlantic Monthly,* Harvard theologian Harvey Cox shared his observations on having been a visiting lecturer at Pat Robertson's Regent University in Virginia. Professor Cox was surprised to find that the conservative Christians at Regent were not monolithic in their political views. He found that while evangelicals, fundamentalists, and charismatics were often lumped together in the press, they in fact "represent distinct tendencies that are frequently at odds with one another."[1]

This is still true today. Harvey Cox is not unlike many observers outside the evangelical movement who are often surprised when they discover just how diverse evangelical intellectual opinions are on political and social issues. The late historian Timothy Smith described evangelicalism as being like a large kaleidoscope that includes not only a diversity of denominations but also Christians from the political right, left, and center. Evangelicals are by no means monolithic in their political views. While they have largely maintained an alliance with political conservatism,

---

1. Harvey Cox, "The Warring Visions of the Religious Right," *Atlantic Monthly,* November 1995, 62.

the movement does have moderate and liberal contingents that are often overlooked.

Evangelical Protestants have a rich and diverse theological heritage that has justified a wide range of approaches to political and civic engagement. There was a time when political involvement by evangelicals was seen as a worldly, or even sinful, activity. Today, political celibacy, if you will, is considered a dereliction of Christian responsibility. This change sparked intense debate among evangelical scholars and leaders in the last half of the twentieth century.

The theological, political, and ethical reflections of four prominent thinkers who helped shape evangelical engagement in the public square over the past fifty years are the subject of this book. J. Budziszewski, a political philosopher at the University of Texas, assesses the contributions of Carl F. H. Henry, Abraham Kuyper, Francis Schaeffer, and John Howard Yoder. His chapter on these men is followed by a response to the life and work of each of them.

While appreciative of the contributions of each of these thinkers, Budziszewski finds fault with each, to a greater or lesser degree, for failing to develop a systematic political theory as compelling as those offered by the secularist establishment. He suggests that evangelical political thought would be improved if it were more informed by the tradition of natural law. He argues that "although evangelicals are rightly committed to grounding their political reflection in revelation, the Bible provides insufficient materials for the task." In addition to the *special* revelation of Scripture, evangelicals should also mine the *general* revelation, or natural law, that God has made evident to both believers and nonbelievers.

Carl F. H. Henry, the founding editor of *Christianity Today*, exemplified both the promise and the problems of evangelical thinkers, suggests Budziszewski. He says that Henry deserves "unbounded appreciation" for being "a gadfly" who "pricked the evangelical conscience in the 1940s" and encouraged evangelicals to enter the political and cultural fray of the wider civic realm. But because he spoke in biblical terms only, his influence with his nonbelieving fellow citizens was limited. Henry's "value was inestimable, but his approach was not helpful." Evangelicals' hostility to natural law rhetoric limits their political effectiveness because it deprives them of ways to engage with nonbelievers.

In response, David Weeks of Azusa Pacific University concedes that Henry downplayed natural law as a "rationalistic enterprise unmoored from God" and did little to provide a "common moral ground" between believers and nonbelievers. Weeks questions, however, whether the kind of distinct, comprehensive political theory Budziszewski advocates is a realistic or desirable goal for evangelicals. Henry was predominantly a theologian who made "social engagement a persistent theme" of his writings. Seeing many of his evangelical brethren as "simplistic, fragmentary, and reactionary," Henry urged them "to understand the limits of earthly justice and to accept civil authority," which had been created by God to maintain order. He urged evangelicals to insist on limited government and to work for the spiritual regeneration of their fellow citizens.

Budziszewski next examines the work of nineteenth-century Dutch theologian and politician Abraham Kuyper. He praises him as the "most impressive, powerful, and challenging" of the four thinkers under discussion. Even Kuyper's arguments that have obvious flaws are "compelling," Budziszewski says. Kuyper was well versed in Catholic social thought and was "really a natural law thinker, even if he didn't know it." His doctrine of sphere sovereignty resembles the Catholic principle of subsidiarity in that it offers a defense of civil society based on a religious understanding of the order of creation.

In response, John Bolt of Calvin Theological Seminary urges "North American neo-Calvinists to get over their hang up about natural law." Bolt contends that it is Kuyper's enthusiasm for America's providentially blessed "experiment in ordered liberty" that makes him most relevant to evangelicals today. Evangelical public theology should focus on "the dignity and worth of the human person" created in the image of God.

Budziszewski next commends Francis Schaeffer for his "freshness" and "gift for making connections" but criticizes his "intemperance" and his lack of an underlying political theory. Schaeffer is credited with awakening evangelicals to the fact that, by the 1970s, secular humanism had become the dominant worldview in law, politics, and education. However, his impatience with the world of politics often drove him to move on too quickly to protest and revolution. Yet Budziszewski commends Schaeffer for recognizing the relationship between special and general revelation and the need for a new civic rhetoric that could exploit the points of contact between believers and nonbelievers.

Respondent William Edgar of Westminster Theological Seminary says that Schaeffer is "notoriously hard to label" and discusses his various roles as a theologian, cultural warrior, political conservative, and pro-life leader. At his best, Schaeffer was a "master persuader" who had an admirable desire "to pry open the culture" and an "instinct for what could make an impact." Though he was sometimes an "alarmist," we should, Edgar urges, "celebrate and emulate the better Schaeffer."

The fourth major thinker considered by Budziszewski is the Mennonite theologian John Howard Yoder, author of the influential book *The Politics of Jesus.* Yoder's influence is felt almost exclusively "on the evangelical left." Yoder found great political significance in the life and work of Christ, and he urged all believers to imitate Christ's renunciation of violence and to eschew all political statecraft. While giving Yoder credit for asking challenging questions, Budziszewski ultimately finds him unpersuasive and his answers problematic. He says that Scripture is clear that "magistrates must wield the sword responsibly to protect others."

Respondent Ashley Woodiwiss of Wheaton College says that Budziszewski gives only a "partial portrait" of Yoder by focusing exclusively on *The Politics of Jesus.* As a "theological ethicist," Yoder was addressing particular problems he identified within the church. He did not advocate that Christians "hide from politics" but wanted to stress that "the church be central to political activity." Further, Woodiwiss argues that Yoder saw the church functioning as a "counter-*polis*, not an anti-*polis*."

In her afterword, Jean Bethke Elshtain of the University of Chicago gives her reflections on Budziszewski's overview as a friendly, nonevangelical outsider. She asks, "As believers and citizens, how do we talk when we enter the public arena?" She emphasizes the obligations of believers to learn to be bilingual when in dialogue with non-Christians about matters of politics and justice and to be prepared to "offer a reasonable defense of their positions" because they play an important "role as interpreters of culture." She concludes that, "because of the consequences of sin," we must become "rather humble about our political philosophies and what we can hope to accomplish through them." She reminds us that "such humility would befit our natures as fallen creatures who are nevertheless called to hope and possibility."

These essays were first presented in September 2003 at a conference sponsored by the Ethics and Public Policy Center held at the Black Point Inn in Prouts Neck, Maine. The conference was supported by a generous grant from the Pew Charitable Trusts; their support, and especially the advice and encouragement of Luis Lugo, is greatly appreciated.

I would also like to thank two colleagues from the Ethics and Public Policy Center for their indispensable assistance. Senior editor Carol Griffith edited the papers with her usual consummate skill. We have worked together for twenty years, and I have lost count of how many scholars and academics have told me how much her editing improved their prose. Laura Fabrycky's diligent assistance in organizing the conference was greatly appreciated. More importantly, her consultation and advice early in the planning process helped to make sure the project and the papers were going in the right direction. Interns Richard Barry and Albert Lee came along at just the right time to provide invaluable assistance.

Through our conferences and publications, the Ethics and Public Policy Center strives to stimulate thoughtful dialogue among political, religious, and cultural leaders. Our aim is to foster and encourage a wiser moral and political debate across ideological perspectives. It is our hope that this book will encourage fresh thinking and constructive dialogue both within the evangelical community and among the wider communities concerned with the important issues addressed here.

1

Evangelicals in the Public Square

J. Budziszewski

Evangelical Christians have been conspicuous in the American public square since colonial days. Although we sometimes think of their low profile during the early twentieth century as the norm, it was actually a short-lived exception. Conventional wisdom dates their reentry into public affairs to the spectacular rise of the fundamentalist Religious Right in the 1970s, but this view is misleading in several ways. In the first place, fundamentalists make up only a part of the evangelical movement. In the second, evangelicals had reentered the public square at least a generation earlier. If a marker is needed, we might use the founding in 1941 of the National Association of Evangelicals, a self-consciously "new evangelical" organization—new in its contrast with fundamentalism but old in its desire to engage the civic culture.

Unfortunately, although evangelicals have long played a part in the public square, they have never developed a clear, cohesive, and Christian view of what politics is all about. According to an old inside joke, their formula is "Ready, Fire, Aim." One expects sarcasm from foes, of course, but even their friends have remarked on the disorderly quality of their political reflection. Historian Mark Noll, himself an evangelical, attributes this shallowness to the origins of the evangelical movement in successive Great Awakenings. Revivalistic leadership is "direct," "personal," and "popular," depending mainly on a speaker's "ability to draw a crowd."[1] It attempts to "simplify the essentials of religion in a way that gives them the widest possible mass appeal."[2] The result is that evangelicals are "intuitionist," trusting their "sanctified common sense" but mistrusting the work of the intellect.[3]

Of course, intuitionism is not all bad. There are two kinds of intellectual. One kind seeks to refine and inform common sense; such were the greatest of the classical thinkers.[4] The intellectual of the other sort, all too familiar in our day, holds common sense in contempt, seeking to replace it with a dehumanizing ideology of his own devising.[5] Intuitionism serves as a blunt defense

1. Mark Noll, *The Scandal of the Evangelical Mind* (Grand Rapids: Eerdmans, 1994), 61.

2. Daniel L. Pals, "Several Christologies of the Great Awakening," *Anglican Theological Review* 72 (1990): 426.

3. Noll, *Scandal of the Evangelical Mind*, 160.

4. See Ralph McInerny, "Are There Moral Truths That Everyone Knows?" in *Common Truths: New Perspectives on Natural Law*, ed. Edward B. McLean (Wilmington, DE: ISI Books, 2000), 1–18.

5. "With the decline of clerical power in the eighteenth century, a new kind of mentor emerged to fill the vacuum and capture the ear of society. The secular intellectual might be deist, sceptic or atheist. But he was just as ready as any pontiff or presbyter to tell mankind how to conduct its affairs. He proclaimed, from the start, a special devotion to the interests of humanity and an evangelical duty to advance them by his teaching. He brought to this self-appointed task a far more radical approach than his clerical predecessors. He felt himself bound by no corpus of revealed religion. The collective wisdom of the past, the legacy of tradition, the prescriptive codes of ancestral experience existed to be selectively followed or wholly rejected entirely as his own good sense might decide. For the first time in human history, and with growing confidence and audacity, men arose to assert that they could diagnose the ills of society and cure them with their own unaided intellects: more, that they could devise formulae whereby not merely the structure of society but the fundamental habits of human beings could be transformed for the better. Unlike their sacerdotal predecessors, they were not servants and interpreters of the gods but substitutes. Their hero was Prometheus, who stole the celestial fire and brought it to earth" (Paul Johnson, *Intellectuals* [New York: Harper & Row, 1988], 1–2).

against the latter;[6] unfortunately, it cannot distinguish between the latter and the former.

Are there no orderly thinkers in evangelical ranks? To be sure, there are. Evangelicals have developed an extensive network of schools and colleges, as well as institutions that are intellectual but nonacademic, and some of these are keenly interested in public policy. Thinkers of evangelical persuasion are also increasingly visible in secularized institutions. Has this raised the quality of evangelical political reflection? Yes and no. A handful of evangelical thinkers do give serious attention to politics. They have explored or developed several points of view, each of which has found a certain constituency among activists and scholars. So far, though, none of them is well known outside these circles, and the broad mass of evangelicals is untouched.

There are at least two reasons for this lack of broader influence. The first is that the typical evangelical is ambivalent. On the one hand, he is convinced that Christ is Lord over every part of life, the public square included. This draws him outward. On the other hand, he tends to think of faith in exclusively individualistic terms, as a "personal" relationship with Jesus Christ. From this perspective, even the church begins to blur; society at large becomes invisible. Although the Great Commission to bring Christ to all people pulls him outward again, it does not pull him far enough. He is apt to imagine that if only everyone were converted, the public square would take care of itself. Sufficiently provoked, he warmly takes part in public affairs, but his participation is impulsive rather than careful and orderly.

6. "I detect today a certain public scepticism when intellectuals stand up to preach to us, a growing tendency among ordinary people to dispute the right of academics, writers and philosophers, eminent though they may be, to tell us how to behave and conduct our affairs. The belief seems to be spreading that intellectuals are no wiser as mentors, or worthier as exemplars, than the witch doctors or priests of old. I share that scepticism. A dozen people picked at random on the street are at least as likely to offer sensible views on moral and political matters as a cross-section of the intelligentsia. But I would go further. One of the principal lessons of our tragic century, which has seen so many millions of innocent lives sacrificed in schemes to improve the lot of humanity, is—beware intellectuals. Not merely should they be kept well away from the levers of power, they should also be objects of particular suspicion when they seek to offer collective advice" (ibid., 342).

His civic muscles are more familiar with the spasm than with the long, steady pull.

The second reason for the lack of broader influence is a lack of development. Among evangelicals, orderly political reflection has not yet risen to its task. I do not mean that it ought to be able to play the secularist game but cannot. From an evangelical point of view, the criteria of theoretical excellence that secular thinkers propose are bizarrely distorted; we do not need a Christian version of John Rawls. As I hope to explain in the following pages, the problem is much deeper, for evangelical political thought has failed to achieve excellence even on its own terms. What keeps it from offering a serious challenge to the dominant political theories of the secularist establishment is that it has failed to ask many of the most essential questions, failed to answer many of the questions it *has* asked, and thrown away half of its resources for answering them.

The former reason, evangelical ambivalence, is not my concern in this study; the latter, a lack of development, is. My purpose here is to consider the current state of orderly political reflection among evangelicals and to suggest how it might be improved. My hope is that in time that reflection will grow powerful enough to inform and illuminate the evangelical engagement with civic culture. This study, then, is a mere prolegomenon. Its intent is not to conclude a discussion but to begin one.

What Makes a Political Theory Evangelical?

A starting point for this discussion is to decide what makes a theory evangelical. How would authentically evangelical political reflection differ from the political reflection of, say, a Marxist, a Mormon, or a Muslim?

Different groups of people may ask different political questions, but anyone pursuing more than the narrowest defensive goals in civic and political life needs to know three things: what politics and government are all about, what he should do about them, and how to explain his aims and views to others in ways they can understand. Everyone active in the public square feels these three needs; they are not unique to Christians. Adequate political theory, therefore, would include at least three elements:

(1) an *orienting doctrine,* or a guide to thought, explaining the place of government in the world as a whole; (2) a *practical doctrine,* or a guide to action, explaining in broad but practical terms how Christians should conduct themselves in the civic realm; and (3) a *cultural apologetic,* or a guide to persuasion, explaining how to go about making the specific proposals of those who share the other two elements plausible to those who do not.

Besides this, adequacy requires that all three elements be as near to the truth as one can get. The difficulty, of course, is that people who hold incompatible worldviews disagree not only about what is true but also about how to *determine* what is true. Buddhists think one thing, utilitarians another, postmodernists something altogether different. There is no need to cave in to epistemological "perspectivism"; there really *is* a truth, not just different points of view *about* truth, and God desires to lead us into it. But if we think we do know something, then it is not "perspectivist" to ask what would make political reflection adequate from our perspective.[7] That perspective is evangelical, and so we ask: What makes a political theory evangelical?

To answer this question, we first need to know how evangelicals themselves are distinctive. Their distinctiveness does not lie in their basic theology, a fact that often comes as a surprise to evangelicals themselves. What evangelicals believe is pretty much what all traditional Christians believe—such things as one God in three persons; his revelation in words and deeds; creation, the fall, and the possibility of redemption; the incarnation of God in Jesus Christ; his atoning death and resurrection; the necessity of personal and communal faith; and the life of the world to come.

Many supposed "distinctives" of evangelical theology appear far less distinctive when examined closely. For example, it is sometimes said that evangelicals hold a "low" ecclesiology and a "low" sacramental theology, and for Baptists and nondenominational evangelicals, this is true. But as an explanation of evan-

---

7. "If we talk of a certain thing being an aspect of truth, it is evident that we claim to know what is truth; just as, if we talk of the hind leg of a dog, we claim to know what is a dog. . . . I should not like to be an artist who brought an architectural sketch to a builder, saying, 'This is the south aspect of Sea-View Cottage. Sea-View Cottage, of course, does not exist'" (G. K. Chesterton, *Heretics* [New York: John Lane, 1905], 293 [chap. 20]).

gelical distinctiveness, it leaves much to be desired. The tens of millions of evangelicals who make up the renewal movement in the historic Protestant denominations often hold views of church and sacrament that are scarcely "lower" than the Roman Catholic view. For example, many evangelical Anglicans acknowledge the real presence of Christ in the Eucharist.

Not even the doctrine of justification by faith, so central to evangelical identity, is as distinctive as it was thought to be during the Reformation. The Roman Catholic Church joined with a prominent group of Lutherans in 1999 in a "Joint Declaration on the Doctrine of Justification," declaring that we are reconciled to God by grace, through faith, not by any merit we have in ourselves. Differences persist between evangelicals and Roman Catholics over details of the doctrine of justification, but they are now probably no deeper than the differences among the varieties of evangelicals on the question.

Yet it is not quite true that there is *nothing* theologically distinctive about evangelicals. Their true distinctiveness lies in what they emphasize, and by far what they emphasize most is the Bible as God's revelation. Although all traditional Christians believe in the truth and authority of Scripture, evangelicals surpass all others in their determination to study and follow it. Their first thought on almost every subject is, What does the Bible say? Though evangelical scholarship has often lagged in other fields of Christian thought, such as systematic theology (and, of course, political theory), in biblical exegesis it excels.

At a minimum, then, one would expect an evangelical political theory to be a *biblically illuminated* political theory. What then does the Bible teach about politics and government? As we are about to see, evangelicals have long found it difficult to approach this question honestly, and the difficulty they experience with it goes far toward explaining why, even after centuries of opportunity, evangelical political reflection leaves so much to be desired.

Projective Accommodation

Historically, the most common fallacy of evangelical political theory has been projective accommodation: accommodating

Scripture to one's own political views by reading those views into the biblical text. The longevity of this habit will make it hard to break. Consider, for example, the use of Scripture by some evangelicals on the patriot side of the American War of Independence. Bitterly opposed to English colonial policy and determined to have God on their side, they projected their pro-republican and antimonarchist views into Scripture through a tendentious interpretation of 1 Samuel 8.

At the time the narrative describes, the Hebrew people were organized in a loose confederation, each tribe with its own elders. The prophet Samuel had grown old, so he appointed his sons as judges over all of them. Unfortunately, his sons took bribes and perverted justice, leading exasperated tribal elders to petition Samuel to appoint a king so that they would be ruled as other nations were. Advised by God, Samuel complied with eloquence and force:

> These will be the ways of the king who will reign over you: he will take your sons and appoint them to his chariots and to be his horsemen, and to run before his chariots; and he will appoint for himself commanders of thousands and commanders of fifties, and some to plow his ground and to reap his harvest, and to make his implements of war and the equipment of his chariots. He will take your daughters to be perfumers and cooks and bakers. He will take the best of your fields and vineyards and olive orchards and give them to his servants. He will take the tenth of your grain and of your vineyards and give it to his officers and to his servants. He will take your menservants and maidservants, and the best of your cattle and your asses, and put them to his work. He will take the tenth of your flocks, and you shall be his slaves. And in that day you will cry out because of your king, whom you have chosen for yourselves; but the LORD will not answer you in that day.

> 1 Samuel 8:11–18

In the end, the elders got their wish, but subjection to a human king was every bit as burdensome as Samuel had warned.

To the patriots, this incident seemed a perfect bludgeon with which to beat the heads of the English. In the words of colonial preacher Samuel Langdon:

The Jewish government, according to the original constitution which was divinely established, if considered merely in a civil view, was a perfect republic. The heads of their tribes and elders of their cities were their counselors and judges. They called the people together in more general or particular assemblies—took their opinions, gave advice, and managed the public affairs according to the general voice. Counselors and judges comprehend all the powers of that government; for there was no such thing as legislative authority belonging to it—their complete code of laws being given immediately from God by the hand of Moses. And let them who cry up the divine right of kings consider that the only form of government which had a proper claim to a divine establishment was so far from including the idea of a king, that it was a high crime for Israel to ask to be in this respect like other nations; and when they were gratified, it was rather as a just punishment of their folly, that they might feel the burdens of court pageantry, of which they were warned by a very striking description, than as a divine recommendation of kingly authority.[8]

The problem with this attempt to accommodate the Bible to republicanism is that divine preference for republics over monarchies is simply not in the text. According to the story, God rebukes the elders not because it is wrong to desire a king but *because the people have a divine king already.* "They have not rejected you," God says to Samuel, "but they have rejected me from being king over them" (1 Sam. 8:7). The irony is that the Tories might have used the same projective technique to buttress the opposite thesis: that God prefers monarchies over republics. After all, later in Israel's history the reign of King David ushered in a golden age, which the biblical writers view as foreshadowing the age of the Messiah.[9] The fact is that the Bible as a whole commends neither republics over monarchies, nor monarchies over republics, nor republics and monarchies equally; to suggest otherwise is to indulge in special pleading, highlighting some texts but suppressing or distorting others. Even for so important

8. Samuel Langdon, "Government Corrupted by Vice, and Recovered by Righteousness" (1775), preached to the Congress of the Massachusetts Bay Colony, May 31, 1775, in *The Pulpit of the American Revolution*, ed. John Wingate Thornton (Boston: n.p., 1860), 233–58.
9. See especially 2 Sam. 8; see also Messianic Psalms 2, 72, 110.

a political judgment as the choice among forms of government, Scripture provides no criterion.

This is not to say that the incident in 1 Samuel 8 has nothing to teach political thinkers. Taken in the context of Israel's history, it teaches many things, important things that are hidden from the gaze of secularists. For example, it illustrates that even a man of God may fall into folly when he follows his personal inclinations, for though Samuel is an authentic prophet, he appoints his corrupt sons as judges. It demonstrates how one sin in government begets another, for the elders respond to the corruption of Samuel's sons by defying God himself. And it shows that rebellion against God brings punishment, for Samuel's warnings do come true. Unfortunately, these were not the lessons that the patriots drew; such lessons did not suit their program.

The Evangelical Dilemma

The problem for evangelical political thinkers is not that the Bible contains no political teachings (for it does) but that the Bible does not provide enough *by itself* for an adequate political theory. Although important general principles about government can indeed be drawn from Scripture, the list of such principles is short. Chief among them are the following:

1. *God is the true sovereign; he ordained all human government for the good of man, whom he made in his image.* "For dominion belongs to the LORD, and he rules over the nations" (Ps. 22:28). "For there is no authority except from God, and those that exist have been instituted by God. . . . Would you have no fear of him who is in authority? Then do what is good, and you will receive his approval, for he is God's servant for your good" (Rom. 13:1, 3–4). "So God created man in his own image, in the image of God he created him; male and female he created them" (Gen. 1:27).
2. *Although God originally chose only one nation, he desires ultimately to draw all nations into the light of his Word.* "It is too light a thing that you should be my servant to raise up the tribes of Jacob and to restore the preserved of Israel; I will give you as a light to the nations, that my salvation

may reach to the end of the earth" (Isa. 49:6). "For there is no distinction between Jew and Greek; the same Lord is Lord of all and bestows his riches upon all who call upon him" (Rom. 10:12). "And the city [of the Messianic age] has no need of sun or moon to shine upon it, for the glory of God is its light, and its lamp is the Lamb. By its light shall the nations walk; and the kings of the earth shall bring their glory into it" (Rev. 21:23–24).

3. *He disciplines the nations according to their deeds.* "If at any time I declare concerning a nation or a kingdom, that I will pluck up and break down and destroy it, and if that nation . . . turns from its evil, I will repent of the evil that I intended to do to it. And if at any time I declare concerning a nation or a kingdom that I will build and plant it, and if it does evil in my sight, not listening to my voice, then I will repent of the good which I had intended to do to it" (Jer. 18:7–10). "They judge not with justice the cause of the fatherless, to make it prosper, and they do not defend the rights of the needy. Shall I not punish them for these things? says the LORD, and shall I not avenge myself on a nation such as this?" (Jer. 5:28–29).

4. *He also disciplines their rulers.* "Blessed be the name of God for ever and ever, to whom belong wisdom and might. He changes times and seasons; he removes kings and sets up kings" (Dan. 2:20–21). "Then after seventy years are completed, I will punish the king of Babylon and that nation, the land of the Chaldeans, for their iniquity, says the LORD, making the land an everlasting waste" (Jer. 25:12). "Therefore, O king, let my counsel be acceptable to you; break off your sins by practicing righteousness, and your iniquities by showing mercy to the oppressed, that there may perhaps be a lengthening of your tranquillity" (Dan. 4:27).

5. *In general, disobedience to human government is disobedience to God; indeed, government deserves not only obedience but honor.* "Let every person be subject to the governing authorities. . . . He who resists the authorities resists what God has appointed, and those who resist will incur judgment" (Rom. 13:1–2). "Pay all of them their dues, . . .

respect to whom respect is due, honor to whom honor is due" (Rom. 13:7).

6. *But there are exceptions: Any governmental edict that contradicts the commands of God must be disobeyed.* "We must obey God rather than men" (Acts 5:29). "Be it known to you, O king, that we will not serve your gods or worship the golden image which you have set up" (Dan. 3:18). "But the midwives feared God, and did not do as the king of Egypt commanded them, but let the male children live. . . . So God dealt well with the midwives; and the people multiplied and grew very strong. And because the midwives feared God he gave them families" (Exod. 1:17, 20–21).

7. *The just purposes of human government include the commendation of good, the punishment of evil, the maintenance of peace, and the protection of the oppressed.* "Be subject for the Lord's sake to every human institution, whether it be to the emperor as supreme, or to governors as sent by him to punish those who do wrong and to praise those who do right" (1 Pet. 2:13–14). "First of all, then, I urge that supplications, prayers, intercessions, and thanksgivings be made for all men, for kings and all who are in high positions, that we may lead a quiet and peaceable life, godly and respectful in every way" (1 Tim. 2:1–2). "Woe to those who decree iniquitous decrees, and the writers who keep writing oppression, to turn aside the needy from justice and to rob the poor of my people of their right, that widows may be their spoil, and that they may make the fatherless their prey!" (Isa. 10:1–2).[10]

8. *In pursuance of these purposes, God authorizes human government to use force on his behalf and in grave cases even to take life, though never deliberately to take the life of the innocent.* "Whoever sheds the blood of man, by man shall his blood be shed; for God made man in his own image" (Gen. 9:6). "Would you have no fear of him who is in authority? Then do what is good, and you will receive his approval, for he is God's servant for your good. But if you do wrong, be afraid, for he does not bear the sword

10. For a particularly dramatic illustration, see also 2 Sam. 12:1–10.

in vain; he is the servant of God to execute his wrath on the wrongdoer" (Rom. 13:3–4).

9. *Yet human government cannot fully or permanently redress wrong, because it cannot uproot sin from the human heart; this can be done only by the saving grace of God through Jesus Christ.* "The heart is deceitful above all things, and desperately corrupt; who can understand it?" (Jer. 17:9). "We have all become like one who is unclean, and all our righteous deeds are like a polluted garment" (Isa. 64:6). "For there is no distinction; since all have sinned and fall short of the glory of God, they are justified by his grace as a gift, through the redemption which is in Christ Jesus, whom God put forward as an expiation by his blood, to be received by faith" (Rom. 3:22–25).

10. *Moreover, the community of redemption is not the state but the church. No matter how much respect is due to the state, the church is never to be identified with it.* "Pilate entered the praetorium again and called Jesus, and said to him, 'Are you the King of the Jews?' Jesus answered, 'Do you say this of your own accord, or did others say it to you about me?' Pilate answered, 'Am I a Jew? Your own nation and the chief priests have handed you over to me; what have you done?' Jesus answered, 'My kingship is not of this world; if my kingship were of this world, my servants would fight, that I might not be handed over to the Jews; but my kingship is not from the world'" (John 18:33–36). "Take heed to yourselves and to all the flock, in which the Holy Spirit has made you overseers, to care for the church of God which he obtained with the blood of his own Son" (Acts 20:28).

These ten principles are sufficient to give a jolt to secularist political thinking. However, they fall far short of an adequate doctrine of politics:

- Granted that all human government is ordained by God, it does not follow that God requires the continuance of the present regime or magistrates; we are told neither how rulers should be chosen nor what forms of government are preferable.

- Granted that God disciplines the nations and rulers, Scripture explicitly denies that all good is reward or that all ill is punishment;[11] only prophets can with certainty discern God's mind in unfolding events.
- Granted that governmental *edicts* that contradict God's must be disobeyed, we are not instructed as to whether an unjust *government* may be resisted.
- Granted that the just purposes of government include commendation of good, punishment of evil, maintenance of peace, and protection of the oppressed, whether government may systematically pursue additional purposes is not spelled out.

In fact, not a single requirement of political theory is satisfied: We are not provided with an adequate orienting doctrine, an adequate practical doctrine, or an adequate cultural apologetic. The ten principles tell us precious little about the place of government in the world as a whole, still less about how Christians should conduct themselves in the civic realm, and almost nothing about how to make Christian cultural aims and aspirations plausible to those who do not share the biblical worldview.

Inflationary Strategies

Of course, another principle or two might be found in Scripture, and the outlines of the principles (whether there are ten, eleven, or twelve) can be filled out somewhat by careful attention to the rest of the Bible. Unfortunately, the "filling out" methods

11. "There were some present at that very time who told him of the Galileans whose blood Pilate had mingled with their sacrifices. And he answered them, 'Do you think that these Galileans were worse sinners than all the other Galileans, because they suffered thus? I tell you, No; but unless you repent you will all likewise perish. Or those eighteen upon whom the tower in Siloam fell and killed them, do you think that they were worse offenders than all the others who dwelt in Jerusalem? I tell you, No; but unless you repent you will all likewise perish'" (Luke 13:1–5). "As he passed by, he saw a man blind from his birth. And his disciples asked him, 'Rabbi, who sinned, this man or his parents, that he was born blind?' Jesus answered, 'It was not that this man sinned, or his parents, but that the works of God might be made manifest in him'" (John 9:1–3).

most popular among evangelicals are inflationary; they try to draw more money than the bank contains.

There are three main inflationary strategies. The first is to *assume that the details of God's code for ancient Israel reflect the divine blueprint for all civil law*.[12] This assumption is illegitimate because the law of Israel was expressly given only to Israel, and although the New Testament confirms the universality of the moral principles that underlie its code[13]—sometimes called by evangelicals "the general equity of the law"—it nowhere universalizes the details. For instance, we should always provide for the poor, but it does not follow that in all times and places farmers should be required to leave the corners of their fields unharvested for the poor to glean.[14] A further complication is that the Old Testament code did not *fully* express God's moral intentions even for the Jews. Jesus made this clear when he prohibited divorce, remarking, "For your hardness of heart Moses allowed you to divorce your wives, but from the beginning it was not so" (Matt. 19:8).[15]

The second inflationary strategy popular among evangelicals is to *assume that the biblical pattern of covenant represents the divine blueprint for all political authority*. This assumption is unwarranted. Certainly, covenant provides the pattern for certain institutions—in particular, the union of husband with wife

12. This widespread strategy assumes its most pronounced form in a doctrine called theonomy, represented by such writers as R. J. Rushdoony, Gary North, Greg L. Bahnsen, David Chilton, and Gary DeMar. See especially R. J. Rushdoony, *The Institutes of Biblical Law* (Nutley, NJ: Craig Press, 1973), to which North contributed three appendixes; see also Greg L. Bahnsen, *Theonomy in Christian Ethics* (Nutley, NJ: Craig Press, 1977), especially chap. 7. A distinctive feature of theonomy is its emphasis on retention of the Old Testament penalties, including capital punishment, for numerous kinds of crimes. Theonomy, in turn, is the most distinctive assumption of a school of political thinking called reconstructionism, which enjoyed a certain influence in some evangelical circles during the 1990s but fell into disarray after the deaths of Rushdoony and Bahnsen.

13. "Now we know that the law is good, if any one uses it lawfully" (1 Tim. 1:8).

14. "And when you reap the harvest of your land, you shall not reap your field to its very border, nor shall you gather the gleanings after your harvest; you shall leave them for the poor and for the stranger: I am the LORD your God" (Lev. 23:22).

15. Apparently God agrees with Thomas Aquinas that law should not try to teach people more quickly than they can bear (*Summa Theologica*, I–II, Q. 96, Art. 2).

and the union of God with his people.[16] But this does not imply that covenant provides the pattern for *civic* institutions. True, the Israelite covenant community was associated with the Israelite political community. True too that kingship in Israel was confirmed by covenant,[17] and the Old Testament records many other instances of covenant between rulers and subjects.[18] Yet nowhere does Scripture teach that God might covenant with another nation in the way he covenanted with Israel, nor does it ever suggest that the relationship between each government and its subjects is *intrinsically* based on covenant or that it *must* be based on covenant. Covenantal theories of authority have abounded in modern times, often from Christian motives, and plausible arguments might be made for at least some of them. But whether these theories are correct or incorrect, they cannot claim derivation from Scripture alone; inevitably they rely equally on extrabiblical considerations.

The third inflationary strategy is to *assume that the policies adopted by biblical rulers reflect God's blueprint for governmental policy in general.* This assumption is ill-advised for three reasons: Not everything recorded in Scripture is approved by Scripture, not everything approved in part is approved in full, and not everything approved in full is intended as a model for all time. We find, for example, in Genesis 41, that Joseph, granted divine foreknowledge of a seven-year abundance to be followed by a seven-year famine, advises the Egyptian ruler to prepare for the coming dearth by warehousing a fifth of the national harvest in each good year. Although the story is sometimes blown up into a biblical warrant for the welfare state, such an interpretation far exceeds what is justified by the narrative itself. To be sure, the tale portrays Joseph's counsel as appropriate to the circumstances. But from this fact, no more follows than that governments should

16. Scripture represents the two unions as analogous; the covenant between God and his people is often portrayed in matrimonial terms. See Song of Songs; Isa. 1:21–26; 50:1; 54:4–9; 62:4–5; Jer. 2:2; 3:1, 6–12; Ezek. 16; 23; Hos. 1–3; Matt. 9:15; 22:1–4; 25:1–13; John 3:28–29; 2 Cor. 11:2; Eph. 5:25–33; Rev. 19:7–9.

17. "So all the elders of Israel came to the king at Hebron; and King David made a covenant with them at Hebron before the Lord, and they anointed David king over Israel" (2 Sam. 5:3). "And Jehoiada made a covenant between himself and all the people and the king that they should be the Lord's people" (2 Chron. 23:16).

18. E.g., Josh. 24:25; Ezra 10:1–5; Jer. 34:8–9.

take extraordinary measures to meet extraordinary disasters, something we might have known anyway. The particular measure that Joseph recommended does not provide a blueprint for dealing with similar disasters in our own time; it was adapted to a form of government, type of agriculture, and system of taxation in kind that we no longer use, that we are not commanded to restore, and that we properly consider inferior to our own. Still less does the story tell us what the *routine* functions of government should be. True, elsewhere in Scripture the community is exhorted to care for the hungry, but does that necessarily mean the *government* of the community? If Peter votes to tax Paul to succor Mary, is that the same as Peter's succoring Mary on his own? Suppose, for argument, that the community's duty does imply a governmental duty. Even so, Scripture does not tell how the duty should be performed. That is a question of prudence.

Besides these three main inflationary strategies, there are a motley of others, most of them less systematic—the whole armory of tendentious interpretation, such as the sword of selective quotation and the shield of taking passages out of context. What all such methods have in common is that they make the normative political teaching of the Bible seem more ample than it is. They read into it principles that are not really there that really come from the intuitions of the interpreter. Mark Noll has identified intuitionism as a basic trait of the evangelical mind, independent of biblicism but just as deeply rooted.[19] In the political thought of evangelicals, much of what passes for biblicism is really intuitionism in disguise.

The Missing Piece of the Puzzle: General Revelation

Although evangelicals are rightly committed to grounding their political reflection in revelation, the Bible provides insufficient materials for the task. This I have called the evangelical dilemma. The missing piece of this puzzle lies in the recognition that the Bible is only part of revelation. "Special" revelation is that which God infallibly provides in actual words to the community of faith. But God has also provided "general" revelation, which

19. Noll, *Scandal of the Evangelical Mind*, 160.

he makes evident not only to believers but to all humankind. General revelation is divulged not through words but by other means: "The heavens are telling the glory of God; and the firmament proclaims his handiwork. Day to day pours forth speech, and night to night declares knowledge. There is no speech, nor are there words; their voice is not heard; yet their voice goes out through all the earth, and their words to the end of the world" (Ps. 19:1–4). The divine Word is imparted even without words. Such is general revelation.

Many evangelicals are unfamiliar with the concept of general revelation. Evangelical theologians are somewhat reluctant to say much about it, not because they think it isn't real—as we have just seen, Scripture itself testifies to its reality—but because they fear that saying much about it might detract from the more perfect revelation of the Bible. This is a strange fear indeed for those whose God declares, "From the beginning I have not spoken in secret" (Isa. 48:16).[20]

In fact, the greater danger lies in *not* talking about general revelation. Of course, the Bible is indispensable; it tells us God's dealings with fallen humans—the plan of salvation and the way in which God has unfolded it in actual history. Yet the Bible takes it for granted that we know certain large truths even prior to its instruction, truths apart from which this instruction would be incomprehensible. Examples of the many truths known from general revelation include the following. For each case I provide scriptural quotations, not to blur the difference between special and general revelation but to show that special revelation takes general revelation for granted:

> *The difference of quantities.* "He cast two pillars of bronze. Eighteen cubits was the height of one pillar, and a line of twelve cubits measured its circumference; it was hollow, and its thickness was four fingers; the second pillar was the same" (1 Kings 7:15).
>
> *The principle of identity, as to both unconditioned and conditioned being.* "God said to Moses, 'I am who I am.' And he said, 'Say this to the people of Israel, "I am has sent me to you"'"

20. See also Isa. 45:19; John 18:19–20; Acts 26:26.

(Exod. 3:14). "But by the grace of God I am what I am, and his grace toward me was not in vain" (1 Cor. 15:10).

The principles of noncontradiction and excluded middle. "Go down and buy grain for us there, that we may live, and not die" (Gen. 42:2). "And if you be unwilling to serve the LORD, choose this day whom you will serve, whether the gods your fathers served in the region beyond the River, or the gods of the Amorites in whose land you dwell; but as for me and my house, we will serve the LORD" (Josh. 24:15). "You did not choose me, but I chose you" (John 15:16).

The link between cause and effect. "Because you sinned against the LORD, and did not obey his voice, this thing has come upon you" (Jer. 40:3). "But you have turned aside from the way; you have caused many to stumble by your instruction" (Mal. 2:8). "If you were of the world, the world would love its own; but because you are not of the world, but I chose you out of the world, therefore the world hates you" (John 15:19).

The basics of natural teleology; for example, the complementarity of the sexes. "Their women exchanged natural relations for unnatural, and the men likewise gave up natural relations with women and were consumed with passion for one another . . . receiving in their own persons the due penalty for their error" (Rom. 1:26–27).[21]

The reality and deity of God himself. "For what can be known about God is plain to them [nonbelievers], because God has shown it to them. Ever since the creation of the world his invisible nature, namely, his eternal power and deity, has been clearly perceived in the things that have been made. So they are without excuse" (Rom. 1:19–20).

God's basic moral requirements. "When Gentiles who have not the law [of Moses] do by nature what the law requires, they are a law to themselves, even though they do not have the law. They show that what the law requires is written on their hearts, while their conscience also bears witness and

21. See also Prov. 8:22, 32 (Wisdom speaking): "The LORD created me at the beginning of his work, the first of his acts of old. . . . And now, my sons, listen to me: happy are those who keep my ways." Plainly, Wisdom's "ways" are norms embodied in the very design of creation.

their conflicting thoughts accuse or perhaps excuse them"
(Rom. 2:14–15).

The Bible assumes that these large truths are known before we
come to the Bible; in the same way, it assumes countless others.
Unless Abraham had already known something of justice, he
could not have debated it with God.[22] Unless the Israelites had
already known the duty of gratitude, the reminder of God's benefits could not have moved them.[23] Unless they had already known
the meanings of marriage, family, life, property, and telling the
truth, the commandments about adultery, parents, murder, theft,
coveting, and bearing false witness (Deut. 5:16–21) would have
been incomprehensible to them. However much such matters
may be denied and derided, they are actually known to everyone.
They are "first" principles of knowledge, the very preconditions
of all subsequent knowledge. History and experience have much
to teach, but they are not self-interpreting; how could we learn
the wages of sin without already knowing "wages" and knowing "sin"? In turn, how could we understand "wages" without
grasping the concept of causality, or "sin" without grasping the
concept of personal responsibility?

To call these first principles part of *revelation* is not a euphe-
mism, for they come from God; they are utterly dependent on his
arrangements in creation. We know them for no other reasons
than the divinely ordained design of the world, the divinely ordained design of the intellect, and the divinely ordained correspondence between them. Creation may be fallen, but it has not
been destroyed; its structures may be resisted, but they cannot
be overthrown; the knowledge of them may be suppressed, but
it cannot be abolished.

The reality of general revelation changes the whole meaning
of how to take revelation seriously. At first it may seem that there
are only two possible ways to study politics and government (or
for that matter any other subject): with revelational guidance

22. "Far be it from thee to do such a thing, to slay the righteous with the
wicked, so that the righteous fare as the wicked! Far be that from thee! Shall
not the Judge of all the earth do right?" (Gen. 18:25).
23. "I am the Lord your God, who brought you out of the land of Egypt, out
of the house of bondage" (Deut. 5:6).

or without it. Considering the duality of revelation, there are really four.

First, one might *acknowledge general revelation but disregard special revelation.* This is the method of both pagan antiquity and the Enlightenment, with this difference: Although the pagans disregarded special revelation through mere ignorance, the Enlightenment thinkers did so through disdain. Although this general-revelation-alone method is suggestive, its value is sharply limited. In the first place, though it acknowledges general revelation, it does not recognize that revelation *as revelation,* and so its understanding of what it acknowledges is inevitably flawed; for example, it cannot grasp the relationship between Creator and creation. In the second place, it never acknowledges general revelation *consistently.* Indeed, it cannot; apart from the promises of special revelation, the burden of doing so is intolerable. General revelation includes the basics of moral law, but clear vision of right and wrong reveals a debt that exceeds anything we can pay. Apart from an assurance that sin can be forgiven—something that utterly transcends what human reason can find out on its own—no human being dares to be completely honest with himself.[24] Consequently, although he has a certain grasp on morality and justice, it is weak and infirm.

The second way is to *proceed in disdain for both general and special revelation.* This is the method of contemporary secularist modernism, which ignores not only the plan of salvation but also the need for it. Reality is deemed to have no structure other than what we choose to recognize. God and humans, power and justice, sin and innocence, male and female, the *who*ness of persons, the *what*ness of things—all these are regarded as matters that we collectively make up and that we can change at will. Of course, secularist modernism cannot really *escape* general revelation but rather reflects it like a carnival mirror—obliquely confessing it in the very act of denying it. This is notoriously the case in logic, where to argue against the rules of reasoning explicitly is to affirm them tacitly. But it is no less true in ethics, where rationalization is the homage paid by sin to guilty knowledge.

24. J. Budziszewski, "The Second Tablet Project," *First Things* 104 (June/July 2002): 23–31.

Third, one might *acknowledge special revelation but be careless of general revelation*. This method—which we have already considered and found wanting—is what most evangelicals think it means to take revelation seriously. Usually, they arrive at this view by taking certain Reformation slogans either further or more literally than the Reformers intended. The original meaning of Scripture alone, for example, was not that only special revelation is *revelational* but that only special revelation is *infallible*; indeed, Scripture itself bears witness to general revelation. The original meaning of total depravity was not that general revelation is destroyed but that it is corrupted. For example, we still possess native knowledge of the reality of God and of his basic moral requirements, but we suppress it, pretending that we do not know what we really do. If our minds really were too damaged to receive general revelation, then they could not understand special revelation either, for special revelation presupposes general revelation and relies on it.

Finally, one might *acknowledge both general and special revelation*. This is the method of the natural law tradition, which was once as familiar to Christians as it is unfamiliar to most evangelicals today. The expression "natural law" refers especially to general *moral* revelation. It includes not only those truths we can't not know about right and wrong but also the first few rings in the spreading ripple of implications. Actually, while pushing natural law out the front door, evangelicals have slipped it in partly through the back door; certain remnants of natural law sift back into evangelical political reflection through various other doctrines, including common grace, orders of creation, conscience, the doctrine of humans as made in the image of God, and the doctrine of general revelation itself. All these doctrines are connected. It is because of God's image that we can receive general revelation, and it is for the sake of his image that he imparts it. His action, in imparting it, is common grace; the pattern of this grace is the orders of creation; and its mode is God's care in sustaining those orders. The purpose of common grace is to chide, to preserve, and to lead us to the greater grace that saves; its interior witness is conscience; and its requirements are the natural law, which is confirmed and illuminated by Scripture.

To these various and scattered doctrines we owe what remains of the great tradition in our political reflections. However, we would do better to follow the example of earlier Christians, including the Reformers, who acknowledged their connection and explicitly affirmed the natural law. The witness of John Calvin is clear:

> Now, as it is evident that the law of God which we call moral, is nothing else than the testimony of natural law, and of that conscience which God has engraven on the minds of men, the whole of this equity of which we now speak is prescribed in it. Hence it alone ought to be the aim, the rule, and the end of all law.[25]

No less plain is the word of Martin Luther:

> Not an individual is there who does not realize, and who is not forced to confess, the justice and truth of the natural law outlined in the command, "All things therefore whatsoever ye would that men should do unto you, even so do ye also unto them" [Matt. 7:12]. The light of this law shines in the inborn reason of all men. Did they but regard it, what need have they of books, teachers or laws? They carry with them in the depths of their hearts a living book, fitted to teach them fully what to do and what to omit, what to accept and what to reject, and what decision to make.[26]

Because the Christian natural law tradition is a work in progress, it would be too much to say that the natural law thinkers of the past provide the last word on politics and government. Many questions remain unanswered, and many answers remain undeveloped. From the beginning, however, the enterprise has recognized the need for all three elements of adequate political reflection: orienting doctrine, practical doctrine, and cultural apologetic. Its orienting doctrine seeks to understand government in the context of the other creational structures; its practical doctrine asks what the general principles of natural law require in concrete circumstances (the determination of which requires experience and cultivated judgment); and its cultural apologetic

25. John Calvin, *Institutes of the Christian Religion*, book IV, chap. 20, sec. 16.

26. Martin Luther, "Sermon for the Fourth Sunday after Epiphany: Rom. 13:8–10," in *The Sermons of Martin Luther*, ed. John Nicholas Lenker, 8 vols. (Grand Rapids: Baker, 1983), 7:73.

relies on the fact that the elements of general revelation are known, at some level, to everyone—even nonbelievers.

Of course, we should not beat nonbelievers over the head with general revelation any more than we should do so with special revelation. The line "Natural law says!" is no more persuasive, by itself, than the line "The Bible says!" But we need not invoke the natural law tradition by name just to make use of it. What the Christian natural law tradition teaches us is what nonbelievers, in fragmentary fashion, already know—whether or not they *know* that they know it, whether or not they *think* that they know it, and even if they would rather *not* know it. Viewed this way, the art of cultural apologetic is less a matter of laying foundations than of digging up and repairing them, less a matter of talking people into truths they do not yet know than of dredging up what they do know but have not acknowledged.

In the words of the apostle Paul, a law is written on the heart. In fallen humans, it is far easier to suppress than we might wish, but it is altogether impossible to erase.

2

Four Shapers of Evangelical Political Thought

J. Budziszewski

The premier influences on American evangelical political reflection have been Carl F. H. Henry, Abraham Kuyper, Francis Schaeffer, and John Howard Yoder. Not all four are American, and not all four are evangelical. Nonetheless, these four have provided both the models and the highest instances of the art so far; they are the cardinal points of the compass by which others have been guided. This chapter takes inventory of their foundational ideas.

My purpose here is not to attempt to discuss everything these four have written about politics, for this is a brief study and their oeuvres are large. The difficulties of selection, however, have been greatly reduced by the fact that for each writer a single book not only provides the main channel of his influence on other evangelicals but also epitomizes his work as a whole. Of course, I mention other works of theirs where it seems important to do so.

Every discussion has a point of view, and my aim is not to be neutral but to be fair. I also offer a modest critique along the lines sketched in chapter 1.

Carl F. H. Henry: Pricker of the Evangelical Conscience

Contemporary evangelicalism has its roots in the 1930s, when conservative Protestants who first called themselves "new evangelicals" began distancing themselves from their fundamentalist brethren. The difference between fundamentalists and new evangelicals lay less in theology than in style. Surrounded by the secularist mass culture, the fundamentalist responded defensively; intimidated by the adversary's intellectual armament, he withdrew from the field of battle. By contrast, the new evangelicals wanted to play offense. Not only were they eager to carry the cultural battle to the enemy's home turf, but they were also convinced that they could win the war of the intellect. Certainly, there had been no shortage of Christian intellectual power in the past, even in the recent past. The more hollow modern life became, the greater the opportunity for Christians to show the superiority of their faith—*provided* that they were prepared to demonstrate its implications in every dimension of life, including politics.

If Carl F. H. Henry is not the *father* of the new evangelical movement—for it has no single originator—then he is certainly one of its uncles. As one of the first faculty members at Fuller Theological Seminary, he helped shape the movement's mind. As founder and first editor of the widely circulated magazine *Christianity Today,* he took the movement to the masses. Even his critics must admit that no other thinker has done more for contemporary evangelicalism. Yet while he wrote or edited more than thirty books, including several that discussed social action, his most influential contribution to evangelical political reflection remains his brief second book, *The Uneasy Conscience of Modern Fundamentalism*, published in 1947.[1]

Henry's first thesis in *Uneasy Conscience* is that contemporary secularist culture is jaded, the sweet savor of modernity having dissolved and left only the taste of wormwood. Society wallows in futility because it is unwilling to acknowledge the whole truth about humans and God. Denying the reality of sin, society continues to entertain grand dreams; denying the need for salvation, it cannot achieve those dreams; unwilling to confess the redeeming God, it finds that life seems to have no significance.

According to Henry, the solution to the doom of modernity lies in Christ alone. Concealed in the mystery of the incarnation—the sublime condescension of a God who took humanity's burden upon himself—is a hope greater than fundamentalism has yet recognized. As sin is not merely individual but social, so is redemption. Moreover, the seeds of renewal have already been planted on earth. God does not want their germination to be deferred until the second coming; he wants them to sprout now. The activists of the social gospel movement caught a hint of this hope. Unfortunately, they perverted it into a humanism that spoke of Christ but meant only man. Though fundamentalists were right to reject this distortion, Henry believes, they have gone too far; they seem to revolt against the social imperative of the gospel itself.[2]

The desperate sickness of fundamentalism requires a radical cure. Above all, evangelicals must rediscover the social teaching of Scripture—and, indeed, the full redemptive meaning of the incarnation. Afterward, they must not only develop the enlarged charity necessary to act on this teaching but also reform their way of presenting faith to the culture. All too often, the evangelical movement has retreated into isolationism.[3] Despite its broad agreement on great doctrines, it has dissipated its energies in pointless schism.[4] When it has at last condescended to turn its face toward the surrounding culture, it has too often paraded points that are "secondary and . . . even obscure" as though they

---

1. Carl F. H. Henry, *The Uneasy Conscience of Modern Fundamentalism* (Grand Rapids: Eerdmans, 1947).
2. Ibid., 32; see also 31n, 37, 51–52, 85.
3. Ibid., 13.
4. Ibid., 63–64.

were the core of its message.[5] Outsiders might almost be forgiven for thinking that the burning question in Christian personal ethics, for example, is whether the pastor and his wife may join in mixed public swimming.[6]

Merely shedding tears for suffering humanity is not enough. Yet it would be equally mistaken, Henry thinks, to jump on the bandwagon of secularist ideologies that ignore both the need and the possibility of redemption. Evangelicals must develop no less than a "world program," a "global manifesto."[7] First they must fill in the implications of the gospel for the "political, economic, sociological, and educational realms, local and international";[8] next they must endeavor to provide the leadership, basic principles, and moral energy for movements of justified reform. Where they find themselves outnumbered, they should not be discouraged; rather, they should follow a twofold strategy of supporting the attack on the evil in question while proclaiming that a permanent solution is possible only in the context of redemption.[9] They should withdraw only from movements whose means or goals are explicitly *anti*-evangelical.[10]

Of course, evangelicals may not succeed in establishing a fully Christian civilization, but they should seek to win as many areas as possible.[11] They must formulate distinctively redemptive responses to statism, totalitarianism, imperialistic warfare, racial hatred and intolerance, family disorders, juvenile delinquency, the exploitive traffic in liquor, inequities in the relationship between labor and management, educational secularism, and "political naturalism" in general.[12] The critical ingredient in every attack on every social evil is the insight that the world can be changed only through change in the individuals who inhabit it—and that individuals can be changed only through the power of Christ.[13] All other approaches are "bubble and froth";

5. Ibid., 10, 63.
6. Ibid., 21.
7. Ibid., 37, 72.
8. Ibid., 68.
9. Ibid., 43, 78–79.
10. Ibid., 80, 87.
11. Ibid., 69.
12. Ibid., 17, 23, 32, 45, 78.
13. Ibid., 27, 33.

nonredemptive humanisms can achieve nothing permanent and are in that sense "sentenced to failure."[14]

Finally, Henry is convinced that unless fundamentalism accepts its medicine, it is doomed to irrelevance. An evangelical movement that fails to recover the prophetic and apostolic passion for the relief of humankind's estate and remains on the wrong side of every major social issue[15] will be unable to win a new "world hearing."[16] Should this happen, it will hardly matter whether society slides further into secularity or instead adopts a subevangelical form of religious belief,[17] for evangelicalism will decline either way: in the former case becoming a tolerated sect, in the latter a persecuted cult.[18] Here lies the burden of the book. The evangelical conscience is uneasy because "no voice is speaking as Paul would, either at the United Nations sessions, or at labor-management disputes, or in strategic university classrooms whether in Japan or Germany or America"; because "the historic Christian message is dismissed arbitrarily as a dead option for dissolving the ills of Occidental culture"; and because fundamentalism has come to mean not "doctrinal fidelity" but "ethical irresponsibility."[19] Yet the book ends on a high note, for "a baptism of pentecostal fire resulting in a world missionary program and a divinely empowered Christian community would turn the uneasy conscience of modern evangelicalism into a new reformation"—this time, says Henry, a reformation with ecumenical rather than schismatic significance.[20]

14. Ibid., 26, 87, 77.

15. Ibid., 13 (from the preface by Harold J. Ockenga).

16. Ibid., 10.

17. What Henry has in mind is liberal Protestantism (ibid., 29–30) or Roman Catholicism (ibid., 9). He did not anticipate the contemporary *rapprochement* between evangelicals and Catholics. Later in life, however, he did recognize that the greatest religious threat to evangelicalism lay not in what he considered a subevangelical form of Christianity but in resurgent neo-paganism.

18. Ibid., 9, 13.

19. Ibid., 34, 26, 19. Fundamentalists acquired their name from *The Fundamentals: A Testimony to Truth*, a series of articles published early in the century as a protest against theological revisionism and given away free to Christian ministers and teachers. In the original sense, then, a fundamentalist was anyone who believed the fundamentals, which included such things as the virgin birth, the physical resurrection of Christ, the inerrancy of the Bible, and the doctrine of substitutionary atonement.

20. Ibid., 89.

The influence of *Uneasy Conscience* can hardly be overstated; it has become an epitome of the evangelical social ethos. In this respect, Henry's argument has triumphed. Yet not only is the program of *Uneasy Conscience* still largely unfulfilled, but evangelicals have often modeled their political outlook on the weaknesses as well as the strengths of its argument. These matters deserve closer attention.

The Burden of Premillennial Defeatism

Henry is deeply disturbed by disputes concerning the second advent of Christ and the establishment of his kingdom. In the first place, these disputes divide evangelicals, distracting them from their central agreements and dissipating their energies in quarrels. In the second place, they undermine the evangelical message. Some preachers give these quarrels more pulpit time than the gospel of redemption itself, he complains; others so fear quarreling that they do not mention the kingdom at all. Alas for them, Henry thinks, because redemption flies on two wings, one individual, the other social; a gospel without the kingdom has only one wing.

But the deepest reason for Henry's distress is that, at the time he writes, none of the disputing parties seems to have thought through its eschatological assumptions. On the one hand are premillennialists and amillennialists, who believe that the kingdom will not be established until after Christ's return. They tend to be either defeatist or escapist, reasoning either that before Christ's return all social reform is futile or that Christ may return any day, so why waste time reforming? On the other hand are postmillennialists, who believe that the establishment of the kingdom will *precede* the second coming; Christ will return after a golden age of world conversion. Their tendency, equally careless, is excessive optimism, imagining that they can bring in the kingdom by their own unaided effort, which is merely liberal optimism with a religious patina.

Against defeatists, Henry lectures that the kingdom in one sense is here already, in another sense is to be further realized before Christ's return, and in yet a third sense is to be fully realized only when Christ returns; defeatists ignore both the first and the second sense.[21] Against escapists, he chides that the imminence of Christ's return does not lessen our duty to speak: "What if we rise tomorrow? We are *here* today."[22] Apart from a few dismissive remarks, he has little to say about the ultra-optimists, probably because, with their naive belief in inevitable progress punctured by two world wars, they have already lost most of their adherents.[23]

Though broadly premillennial himself, Henry feels no desire to convert other evangelicals to the premillennial side. "Nothing is so essential among . . . essentials," he says, "as the relevance of the gospel to the entire world. Whatever in our kingdom views undercuts that relevance destroys the essential character of Christianity as such."[24] Henry is perfectly happy for evangelicals to adhere to their various eschatologies, as long as they give up their obsessions with secondary points and grasp this great redemptive truth.

Unfortunately, Henry's wish has not come true. Premillennialism remains the eschatology of the evangelical majority, and it is the sort of premillennialism that he criticized.[25] Escapism of the "Left Behind" variety is, if anything, on the rise. Defeatism thrives too, if defeatism can be said to thrive. The dramatic rise of fundamentalist political activism over the last thirty years may produce the opposite impression, but defeatism and *a certain kind* of activism are perfectly compatible. For the defeatist sort of activist, political activity is protective, not redemptive; when a defeatist organizes, he does so not to transform the surrounding

21. Ibid., 53.
22. Ibid., 66.
23. Ibid., 49.
24. Ibid., 51–53; quotation on 53.
25. Postmillennialism, contrary to Henry's expectation, experienced a sort of comeback in the 1980s and 1990s—the heyday, such as it was, of the small movement called Christian reconstruction. The reconstructionists were eclectic, combining postmillennialism with theonomy, Van Tilian presuppositional apologetics, Kuyperian sphere sovereignty (to be considered later), and the cultural mandate to reclaim the fallen world in the name of God. Defying the Calvinist stereotype (for they were Calvinists to the man), they were cheerful optimists. Though in principle they conceded that the establishment of the kingdom might take tens of thousands of years, in practice they seemed in a hurry. However, their optimism was as conservative in its tendency as the optimism of the earlier postmillennialists had been liberal.

secularist culture but to defend against it. At bottom, he is willing to let the secularists have the culture, as long as they leave his family alone. For example, though he may lobby the custodians of the public school establishment, he does not really expect to change their philosophy of education; he just wants them to stop using it on his kids. The rise in fundamentalist political activity therefore reflects not a shift from a protective goal to a redemptive goal but an increase in the perceived level of threat. Many kinds of threat provoke the protective response, from fiscal threat, like the Carter administration's challenge to the tax exemption of private religious schools in the 1970s, to purely cultural threat, like the ongoing transformation of public space into a sort of pornotopia. But injustices that are not personally threatening to the activists receive much less of their attention.

The second sign of such defeatism is the tactic these activists choose. Although they have not lost their enthusiasm for personal conversion, they have never developed a cultural apologetic; the reasoning seems to be that until a nonbeliever is converted, there is no point in arguing with him. Therefore, in politics their goal is not to change minds but to push into action people whose minds have *already* been changed, whether the action is to sign a petition, show up at a meeting, or cast a vote. This is called activating the base. It may seem that the base is too small for its activation to have any result. Yet that activation can achieve short-term goals in arenas where small numbers make big differences, such as local party caucuses, low-turnout elections, and elections where the candidates are closely matched. This makes it a difficult mistake to unlearn. Unfortunately, because the base never gets any bigger, *long*-term goals remain out of reach.

The third sign of defeatism is that fundamentalist political activists are easily discouraged. As Paul Weyrich put it, "We got our people elected. But that did not result in the adoption of our agenda."[26] Widespread disillusion soon leads to an ambivalence about the activism itself, epitomized by the writers Cal Thomas and Ed Dobson. Former close allies of Moral Majority founder Jerry Falwell, Thomas and Dobson now argue that

26. Paul Weyrich, "The Moral Minority," in the colloquium "Is the Religious Right Finished?" *Christianity Today,* September 6, 1999, http://www.christianity today.com/ct/9ta.

fundamentalists who tried to build a political movement were "blinded by might," forgetting that true change in society can be accomplished only when sinful hearts yield themselves to God.[27] In this discourse of disappointment, charitable enterprise is still commended, but politics is not taken seriously as a vocation. The possibility of working in politics without losing one's way is dismissed.

Although the discourse of disappointment may seem far removed from the attitude of Carl Henry, in fact this great pioneer bears some responsibility for it. "The evangelical task," he explains, "primarily is the preaching of the Gospel, in the interest of individual regeneration by the grace of God, in such a way that divine redemption can be recognized as the best solution of our problems, individual and social."[28] At the time that he wrote these words in *Uneasy Conscience,* Henry thought he was describing an *approach* to social activism; however, they can equally be read as recommending a *substitute* for it. They seem to say that trying to change laws is a distraction from the real work of evangelism, which alone changes lives. Henry never reveals how evangelism and social activism can work together; he never makes clear how his approach to social reform is different from saying, "Make people Christians and their problems will take care of themselves." Are nuclear weapons proliferating? Convert the national leaders. Are there inequities in the relationship between management and labor? Convert the bosses and workers. Is juvenile delinquency on the rise? Convert the parents and kids.

Surely it would be naive to think that better laws eliminate the need for God's grace. But it is equally unrealistic to suppose that conversion cancels out the need for better laws. Four decades later, Henry reaches this conclusion himself. In a 1987 lecture at Fuller Seminary called "The Uneasy Conscience Revisited," he confesses that although his plea for "a divinely empowered Christian community" that would "turn the uneasy conscience of modern evangelicalism into a new reformation" now seems "almost prophetic,"

27. Cal Thomas and Ed Dobson, *Blinded by Might: Why the Religious Right Can't Save America* (Grand Rapids: Zondervan, 1999).
28. Henry, *Uneasy Conscience,* 88.

there was, for all that, a notable weakness in my concentration on regeneration as the guarantee of a better world. For *Uneasy Conscience* failed to focus sharply on the indispensable role of government in preserving justice in a fallen society. Essential as regenerative forces are to transform the human will, civil government remains nonetheless a necessary instrument to constrain human beings—whatever their religious predilections—to act justly, whether they desire to do so or not.[29]

This new insight is welcome, but there is less to it than meets the eye. Henry remains ambivalent about the uses of the law. From the beginning of his career as a theologian and journalist, Henry acknowledges his debt to his Calvinist mentors;[30] yet he does not seem to absorb John Calvin's teaching about the "three uses of the law."

According to Calvin, the law of God—as well as human statute law, when it is well modeled on the law of God—functions in three ways: (1) as a *mirror*, because by exhibiting God's standard of righteousness, it makes fallen humans aware of their sins and imperfections; (2) as a *curb*, because it restrains the unregenerate through fear of penalties; and (3) as a *teacher*, because it instructs the regenerate in the requirements of sanctity.[31] Surprisingly, Henry's retrospective on *The Uneasy Conscience* makes plain mention of only the second use: "Even at its best, of course, statute law does not impart moral power, but rather compels obedience under the threat of penalty." He does follow this statement with an obscure hint of the third use: "But if law lacks moral force in public life it is not because regenerative powers cancel it, but because secularist society has lost sight of law's revelatory foundation and heritage."[32] The first use, however, goes unmentioned.

29. "The Uneasy Conscience Revisited" became the concluding chapter of Henry's book *Twilight of a Great Civilization: The Drift toward Neo-Paganism* (Westchester, IL: Crossway, 1988), 163–82; quotation on 167.

30. Gordon Clark, William Harry Jellema, and Cornelius Van Til, whom the dedication of his first book called the "three men of Athens."

31. John Calvin, *Institutes of the Christian Religion*, book II, chap. 7, sec. 6–12.

32. Henry, *Twilight of a Great Civilization*, 167.

This is especially surprising because, according to Calvin, the first use of the law—as a mirror—has two branches.[33] In the first branch, the mirror of the law accuses sinners so that when God at last condemns them, they cannot claim ignorance of the standard by which they are judged. As Augustine had written, "If the Spirit of grace be absent, the law is present only to convict and slay us."[34] But in the second branch, the mirror of the law prompts sinners to flee to the refuge of God's grace. Again Calvin quotes Augustine: "God enjoins what we cannot do, in order that we may know what we have to ask of him."[35] Paul too is called on for support. In ancient Greek society, a certain class of servant—the *paidagogos,* or child-master—guarded and escorted children on the way to school. In an arresting simile, Paul had called Christ the school, the law the child-master.[36]

If the second branch of the first use is real, then statute law that is well modeled on God's law ought to serve the same use today: not as a means of salvation but as a preparation for it. The purer the laws, the more vividly citizens might conceive the ideal of justice; the more vividly they conceive it, the more sharply they might feel their sin; the more sharply they feel their sin, the more deeply they might long for the One who can do for them what government never can. According to

33. Calvin's account would have been clearer if he had written of four uses of the law, not three.

34. Augustine, *De correptione et gratia* ("On Admonition and Grace"), quoted in Calvin, *Institutes,* book II, chap. 7, sec. 7. I am using the Henry Beveridge translation of the *Institutes* (Grand Rapids: Eerdmans, 1989), 305.

35. Augustine, *De correptione et gratia,* quoted in ibid., sec. 9 (Beveridge, 307).

36. Paul's remark is in Gal. 3:23–24; Calvin cites it in ibid., sec. 11 (Beveridge, 308). In the NKJV, the verses are rendered, "But before faith came, we were kept under guard by the law, kept for the faith which would afterward be revealed. Therefore the law was our tutor [*paidagogos*] to bring us to Christ, that we might be justified by faith." Literally, a *paidagogos* is a "boy-leader." *Strong's Concordance* defines him as "a servant whose office it was to take the children to school." *Thayer's Greek Lexicon* remarks, "Among the Greeks and the Romans the name was applied to trustworthy slaves who were charged with the duty of supervising the life and morals of boys belonging to the better class. The boys were not allowed so much as to step out of the house without them before arriving at the age of manhood."

this view, godly law is not subevangelical but authentically preevangelical.[37]

To fully assimilate this point would transform how evangelicals think about politics. Why does Henry overlook it? Probably because of an even deeper difficulty in his thought, to which we now turn.

Vigorous Ambivalence

David L. Weeks points out that Henry affirms the reality of general revelation but then turns and undermines it.[38] Weeks is correct; Henry's ambivalence about general revelation is deep, vexing, and lifelong. The problem is not that his embrace of general revelation is halfhearted, for as Weeks points out, it is "vigorous."[39] The problem is that his undermining moves are just as vigorous.

This vigorous ambivalence toward general revelation undermines all three parts of Henry's political reflection. In his orienting doctrine and his practical doctrine, it deprives him of necessary principles; in his cultural apologetic, it denies him insight into what fallen humans already know. His hostility to the natural law tradition further weakens his thought by cutting him off from the single greatest historical deposit of Christian reasoning about general revelation and the single greatest channel of its continuing life.

---

37. Calvin explains that the vision of their sins in the mirror of the law affects people in different ways, shaming some into seeking God's grace but enraging others so that they desire to transgress even more. "Nay, the more they restrain themselves, the more they are inflamed, the more they rage and boil, prepared for any act or outbreak whatsoever, were it not for terror of the law" (ibid., sec. 7 [Beveridge, 307]). Paul seems to agree here too, for although he says in one place that the law escorts us to Christ, he explains in another place that law somehow increases sin (Rom. 5:20; 7:7–13). But it is too simple to say, with Calvin, that these two distinct effects operate in two distinct categories of people. Looking into the mirror of the law, I may see my sin and be stirred to resentment, but I may also see my resentment and be moved to horror. For further reflection, see J. Budziszewski, *The Revenge of Conscience* (Dallas: Spence Publishing, 1999), chap. 2; and idem, *What We Can't Not Know: A Guide* (Dallas: Spence Publishing, 2003), chap. 7.

38. David L. Weeks, "The Uneasy Politics of Modern Evangelicalism," *Christian Scholars Review* 30, no. 4 (Summer 2001): 403–18.

39. Ibid., 414.

Worse yet, Henry has too little patience with the idea of natural law to get it right. In one place, he writes that "any case for natural law must be made on natural foundations and independently of supernatural considerations"[40]—ignoring the fact that the mainstream of the Christian natural law tradition agrees with him that human beings naturally know the reality of the supernatural God. Even more embarrassingly, he describes the natural law position as "the highly debatable view that, despite the Fall, there survives in all humanity a shared body of theological and moral *doctrine*"[41]—ignoring not only the difference between whether we know and whether we *admit* that we know but also the difference between the natural law and the *theory* of natural law. This is like confusing gravity with the theory of gravitation: The former is known by everyone, the latter by only a few. Unfortunately, Henry's numerous misinterpretations of the natural law tradition have influenced other evangelicals to neglect it too. We should hardly be surprised that his dream of an evangelical public philosophy remains unfulfilled.

Henry's ambivalence about general revelation is painfully obvious in everything he writes. On the one hand, he insists that "politics must go beyond might and expediency to include moral principle and shared conscience."[42] The basis for shared conscience is general revelation, which is "inextinguishable."[43] "Penetrat[ing] the very mind of man even in his revolt,"[44] it "supplies an inner contact point between Christians and the secular community for bringing into relationship the good in the Christian revelational understanding and the general or public conception of the good."[45] On the other hand, he insists that for fallen humans a "right perception of the truth becomes impos-

40. See especially Carl F. H. Henry, "Natural Law and a Nihilistic Culture," *First Things* 49 (January 1995): 54–60.

41. Carl F. H. Henry, *Toward a Recovery of Christian Belief* (Wheaton: Crossway, 1990), 56, emphasis added.

42. Carl F. H. Henry, *Has Democracy Had Its Day?* (Nashville: ERLC Publications, 1996), 52.

43. Henry, *Toward a Recovery of Christian Belief*, 58.

44. Carl F. H. Henry, *God Who Speaks and Shows: Preliminary Considerations*, vol. 1 of *God, Revelation, and Authority* (Waco: Word, 1976), 400.

45. Carl F. H. Henry, *The Christian Mindset in a Secular Society* (Portland, OR: Multnomah, 1984), 121. For his views on the "point of contact" controversy generally, see also ibid., 395–409.

sible."[46] To be sure, there are "certain truths and principles by which states and their political interests stand or fall"[47]—elsewhere he identifies them as the Ten Commandments[48]—but these are "specifically biblical absolutes." Along with the principle of neighbor love, they are "not demonstrable."[49]

Can the curtain of this ambivalence be lifted? Perhaps. In one of the places where Henry comments on the inextinguishability of general revelation, he also remarks that "the light of general revelation may in different contexts survive in different patterns and intensities, depending upon the degree and depth of human animosity."[50] The remark indicates plainly that some parts of general revelation *fail* to survive. But if this is what Henry believes, then when he calls general revelation "inextinguishable," he is not denying that some *parts* can be destroyed; he is only denying that they *all* can be destroyed. It turns out that he does consider *some* parts indestructible—but only a few of them.

Regarding God, he thinks the indestructible parts of general revelation include both certain formal content, such as the fact that there is "a distinction between God and the not-God," and certain material content, for example, that "God exists." Regarding general *moral* revelation, however, Henry appears to concede indestructibility only to the formal parts. He admits that human beings know that the distinction between good and evil is "genuine and inescapable" and that "knowing . . . the good puts one in touch with divinity." But he seems to see no reason why anyone should know *specific* goods and evils—say, the good of loving a neighbor or the evil of murdering him—apart from Scripture.[51] Not to put too fine a point on it, this is false. However poorly followed, parallels to the principle of neighbor love and the precepts of the Decalogue are found in the cultures of

46. Henry, *God Who Speaks and Shows*, 329.
47. Henry, *Has Democracy Had Its Day?* 53.
48. "The universe is put together on moral lines; any attempt to build a civilization on other lines, whether before or after the coming of Jesus Christ into the world, foredooms itself. The ten commandments disclose the only secure foundation for a society without the seeds of dissolution; all cultures, cut loose from these principles, have in them the vitiating leaven of decay" (Henry, *Uneasy Conscience*, 39).
49. Henry, *Has Democracy Had Its Day?* 53.
50. Henry, *Toward a Recovery of Christian Belief*, 58.
51. Ibid., 57–58.

every time and place.[52] Henry has painted himself into a corner. Can he be extricated?

Another interpretation is possible: that Henry *intends* to say merely the same thing about the ineradicable parts of our knowledge of morality that he says about the ineradicable parts of our knowledge of God but does not make himself clear. After all, whether something is "demonstrable" is not the same as whether it is known; Henry did not consider the truth of Scripture demonstrable either. But if he does consider the knowledge of God and morality to be parallel, then we have another problem, for what really is his view of the knowledge of God? As he writes in his first book and maintained throughout his career, "One cannot properly picture man's knowledge of God, in the unregenerate state, unless justice is done to the elements of truth in the insistence both that he knows, and that he knows not, the one true God."[53] My working hypothesis is that Henry also thought that humans "know and know not" the basics of moral law.

If so, then Henry's task should be to discover (1) which particulars unregenerate humans know about God and moral law, (2) in what sense they know them, and (3) in what sense they do not. Compare the advice Henry gives his fellow evangelicals in a parallel case. As we saw earlier, having remarked that "no study of the kingdom teaching of Jesus is adequate unless it recognizes His implication both that the kingdom is here, and that it is not here," Henry immediately goes on to declare, "The task of the Bible student is to discover (1) in what sense it is here; (2) in what sense it is to be further realized before the advent of Christ; and (3) in what sense it will be fully realized at the advent of Christ."[54] Henry ought to apply the same advice to "knowing and not knowing" that he applies to "here and not here."

Unfortunately, he never does, and this neglect is fatal. If we know neither what particulars the conscience of unregenerate humans contains nor in what sense it contains them, then their conscience is inaccessible to appeal. True, Henry did speak of appeal to "shared conscience." However, according to his terms,

52. See, for example, the famous cross-cultural appendix to C. S. Lewis, *The Abolition of Man* (New York: Macmillan, 1947).

53. Carl F. H. Henry, *Remaking the Modern Mind*, 2nd ed. (Grand Rapids: Eerdmans, 1948), 207.

54. Henry, *Uneasy Conscience*, 53.

such language could have stable meaning only in a fully Christianized society. What then becomes of Henry's call for a Christian program of social reform? Can it really mean anything but "evangelize"?

Christian natural lawyers had wrestled with the problem of shared conscience centuries earlier. Over time they came to realize that conscience is really two things, not one. *Synderesis,* which we may call deep conscience, is the universal interior witness to the foundational principles of moral law, along with their first few rings of implications. Here is where the general principles of the Decalogue are enthroned; we *can't not know* the wrong of such things as murder, adultery, and theft. *Conscientia,* which we may call surface conscience, is conscious moral belief, especially about the details of morality. This is the realm in which deep conscience is applied to particulars. The foundational principles are inextinguishable; they cannot be blotted from the heart. The only way to tamper with them is self-deception, and even then they are only repressed, not destroyed. Conscious moral belief is another matter. Here knowledge can certainly be blotted out, not only through honest mistake but also through such things as sloth, corrupt custom, malice, fear, and depraved ideology. This is the biblical view too. For example, according to Paul, the problem with the pagans who do not worship God is not that they do not know the truth but that they suppress it. Experience unhappily concurs. We know things we do not know we know; we know things we try not to know. What we really know is one thing, and what we think we know is another.

Shared conscience, then, at the deep level is already a reality, but at the surface level is yet to be realized. The way to prick and goad the shared conscience of a culture whose *conscientia* is depraved and uneasy is to appeal right past *conscientia* to the *synderesis* that lies beneath, not merely challenging logical errors (important though that is) but dispersing the smoky haze of self-deception. It might go without saying that to dare such a thing the evangelical movement must follow the example of the great tradition by finding out *what it is* that *synderesis* includes, *what it is* that unregenerate humans "know but do not know." Following Henry's example, it has yet to look.

Abraham Kuyper: Preceptor of the Neo-Calvinist Magisterium

A Dutch theological liberal would seem unlikely to become a major influence on conservative American evangelicals of the following century, but Abraham Kuyper was an unlikely sort of person. It was the shocking encounter with the biblical faith of one of his parishioners that led him to rethink his theology and become an evangelical Calvinist. In subsequent years, he founded or helped organize a Christian political party, a Christian university and Christian school movement, several Christian newspapers and labor unions, and a Catholic-Protestant coalition, at the head of which he served as prime minister of the Netherlands from 1901 to 1905.

Kuyper's political thought reached American evangelicals through Dutch immigrants as well as through talks he gave in the United States, especially the celebrated L. P. Stone Foundation Lectures at Princeton Theological Seminary in 1880.[55] What Kuyper proposed was a principled pluralism—not mere interest-group politics but a celebration of the independent worth of the various forms of social life that fill the abyss between the state at the top and the individual at the bottom. These he called spheres, and the corresponding political principle he called sphere sovereignty.[56] Despite the importance of the idea, Kuyper says surprisingly little about it and never develops it in detail. The two main statements of it are his inaugural address at the Free University of Amsterdam, *Souvereiniteit in Eigen Kring* ("Sphere Sovereignty"),[57] and the third Stone Lecture, "Calvinism in Politics." Although the former has been called Kuyper's summa,[58] the latter, given eighteen years later, is presumably the more mature expression of his thought, and because it has long been available in English, it has also had far more influence on

55. Published as Abraham Kuyper, *Lectures on Calvinism* (1931; repr., Grand Rapids: Eerdmans, 2002).
56. We find later that the meaning of "sphere" is more ambiguous than this phrase suggests.
57. A translation of *Souvereiniteit in Eigen Kring* ("Sphere Sovereignty") may be found in James D. Bratt, ed., *Abraham Kuyper: A Centennial Reader* (Grand Rapids: Eerdmans, 1998), 463–90.
58. Ibid., ix.

American evangelicals. For both reasons, it deserves most of our attention.

Sphere sovereignty was part of a broader movement of thought, for arguments in defense of civil society had been offered previously by a variety of thinkers. As Russell Hittinger points out, the great majority of these writers praised it primarily in instrumental terms—for its contribution to the state. Even Alexis de Tocqueville took this view, says Hittinger, for "his famous discussion of intermediate associations in *Democracy in America* is framed almost entirely in terms of how they remedy the destructive consequences of modern democracy, especially its bent toward centralization and uniformity."[59] By contrast, certain nineteenth-century Christian thinkers were developing an understanding of civil society that emphasized its intrinsic value. On the Catholic side, the most important such writers were Wilhelm Emmanuel von Ketteler, Bishop of Mainz, and Pope Leo XIII; on the Calvinist side, the most important was Kuyper himself. What Kuyper calls sphere sovereignty and what Catholic and most other natural law thinkers call subsidiarity have certain important differences, to which we will return. Keenly aware of what was happening among Catholic thinkers, Kuyper remarked in 1891:

> We must admit, to our shame, that the Roman Catholics are far ahead of us in their study of the social problem. Indeed, very far ahead. The action of the Roman Catholics should spur us to show more dynamism. The encyclical *Rerum Novarum* of Leo XIII states the principles that are common to all Christians, and which we share with our Roman Catholic compatriots.[60]

Kuyper even encouraged his Catholic coalition partners to study the works of Leo XIII and von Ketteler more closely.

59. Russell Hittinger, *The First Grace: Rediscovering the Natural Law in a Post-Christian World* (Wilmington, DE: ISI Books, 2003), 269.

60. First footnote to Abraham Kuyper, "The Social Problem and the Christian Religion," 1891, trans. by James W. Skillen as *The Problem of Poverty* (Grand Rapids: Baker, 1991), 24.

The Three Spheres

Various parties claim Kuyper's mantle, and just what he is getting at with the idea of sphere sovereignty is described by writers in different ways. We make the best start by returning to the argument as Kuyper expressed it in "Calvinism in Politics." According to Kuyper, the "dominating principle" of Calvin's theological system was not the soteriological but the cosmological, not justification by faith but "the Sovereignty of the Triune God over the whole Cosmos, in all its spheres and kingdoms, visible and invisible."[61] Kuyper's purpose in the lecture is to explain God's sovereignty in each of the three human spheres of state, society, and church.

However great the dignity of the state, says Kuyper, "authority over men cannot arise from men." The authority of the state is a delegated authority, for "all authority of governments on earth originates from the sovereignty of God alone."[62] Within the state, the magistrate is the "instrument" of that "common grace"[63] by which God restrains evil, shields good, and preserves his human creation from total destruction.[64] For denying God's sovereignty, Kuyper blasts both the "atheistic" French theory of popular sovereignty and the "pantheistic" German theory of state sovereignty—seemingly opposed but "at heart identical" in maintaining the sovereignty of man instead of God.[65] However, his purpose is to criticize theories of authority, not forms of government. Thus, he is careful to explain that he is neither proposing a theocracy (for God has not directly intervened in any

61. This is an oblique criticism of Lutheranism. In the first Stone Lecture, "Calvinism as a Life System," Kuyper says, "But when the question is put, Who had the clearest insight into the reformatory principle, worked it out most fully, and applied it most broadly, history points to the Thinker of Geneva and not to the Hero of Wittenberg. . . . Luther's starting-point was the special soteriological principle of a justifying faith; while Calvin's, extending far wider, lay in the general cosmological principle of the sovereignty of God" (Kuyper, *Lectures on Calvinism*, 22).

62. Ibid., 82.

63. Ibid. Kuyper wrote a three-volume treatise on common grace, *Gemeene Gratie*. A translation of the introduction by Ruben Alvarado can be found in *Christianity and Society* 8, no. 4 (October 1998): 21–23. Translations of other portions by John Vriend can be found in Bratt, *Abraham Kuyper*, 167–201.

64. Kuyper, *Lectures on Calvinism*, 83.

65. Ibid., 85, 90.

government since ancient Israel) nor opposing a republic (for wherever it is feasible for the people to choose their magistrates, it is also a blessing).[66]

As in one way God delegates sovereignty to the state, so in another way, Kuyper maintains, God delegates sovereignty to society. However, state and society differ in three major ways. First, society is not a single sphere, like the state, but a throng of smaller spheres: "the family, the business, science, art and so forth."[67] Second, whereas the unity of the state is "mechanical" or contrived, the unity of each social sphere is "organic" or spontaneous, arising from the order of creation. Third, God delegates sovereignty not to all of these social spheres at once but to each of them individually; every form of social life is sovereign within its own domain.[68] This has tremendous implications for the state, because wherever another sphere is sovereign, the dominion of the state cannot extend. Therefore, the purpose of the state is not to *rule* the social spheres (for internally they rule themselves) but to umpire the relations among them. Kuyper explains:

> [The state] possesses the threefold right and duty: 1. Whenever different spheres clash, to compel mutual regard for the boundary-lines of each; 2. To defend individuals and the weak ones, in those spheres, against the abuse of power of the rest; and 3. To coerce all together to bear personal and financial burdens for the maintenance of the natural unity of the State.

When the state confines itself to this role, Kuyper says, it does well; it "may never become an octopus" but must "honor and maintain every form of life which grows independently in its own sacred autonomy."[69] Unfortunately, since the state is a mechanical contrivance rather than a spontaneous institution like the family, it has no sense of its own limits and tends to overreach. Therefore, the various social spheres must fight back using, for example, "the rights of the citizens over their own purses"[70]—in

66. Ibid., 83.
67. Ibid., 90.
68. Ibid., 95: "Dominion is exercised everywhere; but it is a dominion which works organically; not by virtue of a State-investiture, but from life's sovereignty itself."
69. Ibid., 96–97.
70. Ibid., 97.

other words, the right to refuse taxation. However, the social spheres dislike mechanically imposed authority so much that they try to shake it off completely, so the state must assert itself too. According to Kuyper, "All healthy life of people or state has ever been the historical consequence of the struggle between these two powers."[71]

At last Kuyper turns to the sphere of the church, where his primary purpose is to vindicate the liberty of religion. "The difficulty," he says, "lies in the unanimous advice of Calvin and his epigons, who demanded intervention of the government in matters of religion."[72] Kuyper concedes that their view was a reasonable conclusion from the inherited premise that "the Church of Christ on earth could express itself only in one form and as one institution." But the premise is false (as he thinks Calvinists, of all people, should agree), for "Calvinism itself has ruptured the unity of the church." The moment the premise is denied, everything deduced from it "drops out of sight."[73] The government must not give different legal standing to different churches but must honor "the complex of Christian churches as the multiform manifestation of the Church of Christ on earth."[74]

Someone might object that the multiplicity of churches is beside the point, because every church but Calvin's is in error. In this case, Kuyper accepts the premise but not the conclusion. First, one must discriminate according to the gravity of the error; the deviations of other churches are as nothing compared with rampant atheism.[75] Second, even in the gravest religious offenses—blasphemous denial of the sovereignty of God himself—the magistrate should not punish religious error *as such* but as an attack on the basis of his own delegated authority. In

71. Ibid., 93.
72. Ibid., 99.
73. Ibid., 101.
74. Ibid., 106.
75. Ibid., 102: "Calvin himself wrote down the premises of the correct conclusion, by his acknowledgement that against atheists even the Catholics are our allies; by his open recognition of the Lutheran church; and still more emphatically by his pertinent declaration . . . 'There exists a threefold departure from the Christian truth; a slight one, which had better be left alone; a moderate one, which must be restored by a moderate chastisement; and only manifest godlessness must be capitally punished.'"

other words, he is not to enforce religious truth except insofar as it is presupposed by the authority of the state itself.[76]

If someone is still not convinced of the state's incompetence to choose which Christian church is the true one, Kuyper has what appear to be three more arguments, though they turn out to be one and a half. First, in an allusion to Paul's remark that the magistrate "does not bear the sword in vain" (Rom. 13:4), Kuyper adds that he bears "not the sword of the spirit" but "the sword which wounds."[77] We may agree that the two swords are different, because elsewhere Paul identifies the sword of the Spirit with the Word of God. However, Paul does not comment on whether the former sword may be put in the service of the latter, so his remark does not count as an independent argument on Kuyper's side. Second, Kuyper declares that the government "lacks the data of judgment" to decide among Christian churches.[78] If true, the point would be compelling, but he could hardly have meant his words literally; the same data are available to the government as to everyone else, and Kuyper is no agnostic. I suggest that what he really has in mind is not a lack of information but a division of opinion, because elsewhere he remarks that, in every regime but an absolute monarchy, religious disunity among the people is reflected in religious disunity among the magistrates.[79] Although this is a bona fide argument, it is merely pragmatic, not principled.

76. Ibid., 103: "As regards blasphemy, the right of the magistrate to restrain it rests in the God-consciousness innate in every man; and the duty to exercise this right flows from the fact that God is the Supreme and Sovereign Ruler over every State and over every Nation. But for this very reason the fact of blasphemy is only then to be deemed established, when the intention is apparent contumaciously to affront this majesty of God as Supreme Ruler of the State. What is then punished is not the religious offence, nor the impious sentiment, but the attack upon the foundation of public law, upon which both the State and its government are resting."

77. Ibid., 106.

78. Ibid., 105.

79. My conjecture is based on this remark of Kuyper's (ibid., 104): "In the absolute monarch the consciousness and the personal will are one, and thus this one person is called to rule his people after his own personal conception of the ordinances of God. When on the contrary the consciousness and the will of many cooperate, this unity is lost and the subjective conception of the ordinances of God, by these many, can only be indirectly applied."

Kuyper's third argument is genuinely principled and has just as much force in monarchies as in republics. "Every magisterial judgment" concerning which of the churches is true "infringes the sovereignty of the church,"[80] he says. But there is a difficulty: The claim is not freestanding. It depends on Kuyper's *previous* judgment that "the manifestation of the Church of Christ on earth" is "multiform." He is not saying that although the Calvinists are the only real church, Lutherans and Catholics usurp the name of "church." Rather, he is saying that although both Lutherans and Catholics are in error about Christian truth, they have an equal claim with Calvinists to call themselves part of the church, for otherwise they could not be subsumed in the autonomy of its sphere. In the final analysis, then, Kuyper's principle that the state is incompetent to make distinctions in legal standing among ecclesiastical organizations rests on his ecclesiology—on his doctrine of the nature of the visible church.

His final point about religious liberty is that just as the sovereignty of the state is limited by the sovereignty of the church,[81] so the sovereignty of the church is limited by the sovereignty of individual conscience. In particular, "no citizen of the State must be compelled to remain in a church which his conscience forces him to leave."[82] Except for this example, Kuyper does not explore which decisions are immunized by conscience and which are not; he is explaining not a juridical framework but a vision. Personal liberty exists to enable every man "to serve God according to his own conviction and the dictates of his own heart."[83] However, like the sovereignty of every other sphere, the sovereignty of conscience is delegated. To say that a man is "a king in his conscience, a sovereign in his own person" is to say

---

80. Ibid., 105.
81. This limitation works in the other direction too: "The sovereignty of the State and the sovereignty of the Church exist side by side, and they mutually limit each other" (ibid., 107).
82. Ibid., 108. Contrast the attitude of Islam. According to Abdur Rahman I. Doi, "The punishment of death in the case of apostasy [conversion out of Islam] has been unanimously agreed upon by all the four schools of Islamic jurisprudence" (*Shari'ah: The Islamic Law* [Kuala Lumpur, Malaysia: A. S. Noordeen, 1989], 266).
83. Kuyper, *Lectures on Calvinism*, 109.

not that within the precincts of conscience he is answerable to no one but that there he is answerable to God alone.[84]

Mysteries of the Spheres

Because of the elegant geometry of the metaphor of independent spheres, the idea of sphere sovereignty seems clear. Examined closely, though, the pristine water clouds. Let us consider some of the difficulties.

The first great difficulty is that, like Carl Henry, Kuyper is ambivalent about a human being's relationship to the state. On one page he endorses Aristotle's view of man as a *zoön politikon,* a naturally political animal. In this vein, he declares that "the impulse to form states arises from man's social nature"[85] and later on asserts the "natural unity of the state."[86] On the other hand, he holds that "every state-formation" is "something unnatural," "something against which the deeper aspirations of our nature rebel,"[87] and that magistrates "do not harmonize with our nature."[88]

The reason for this tension is that Kuyper is blurring two ideas of what it means to be a political animal. What Aristotle meant is that an individual human being comes into his own only in a commonwealth; partnership in goodness under law is a necessary element in the individual good. Historically, Christians have agreed, even when, with Augustine, they have found it necessary to stress the deep rift between the city of God and the city of man and to emphasize that our true commonwealth is in heaven. By contrast, what Kuyper means is merely that the human race has a "genealogical" unity in its common descent from Adam.[89] Had sin not intervened, some sort of "political life" would have "evolved itself, after a patriarchal fashion," from domestic life, embracing the whole world.[90]

84. Ibid., 107.
85. Ibid., 79.
86. Ibid., 97.
87. Ibid., 80.
88. Ibid., 81.
89. Ibid., 79.
90. Ibid., 80.

In what sense this would truly have been "political" Kuyper does not say; anyhow, this possibility has been lost to us. Sin has "divided humanity" into the "different sections" we call states,[91] and instead of patriarchs, we have magistrates. Patriarchal rule would have been "organic": It would have arisen spontaneously from the nature of our social bond, and we would have been at one with it. By contrast, the rule of magistrates is "mechanical": Because it is a mere contrivance for "compelling order and guaranteeing a safe course of life," it never arises spontaneously and in fact seems alien to us.[92] Yet Kuyper says we deceive ourselves if we imagine that we can recover our primordial unity by dissolving the state, for "a sinful humanity, without division of states, without law and government, and without ruling authority, would be a veritable hell on earth."[93]

Another source of perplexity is just what kind of theory Kuyper thinks he is developing. He says in another work that "on almost every point in regard to the social question, God's Word gives us the most positive direction."[94] Considering this view, one would expect him to unfold his theory from special revelation. Actually, despite a few scriptural allusions, he is really unfolding it from *general* revelation, whether or not he realizes he is doing so. The Bible certainly testifies to a creational charter for the family, for man and woman were made for each other and were commanded to multiply, fill the earth, and exercise dominion over all other living things. However, the only other spheres explicitly chartered by Scripture are the state and the church,[95] which Kuyper expressly distinguishes from society. Although he might claim an analogy between the family and the rest of the social spheres, analogies between ideas internal to Scripture and ideas external to it are plainly not based on Scripture *alone*. They are inferences, not from what the Bible tells us about the order of creation but from what we can observe about it. What then does

91. Ibid., 79.
92. Ibid., 80. See also 82: "I do not speak of the family, for here organic, natural ties rule; but in the sphere of the State I do not yield or bow down to anyone, who is man, as I am."
93. Ibid., 81.
94. Kuyper, "Social Problem and the Christian Religion," 68.
95. For the state, Rom. 13:1–5; 1 Pet. 2:13–17; for the church, Matt. 16:18; 28:18–20.

Kuyper infer? As he says elsewhere, "We do not have to organize society; we have only to develop the germ of organization that God himself has created in our human nature."[96] In fact, he is developing a theologically motivated theory of natural law.

If that is what he is doing, more power to him. But now we meet another problem. Having neglected the foregoing tradition of natural law, Kuyper must work up his theory from scratch, and considering the magnitude of the task, it is not surprising that in various ways he slips. The single greatest problem is that he cannot decide just what he has in mind when he speaks of social spheres. It isn't just that there are different kinds of spheres but also that he gives the term *sphere* several incompatible senses, each having different implications for the shape of the state. Moreover, some of his spheres intersect. This makes it impossible for the state to carry out what he thinks is its main duty, because it can "compel mutual regard for the boundary-lines" of clashing spheres only if they do, in fact, have boundaries.

According to Kuyper, the "primordial"[97] social sphere is a relationship of marriage and blood—that is, a family—wherein sovereignty is spontaneously exercised by parents.[98] More generally, he uses the expression "social sphere" for any activity that employs our natural powers, such as science, art, commerce, seafaring, manual labor, and philanthropy, as well as for any association founded to pursue such an activity, such as a business, a shop, or a university.[99] Within social spheres in the latter two senses, Kuyper holds that sovereignty is spontaneously exercised by "genius"—by superiority in the use of the powers distinctive to the activity. The supposition here is that scientists defer to superior scientists, artists to superior artists, and so on.[100] But this does not seem true; the autonomy of a shopkeeper, for

96. Kuyper, "Social Problem and the Christian Religion," 69.

97. Kuyper, *Lectures on Calvinism*, 91.

98. Ibid., 96: "Paternal authority roots itself in the very lifeblood and is proclaimed in the fifth Commandment."

99. Ibid., 90, 94–95.

100. In science, for example, the "sovereignty of genius is a gift of God, possessed only by His grace. It is subject to no one and is responsible to Him alone Who has granted it this ascendancy." In art, "Every maestro is a king . . . only by the grace of God. And these maestros also impose authority, and are subject to no one, but rule over all and in the end receive from all the homage due to their artistic superiority" (ibid., 95).

instance, rests on his ownership of the shop, not his genius in maintaining it. And what about the family? We have treated it as *sui generis,* but it could just as easily be classified here; after all, it too is founded on a natural power, the power of generation. Must we then conclude that generative superiority is the ruling principle in families? If this were the case, then we could not expect children to defer to their parents, or the younger to defer to the older. Rather, the less prolific would spontaneously defer to the more prolific. But of course this is not what Kuyper thinks, nor do we find it in the world.

Then again, Kuyper uses the expression "social sphere" for an organization founded to enforce standards for such activities, such as a craft guild, a trade union, or an academy of fine arts. Kuyper seems to think that sovereignty within organizations like these is exercised by those who are competent to exercise the requisite kind of judgment.[101] But then what do we make of universities? The academy is founded to exercise the natural powers of thought and investigation, but it also sets standards for this pursuit.[102] Therefore, it might be a sphere of either the type wherein sovereignty is exercised by genius or the type wherein sovereignty is exercised by competent judges. Now genius in investigation seems to be a very different thing from excellence in judgment; yet two sovereignties cannot coexist in a single social sphere. So which one wins? Not only has Kuyper no answer, but he overlooks the question. Yet another Kuyperian usage for "social sphere" is a territorial commune of narrower jurisdiction than the state, such as a village or a city. Here the basis for sovereignty is that the social life of a city and a village "arises from the very necessities of life, and . . . must therefore be autonomous."[103] But to say that a city or a village is *necessarily* sovereign is neither to explain nor to justify its sovereignty; it is only to assert it.

101. Ibid., 96: "The University exercises scientific dominion; the Academy of fine arts is possessed of art power; the guild exercises a technical dominion; the trades-union rules over labor—and each of these spheres of corporations is conscious of the power of exclusive independent judgment and authoritative action, within its proper sphere of operation."

102. Ibid., 92, 96.

103. Ibid., 96.

The sixth sort of thing that Kuyper considers a social sphere is a social class or order, such as the class of laborers or the order of nobles. He mentions the sovereignty of classes and orders only in passing, as if it were perfectly clear.[104] It is not clear at all. Probably he means something like group representation in the legislature.[105] However, the idea of sovereignty within the sphere would seem to imply internal autonomy, not external representation. Therefore, either Kuyper is mixing apples and oranges,[106] or else he does not know that the lowly defer to the high. Amazingly, though, in his final way of using the expression "social sphere," he goes all the way to the opposite extreme. I refer to his idea of a social sphere as a circle of personal influence, wherein sovereignty is exercised by a dominant personality. Here are his words:

> There is no equality of persons. There are weak, narrow-minded persons, with no broader expanse of wings than a common sparrow; but there are also broad, imposing characters, with the wing-stroke of the eagle. Among the last you will find a few of royal grandeur, and these rule in their own sphere, whether people draw back from them or thwart them; usually waxing all the stronger, the more they are opposed. And this entire process is carried out in all the spheres of life. . . . Everywhere one man is more powerful than the other, by his personality, by his talent and by circumstances. Dominion is exercised everywhere; but it is a dominion which works organically; not by virtue of a State-investiture, but from life's sovereignty itself.[107]

The language is almost Nietzschean, and it is flatly impossible to reconcile with Kuyper's own principle that in every sphere the weak should be protected from the strong.

104. Ibid., 97–98: "But in whatever way the form may be modified, it remains essentially the old Calvinistic plan, to assure to the people, in all its classes and orders, in all its circles and spheres, in all its corporations and independent institutions, a legal and orderly influence in the making of the law and the course of government, in a healthy democratic sense."

105. Ibid., 98.

106. As maintained by George Harinck, "A Historian's Comment on the Use of Abraham Kuyper's Idea of Sphere Sovereignty," *Journal of Markets and Morality* 5, no.1 (Spring 2002), http://www.acton.org/publicat/m_and_m/2002_spring/harinck.html.

107. Kuyper, *Lectures on Calvinism*, 95.

The final difficulty of Kuyper's theory concerns the sphere of the church. As we saw, his discussion of religious liberty yields two principles. For convenience, I list them in a different order than before. (1) No citizen may be compelled to remain in a church that he considers mistaken, and (2) different churches must be granted equal legal standing. These correspond roughly to the free-exercise and establishment clauses of the First Amendment to the U.S. Constitution.

Even Kuyper's own premises demand revision of principle 1; it is too narrow. His argument is that compulsory church membership invades the sphere of conscience, but he considers conscience a gift of common grace, not a possession of Christians alone but an heirloom of the family of man. For consistency, then, he should have said that no citizen may be compelled to remain in a *religion* that he considers mistaken. What about the other side of the coin? Should he also have said that no citizen may be *prevented* from remaining in a religion—that no such group may be compelled to disband? That depends on what we mean by "religion." If we understand by the term any group whose understanding of God is broadly compatible with the two tablets of the Decalogue, then the answer is probably yes. We may call such religions "decalogical." But if we mean by the term any group that *calls* itself a religion, the answer is surely no.[108] Worldwide, the last two centuries have seen the rise and fall of cults devoted to assassination, human sacrifice, and systematic terror. By the common grace of conscience, there are some things that every human being should be expected to recognize as wrong.

---

108. To speak more generally, the term *religion* is used in two senses. In the first, it refers to rock-bottom assumptions and unconditional loyalties of any sort whatsoever; this is the sense in which we say, "That fellow's religion is money" or "Philosophical naturalism is the established religion of American higher education." In the second, it refers to the worship and service of the God who created the universe and its moral order. This is the sense in which the framers of the First Amendment to the U.S. Constitution declared that the free exercise of "religion" shall not be prohibited by Congress. Unfortunately, contemporary American jurisprudence cannot tell these senses apart. For example, the Supreme Court relies on the first sense when it says that religion is whatever a conscientious objector believes sincerely (*United States v. Seeger*, 380 U.S. 163 [1965]), but it relies on the second when it says that the government must be neutral between religion and nonreligion (*Abington v. Schempp*, 374 U.S. 203 [1963])—for otherwise any doctrine might count as religious.

Principle 2 is also too narrow, but the cost of fixing it is higher: It cannot be changed unless the premises are changed too. When Kuyper says that no government, not even a monarchy, may give one church a different legal standing than it gives another, in this case he really does mean churches. We know this because the argument depends on ecclesiology, on his view that the manifestation of the church of Christ on earth is multiform. In other words, Kuyper is not trying to say that Calvinism and Judaism should have the same legal standing because both are religions, whether in the decalogical or any other sense. What he is trying to say is that Calvinism and Catholicism should have the same legal standing because both are manifestations of the church of Christ on earth. The problem is that if principle 1 is grounded in the common grace of conscience, then it is hard to see why principle 2 should not be grounded in it too. After all, if the state fuses itself with a religion that is at odds with my own, then my conscience is defiled whether I am compelled to belong to it or not; either way I am compelled to belong to the state, and the two are one. By this reasoning, we should prohibit not merely state churches but also state religions. It would be just as wrong to make an official church out of generic Christianity as it would be to make one out of Calvinism—and it would be wrong from a Christian point of view.

The altered principle is still Kuyperian in one respect. Although it is antiestablishment, it is not liberal; although it opposes official state religions, it does not demand government neutrality toward religion.[109] Substantive neutrality is impossible in any case. The very promise *not* to elevate any religion to official status violates neutrality; it discriminates against religions that demand official establishment and in favor of religions that oppose it. For another illustration, consider the question of proselytizing. Here there are two ways to level the playing field: allow all to proselytize, or do not allow any to proselytize. A universal ban on proselytizing is intolerable to Christians because it conflicts with the Great Commission, but a universal liberty to proselytize is intolerable to Muslims in the *dar al-Islam* because it conflicts

109. Kuyper rejects "the false idea of neutrality" (*Lectures on Calvinism*, 105). Human beings have a common ground in common grace; it is not a *neutral* ground because any human being can reject it, and some do.

with *shari'ah*. Although both policies treat religions equally, neither treats them with neutrality.

It seems, then, that ecclesiology has a place in the doctrine of religious liberty after all, but not the place Kuyper gives it. While the legal equality of decalogical religions is grounded on the common grace of conscience, the choice among *different equalities* must take into account the divine mission of the church to bring the gospel of Christ to the world.[110]

The Other Principled Pluralism

The influence of Kuyper's vision in the Reformed wing of American evangelicalism is not difficult to understand. In our day, pluralism usually means relativism; by contrast, the Kuyperian movement prides itself on its "principled" pluralism. Unfortunately, the tendency of most Kuyperian thinkers has been to make the originating vision ever more elaborate, to push it ever more in the direction of a full-fledged juridical doctrine. For all of the reasons discussed above, it is precisely as a juridical doctrine that sphere sovereignty cannot work. Kuyper's spheres overlap even when they do not overreach. Each overlap produces a clash between incompatible sovereignties, so the chief role of the state as umpire becomes moot. The whole discussion of the natural, the organic, and the spontaneous is confused. The spontaneous comes into conflict with the just, for Kuyper is simultaneously committed to the protection of the weak and the "dominion" of the strong, a dominion that works "organically, not by virtue of a State-investiture, but from life's sovereignty itself."[111] His religious pluralism is less pluralistic than it looks, not only because he does not consistently follow his premises, but also because some of his premises are wrong.

The principled and pluralistic way for a principled pluralism to avoid such embarrassments is to invite collegial discussion with comparable traditions. One might have thought that Kuyper

110. Compare the view presented in the Vatican II document *Dignitatis Humanae*, which grounds religious liberty in general on the *imago Dei* but grounds the liberty of the church in particular on its divine redemptive mission. For discussion, see Hittinger, *First Grace*, 215–41.

111. Kuyper, *Lectures on Calvinism*, 95.

would have done so, for he admits that there is a comparable tradition—the pluralism of von Ketteler and Leo XIII—and he even led a Protestant-Catholic coalition in Dutch politics. Unfortunately, he seems more interested in criticizing Catholicism than in entering into serious dialogue about civil society, and even his rare compliments to Catholics are backhanded.[112] Another reason for his resistance to mutual critique may have been the conviction that none was needed. Had he not developed his doctrine of civil society from Scripture alone? Yet as we have seen, this was an illusion. Sphere sovereignty is not a sheer inference from Scripture but an elaboration upon it.

Constructive engagement between proponents of subsidiarity and proponents of sphere sovereignty has developed only recently,[113] and although there are signs of convergence,[114] the dialogue partners have a lot of catching up to do. Behind the principle of subsidiarity is the recognition that human beings are naturally social. There arise among us myriad forms of solidarity and association—marriages, families, neighborhoods, religious congregations, labor unions, professional groups, and so on—right on up to those institutions for public justice that we call government. But we are social not only in the sense that we *do* participate in them but also in the sense that for a fully

112. In the final Stone Lecture, for example, where he includes von Ketteler among Catholics whom he admires, Kuyper uses them to illustrate the principle that "in order to appreciate the noble, energetic traits of the Romanists," one must observe them "not in their own countries" but in "regions where, deprived of a controlling influence, they adjust themselves to the polity of others" (ibid., 185).

113. One important occasion of its development was the conference "Commemorating Over a Century of Christian Social Teaching: The Legacy of Abraham Kuyper and Leo XIII," cosponsored by the Acton Institute and Calvin Theological Seminary and held at Calvin College in 1998.

114. Both sides acknowledge this. "Catholic social thought has tended to stress the connection between the state and other social communities first, and the distinction between them second. The advocates of sphere sovereignty have emphasized the distinction first and then the connection. However, the trends may be converging. In recent decades Catholic social thought has tended to emphasize more strongly the limited role of the state in the economy and social life, while contemporary neo-Calvinist political theorists are finding a more developed notion of the common good" (Keith Pavlischek and Kenneth Grasso, "Evangelicals and Catholics Thinking through Politics Together," *Public Justice Report* 21, no. 4 [1998], http://www.cpjustice.org/stories/storyReader$754).

human life we *must*. It is through communion with others that we learn the virtues, through solidarity that we find out the meaning of hope, love, and trust. Without association, God's very image in us would be incomplete, because God is social in his own being: Although Father, Son, and Holy Spirit are one God, they are not a solitary person but a blazing eternal union of three in one.

Not all of our forms of association are natural institutions in the way that the family is, with inbuilt designs of their own. Moreover, all of them—even the family—are elaborated by human culture. Yet in a more general way, their diversity and profusion are provided for by created human nature, and when all goes well, each contributes in its own way to the unfolding of this nature. In its positive form, then, the principle of subsidiarity declares, So it shall be: Every form of social activity should furnish help (*subsidium*) to the members of the community in the manner that befits its calling. But if forms of communion among persons really do have something like callings,[115] as persons do, then they also have rights to respond to their callings as persons do. Here we discover a problem, for because of sin, associations that have greater sway and scope may usurp the proper work of associations that have less. In its negative form, then, the principle of subsidiarity declares, This is not to be: For any form of social activity to destroy or absorb what another can do by its own initiative and industry is a profound evil, an injustice, and a disturbance of the order intended by God.[116] Although this applies to every form of social activity, the state in particular must recognize that its purpose is "to protect the flourishing of societies other than the state itself,"[117] not to usurp their place.

115. More strictly, *munera* (singular *munus*). Russell Hittinger remarks, "My guess is that the idea of *munus* holds together the Aristotelian notion of an *ergon* or characteristic function with the more biblical concept of vocation or mission. In so doing, it gets at something not well developed by conventional Thomism" ("Social Pluralism and Subsidiarity in Catholic Social Doctrine," *Providence Studies in Western Civilization* 7, no. 1 [2002]: 57).

116. My division of the principle into positive and negative forms is suggested by the language of the encyclical letter of Pope Pius XI, *Quadragesimo Anno* (1931), at section 79. See also the encyclical letter of John Paul II, *Centesimus Annus* (1991).

117. Hittinger, *First Grace*, 241.

Subsidiarity is not a finished theory. Its proponents have yet to explain exactly how the callings of the various forms of social activity may be recognized, and critique from sphere sovereigntists may help keep subsidiarists on their toes.[118] On the other hand, subsidiarists who tackle the problem have an immense advantage in that they can call upon the natural law tradition for help.[119] Nor are they burdened, as Kuyper was, with the supposition that each form of social activity is equally spontaneous, distinct from all the rest, and unambiguously ruled by a norm unique to itself.

Evangelicals can broaden and deepen their understanding of the plural structure of society; indeed, they already have. However, insofar as further progress depends on a broadening and a deepening of dialogue with Catholics who are engaged in a parallel enterprise, the greatest obstacle to progress is sectarian prejudice. The fact that so few evangelicals learn about Catholic social thought by reading orthodox Catholic thinkers is a weariness and vexation of spirit. Most learn about it only from one another, with an occasional glance in the direction of Catholic dissidents. This is not the way to hold a conversation. Pray God we will learn to hold it differently.

118. For discussion of the strengths, weaknesses, and prospects of subsidiarist theory as viewed from the inside, see Kenneth L. Grasso, "The Subsidiary State: Society, the State, and the Principle of Subsidiarity in Catholic Social Thought" (paper presented at the Civitas Annual Symposium, "Civil Society and Christian Social Thought: Three Views," sponsored by the Center for Public Justice, Baylor University, March 22–23, 2002).

119. Among sphere sovereigntists, greater energy has been poured into finding ways around natural law; see especially the "cosmonomic" philosophy of Herman Dooyeweerd, *A New Critique of Theoretical Thought*, 4 vols., trans. David H. Freeman and William S. Young (Lewiston, NY: Edwin Mellen, 1997). As Jonathan Chaplin observes, "Dooyeweerd claims that the notion of a structural principle differs sharply from the Thomist notion of the telos of an essential form, but it would not be greatly misleading to describe his own notion as expressing a Calvinist, as compared to a Thomist, teleology" (Jonathan Chaplin, "Civil Society and the State: A Neo-Calvinist Perspective" [paper presented at the Civitas Annual Symposium, "Civil Society and Christian Social Thought: Three Views," sponsored by the Center for Public Justice, Baylor University, March 22–23, 2002]). Dialogue between neo-Calvinists and neo-Thomists is still too rudimentary for consensus on whether this new teleology reinvents the wheel, improves the wheel, proposes a square wheel, or is interested in something altogether different from wheels. For an account of sphere sovereignty from a Dooyeweerdian perspective, see Chaplin, "Civil Society and the State."

Francis Schaeffer: Sentinel at the Secularist Border

When I first began teaching political theory and my students asked why I did not teach them about a mysterious document called the *Humanist Manifesto,* I thought I had stumbled across the Southern evangelical version of the Roswell flying-saucer myth;[120] no such document had been mentioned in my graduate studies. My students had heard of the *Manifesto* because their pastors had read Francis Schaeffer, the founder of the L'Abri community who had been called by *Time* magazine the "missionary to the intellectuals" and by *Newsweek* the "guru of fundamentalism."[121] Card-carrying secular humanists really did exist, I found, and there had been not one *Humanist Manifesto* but two—the first in 1933, the second on its fortieth anniversary in 1973.[122] Their signatories seemed to include almost everyone who was anyone, from John Dewey, the preeminent American philosopher of the first half of the century, to Betty Friedan, the inventor of an idiom for American feminism. To be sure, these flaccid committee products made a dull read. On the other hand, they provided a fascinating comparison, showing how an antireligious worldview became an unofficially established religion but had to stop calling itself a religion in order to finish the job. *Manifesto I* insisted that secular humanism *is* a religion. *Manifesto II* equivocated. A third manifesto, released just in time for the millennium,[123] not only insisted that secular humanism is *not* a religion but also pinned the blame for the supposed calumny on unnamed political and religious foes—which brings us back to Francis Schaeffer.

It was Schaeffer who first made evangelicals aware of the culture war, an odd sort of war in which, he complained, so far only the other side had shown up to fight. Although no evangelical

120. This paragraph borrows and adapts from J. Budziszewski, "The Humanist Manifestos (1933, 1973, 1999)," *First Things* 101 (March 2000): 42–43.

121. *Time,* January 11, 1960, 48; *Newsweek,* November 1, 1982, 88, cited in James Emery White, *What Is Truth? A Comparative Study of the Positions of Cornelius Van Til, Francis Schaeffer, Carl F. H. Henry, Donald Bloesch, and Millard Erickson* (Nashville: Broadman & Holman, 1994), 62n.

122. Reprinted in Paul Kurtz, ed., *Humanist Manifestos I and II* (Buffalo, NY: Prometheus, 1973).

123. Paul Kurtz, ed., *Humanist Manifesto 2000: A Call for a New Planetary Humanism* (Amherst, NY: Prometheus, 2000).

writer did more to activate and politicize evangelicals, Schaeffer was not an organizer but an apologist, cultural critic, and internal judge of the evangelical movement itself. His books and speeches addressed topics from pollution to aesthetics to postmodern urban life. *How Should We Then Live?* challenged evangelicals to apply a biblical worldview to every department of life.[124] *Whatever Happened to the Human Race?* written with C. Everett Koop opened the eyes of evangelicals to abortion and related forms of dehumanization, catapulting them into the movement for the sanctity of life.[125] The most influential of Schaeffer's more than twenty books was *A Christian Manifesto* (1981), which argued that although Christians have rightly become disturbed about a variety of cultural problems, "they have seen things in bits and pieces instead of totals."[126] Let us consider the argument of *A Christian Manifesto* more closely.

What Schaeffer means is that the problems that have troubled Christians are not isolated but are symptoms of a much broader and deeper problem: the replacement of the previously dominant worldview, which was at least "vaguely Christian,"[127] with an antithetical worldview, secular humanism. As Schaeffer uses the term, being a humanist is not the same as being human, being humanitarian, being interested in the humanities, or being a member of the Humanist Society.[128] To be a humanist is to recognize no knowledge beyond what human beings can discover by their own unaided efforts, no standards beyond what their own fallen desires suggest—a stance that is ultimately dehumanizing. For not "blowing the trumpets" of warning, Schaeffer particularly faults those Christians whose training and occupation have equipped them to recognize the transformation. He blames lawyers especially,[129] viewing law as the vehicle through which humanism has won its most important victories and might yet

124. Francis Schaeffer, *How Should We Then Live?* (Tappan, NJ: Revell, 1976).

125. Francis Schaeffer, *Whatever Happened to the Human Race?* (Tappan, NJ: Revell, 1979).

126. Francis Schaeffer, *A Christian Manifesto*, rev. ed. (Wheaton: Crossway, 1982), 17.

127. Ibid.

128. Ibid., 23–24.

129. Ibid., 47.

win the war.[130] Secondary blame goes to liberal theologians for claiming that Christianity and humanism can be synthesized, when in fact their syntheses are merely humanism in disguise.[131] Educators are censured too.[132] Yet Schaeffer holds that, even at this advanced stage in cultural transformation, the tide can be turned if Christians will only recognize what is happening.

The most striking part of Schaeffer's argument is his claim that so far humanists have grasped what is at stake in each battle much better than Christians have.[133] Whereas humanist leaders have understood that they were fighting for one view of total reality against another, Christians and Christian leaders—seduced by pietism into compartmentalizing their faith—have acted as though nothing more were at stake than a few particular truths, like Christ's virgin birth or his substitutionary death and resurrection.[134]

Yet Schaeffer thinks humanists are even more deeply confused, for their confusion is not strategic but ontological. Not only are they confused about *final* reality, because of their denial of God, but they are confused about *human* reality, because of their failure to recognize humans as created in God's image.[135] Although they often speak of freedom and the rights of the individual, they do not believe in a God who could ground these rights; for them, man is merely "an intrinsically competitive animal" in a world in which the strongest is on top.[136] For this reason, their theories actually revolve not around the individual and his rights but around collectivities, such as state and society. Without moral absolutes, the concept of freedom is uncontained; it ends either in chaos or in an authoritarianism that promises to end the chaos,[137] for having given rights and "freedoms" no other authority than its own, the humanist state may take them away again.

130. Ibid., 49.
131. Ibid., 21, 50.
132. Ibid., 50.
133. Ibid., 20.
134. Ibid., 18–19. Schaeffer may have been thinking here of broadsides like *The Fundamentals: A Testimony to Truth,* cited earlier.
135. Ibid., 25–27.
136. Ibid., 26.
137. Ibid., 29–30.

Furthermore, because humanists deny moral absolutes, their law is based on nothing more than the perceived needs of the moment. The inevitable end of this sort of thinking is brute force—power without principle—and to see this, says Schaeffer, we have only to consider the definition of law proposed by former Supreme Court associate justice Oliver Wendell Holmes Jr.: "the majority vote of that nation that could lick all others."[138] This is worse than a return to paganism, for Schaeffer admits that a certain flawed concept of justice existed outside the Judeo-Christian world. Secular humanism is something new and much more dangerous. The worst that could be said of the pagans was that they *did not know* that humans are created in God's image; because of this ignorance, their concept of justice was defective. By contrast, secular humanists *have heard* that humans are created in God's image *but deny it*; because of this denial, ultimately their concept of justice vanishes altogether.

By contrast, biblical culture has consciously built on the recognition of God's image in humans. In the law of Moses, God commanded justice, demonstrating that on which he wanted human law to be based. In the atonement, says Schaeffer, God went even further. Explicating a comment of the early English legal scholar Henri de Bracton, Schaeffer explains that although God could have chosen a method of crushing Satan that depended on his power alone, God took the just penalty for our sin on himself, thereby showing that "power is not first, but justice is first in society and law." According to Schaeffer, the Reformation made the biblical basis of justice even clearer by insisting that "authority" must be based on Scripture alone. "This not only had meaning in regard to doctrine," he says, "but clarified the base for law." He also examines the Judeo-Christian roots of Western legal tradition, focusing on English common law and the U.S.

138. Ibid., 27. Taken from Oliver Wendell Holmes Jr., "Natural Law," *Harvard Law Review* 62 (1918): 40. The full quotation reads as follows: "I used to say, when I was young, that truth is the majority vote of that nation that could lick all others." Though this seems to express a former rather than a present sentiment, Holmes quotes the sentiment to approve it. His corresponding belief that rights have no deeper basis than the will of the state is reflected in the majority opinion in *Kawananakoa v. Polyblank*, 205 U.S. 349 (1907), of which he was the author, which declares, at 353, "There can be no legal right against the authority that makes the law on which the right depends."

Constitution.[139] In the West, Schaeffer thinks, we have grown so accustomed to the balance of "form" and "freedom"—duties to society and respect for the individual made in the image of God—that we take it for granted, "as though it were natural." But this balance is not the norm for fallen humans; it is a highly unusual, geographically limited outworking of the implications of the biblical worldview.[140]

According to Schaeffer, two symptoms of secular humanist ascendancy are the distortion of the Constitution and the distortion of the language. Constitutional separation of church and state, he says, originally meant that government was not allowed to repress religion or interfere with it. By contrast, today it has come to mean that only nonreligious values are allowed to have influence in government; thus, what once supported religion has now been turned against it.[141] Similarly, the term *pluralism* originally meant that the religious liberty upheld by Christians was not for Christians alone, that Christians must work like everyone else to show the truth of their beliefs. By contrast, today it has come to mean that moral choices, either in law or in individual conduct, are just a matter of personal preference, unrelated to truth. The term that once signified freedom to discover the truth now signifies that there is no truth.[142]

Looking forward (from the early 1980s), Schaeffer sees two possibilities for the United States. What he calls track 1 is to roll back the humanist march through the institutions. He thinks that the rise of political conservatism has "opened a window" of opportunity, making rollback thinkable for the first time in many years.[143] On track 1, the great danger lies in confusing the cause of this conservatism with the cause of Christ. What conservatives like to call the "Silent Majority" is an uneasy alliance of two quite different groups: "the majority of the Silent Majority," who want nothing more than to be wealthy and untroubled by the problems of other people, and "the minority of the Silent Majority," who stand on "some kind of principle, often with at least a memory of

139. Schaeffer, *Christian Manifesto*, 28.
140. Ibid., 25; see also 29, 71.
141. Ibid., 34–36, 42.
142. Ibid., 45–47.
143. Ibid., 73–75.

Christianity" even if they are not in fact Christians.[144] Although the latter group may hold firm, the former group could easily be seduced by the promise, or even the illusion, of "improved economic numbers."[145] "We must remember," Schaeffer says:

> that although there are tremendous discrepancies between conservatives and liberals in the political arena, if they are both operating on a humanistic base there will really be no final difference between them. As Christians we must stand absolutely and totally opposed to the whole humanist system, *whether it is controlled by conservative or liberal elements.* Thus Christians must not become officially aligned with either group just on the basis of the name it uses.[146]

Should the window of opportunity finally close, says Schaeffer, track 1 will be finished. Humanists will consolidate their hold on government,[147] shorten the legal leash on our social institutions, and try to bring even religious groups to heel. Protestants, Roman Catholics, and Jews will all suffer.[148] If the window closes, if the state forfeits legitimacy by renouncing its duty to God and deliberately subverting the just liberties of the citizens, then, Schaeffer argues, the only alternative is track 2: graduated resistance to illegitimate authority, beginning at the lowest level possible. In the face of determined and systematic injustice, he says, resistance is not only a right but a positive moral duty.[149] Schaeffer draws his doctrine of graduated resistance mostly from a political work by the early modern Calvinist thinker Samuel Rutherford titled *Lex Rex*. At a number of points, the theory parallels the better-known argument of John Locke's *Second Treatise of Government,* which strongly influenced the American revolutionaries. Schaeffer argues that the resemblance is more than accidental, because Rutherford was one of Locke's sources.

If a law is unjust, then the first remedy is to seek legal means of redress. If these have been exhausted, the next remedy is nonviolent civil disobedience. In the case of direct commands

144. Ibid., 77.
145. Ibid., 79.
146. Ibid., 77–78.
147. Ibid., 80.
148. Ibid., 82–86.
149. Ibid., 124.

to do evil, civil disobedience means simply refusing to obey and peacefully accepting the legal penalty for refusal. What about permissive injustices like abortion, where the law *allows* fundamental evil but does not command it? It may seem that these are beyond the reach of nonviolent civil disobedience, but this is not true. Suppose, for example, that although the government does not require abortions, it subsidizes them through compulsory taxation; there is no direct command "Commit abortion," but there is an ancillary command, "Pay taxes to support abortion." Nonviolent civil disobedience might include refusing to pay the portion of taxes that is used to support the subsidy. A more recent example might be that, although the government does not require abortions, in various ways it hinders the expression of opposition to them, for example, by prohibiting peaceful protests within thirty feet of abortion facilities. Nonviolent civil disobedience might include peacefully protesting even inside the thirty-foot limit.[150]

The reason Schaeffer speaks of *graduated* resistance is that sometimes nonviolent civil disobedience is not enough. There are several cases. In the first case, the government violates the religious liberties of particular individuals or groups. According to Schaeffer, the oppressed parties should employ all legal means of protest and appeal. If that fails, they should attempt to flee. If even flight is impossible, then in the last resort they may use force in self-defense.[151] In the second case, some parts of the government subvert the constitutional powers of other parts of the government. Here, says Schaeffer, even armed resistance might be appropriate. However, vigilantism is never right; resistance should be undertaken only under the direction and protection of those officials who do remain true to the Constitution. The reason is that, although unjust government is an abomination, government *as such* is ordained by God. A private individual has no authority to undertake revolution. An official of the government itself, however, has a duty to uphold the just constitutional order of which he is a part.[152]

150. Ibid., 106, 108–9.
151. Ibid., 103–4.
152. Ibid.; see also 109–10.

Schaeffer tempers his argument for resistance in two ways. The first is to point out that some people might abuse it.[153] One such danger comes from liberation theologians, who often fail to recognize the fallenness of humans and always confuse the program of socialism with the kingdom of God.[154] Another such danger arises from the unusual prevalence of unstable persons in our disordered era. As Schaeffer explains:

> There are so many kooky people around. People are always irresponsible in a fallen world. But we live in a special time of irresponsible people, and such people will in their unbalanced way tend to do the very opposite from considering the appropriate means at the appropriate time and place. Anarchy is never appropriate.[155]

Abuse of the doctrine of resistance must be firmly resisted, says Schaeffer. However, not even the "very real" risk of abuse changes the "bottom line," the right and duty to resist unlawful acts of government.[156]

The second way in which Schaeffer tempers his argument is to emphasize that it is not enough for Christians to oppose evils through changes in law and politics. They must also offer just and compassionate alternatives to these evils, even when doing so is costly in money, time, and effort. For example, they should not quarrel over whether it is better to change the abortion law or to establish crisis pregnancy centers; they should do both. In the same spirit, Schaeffer softens his sharp criticism of liberation theologians with a reminder of the duty of Christians to use their possessions to care for the needy. In some measure, the errors of liberation theologians are a reaction to the failures of ordinary Christians.[157]

Schaeffer and his *Christian Manifesto* deserve great credit for awakening evangelicals to the fact that humanism is of an encroaching nature and that the culture is slipping out from under

153. These two possibilities of abuse are mentioned as part of a longer discussion of why discussion of resistance, however necessary, is so frightening (ibid., 120–30).

154. Ibid., 124–26.

155. Ibid., 126.

156. Ibid., 126–30.

157. Ibid., 124–26.

their feet. True, his analysis of the species *Homo secularisticus* is blunt. Reading him, one might easily get the impression that its subspecies are like peas in a pod—be they rationalists who believe that reason rules or materialists who believe that matter does,[158] be they Marxists committed to the destruction of class or utilitarians committed to pleasure.[159] All such differences are treated as unimportant. Then again, for Schaeffer's purposes, perhaps they are. Life may indeed be more bearable under certain sorts of humanism than under others—but only while they last, and none of the subspecies can reproduce after its kind. The reason lies in a cardinal principle of Schaeffer's thought: Because we are made in God's image, no humanist can live *consistently* with the implications of his own godless theory, no matter how different his variety of godlessness may be from others.[160] We will return to this point later. For the moment, suffice it to say that if it is true, then every humanism must eventually give place to a different one, and the cumulative movement must inevitably be toward despair.

The Political Response to Encroaching Humanism

After forty-two pages of argument in favor of resistance, Schaeffer opens the final chapter of *A Christian Manifesto* with a surprising confession: "What does all this mean in practice to us today? I must say, I really am not sure all that it means to us in practice at this moment."[161] If he does not know what to do, then one might wish he had waited a bit longer before sitting down to write about it; it is irresponsible to propose such a drastic response before thinking it through.

Even supposing that the doctrine of graduated resistance is correct, there are deep problems with Schaeffer's argument. One of the deepest is his impatience with ordinary politics. He admits that resistance should not be considered until legal means of re-

---

158. Ibid., 44–45.

159. Ibid., 26, 112.

160. As he remarks in another book, "No one can live logically according to his own non-Christian presuppositions" (Francis Schaeffer, *The God Who Is There*, in *A Christian Worldview*, 2nd ed., vol. 1 of *The Complete Works of Francis Schaeffer* [Wheaton: Crossway, 1982], 137).

161. Schaeffer, *Christian Manifesto*, 131.

versing injustices have been exhausted. Yet he has almost nothing
to say about the everyday work of reversing them by trying to get
better laws, better judicial decisions, and better public officials.
Instead, he moves on to protest, resistance, and revolution. Although he is well aware of the ways in which secular humanists
have used small changes in law to bring about small changes in
public opinion that prepared the way for larger changes in law,
the possibility that Christians could use the same method hardly
seems to have occurred to him. If a few evangelical activists
have come to think differently, they have done so not because
of Schaeffer's influence but in spite of it. Steady, plodding incre-
mentalism is not the frame of mind that his book encourages.
It is written as though the only two political possibilities were
quietism and upheaval—as if one had a car that could run at
zero or at eighty but not at any speed in between.

Perhaps Schaeffer's blind spots are not surprising; his stock-
in-trade was apologetics, not political activism. But if the book
is about politics, and if apologetics is about how to challenge
entrenched worldviews, then why doesn't Schaeffer discuss how
to challenge entrenched worldviews *in* politics? Given his concern
about the courts, the legislatures, the press, one would expect him
to ask how to make the case for Christian principles to hostile
judges, nonbelieving voters, and skeptical reporters. He simply
does not do this. How can this gap in his thinking be explained?
Is he already convinced that ordinary politics will fail? Does he
think it is hardly worth trying? That is not what he says; in fact,
he urges Christians to act quickly while the window of political
opportunity is still open. Why then he has so little to say about
what to do while this window remains open is a mystery.

When we come to the higher rungs on the ladder of graduated
resistance, the problems continue. Consider nonviolent civil disobedience. If the government directly commands us to commit
fundamental evil, disobedience is obligatory. That which God
forbids, we must not do. Easy. But the decision to disobey ancillary commands is not so easy; it requires a case-by-case exercise
of prudence, and prudence is not Schaeffer's strong point.

Suppose we are considering whether to stage a silent prayer
vigil inside the government-mandated thirty-foot no-protest
zone around an abortion facility. All sorts of things must be
considered. For example, can we be sure that the protest will

be peaceful? As Schaeffer admits, the world is full of kooks, and protests are magnets for unsavory characters. Worse yet, pro-abortion forces are known to employ *agents provocateurs* to stir up trouble that can then be blamed on the pro-life protestors. Even if the protest does remain peaceful, is it more likely to persuade or to alienate the public? Freedom rides and lunch-counter sit-ins seemed persuasive in the 1960s, but the civil rights movement is a misleading analogy. One reason is that public demonstrations were a relatively unfamiliar means of protest in the 1960s; today they have been discredited by overuse. Another reason is that in the 1960s many reporters supported the civil rights movement and gave protestors favorable cover-age; today the media are overwhelmingly pro-abortion and are inclined to show protestors in an unfavorable light. The final reason is that public sympathy has been affected differently by the two protest movements. When 1960s civil rights protestors patiently endured being beaten with riot sticks, bitten by police dogs, sprayed with high-pressure water hoses, and spat upon by onlookers just to sit at a "whites only" lunch counter, they came across as victims. But when pro-life protestors hold a silent vigil around an abortion facility entrance so that a woman must run an intimidating gauntlet to get to the door, they come across as bullies. This is, of course, unfair; they aren't threatening her, and the only reason she runs that gauntlet is to end the life of the child she is carrying. But sympathy is aroused mostly by what we can see. Observers can see only the trembling woman; they cannot see the baby she is carrying to its death.

Or consider the next higher rung, the use of force. An illus-tration will make clear the sort of thing that Schaeffer has in mind. Suppose the Supreme Court usurps the legislative power that rightly belongs to Congress. Schaeffer insists that private citizens have no authority to begin a revolution, but Congress itself could unseat the usurping court, and it could call upon citizens for assistance. Simple. Or is it? This is an irregular, extra-constitutional check. Schaeffer writes as though he were completely unfamiliar with the system of checks built into the Constitution itself. Congress should not need *force* to resist ju-dicial usurpation of the legislative power. It might impeach the offending justices; if that is not enough, it might employ its Article 3 powers to redefine the appellate jurisdiction of the Supreme

Court. What we find, however, is that the Supreme Court *has* usurped the legislative power; yet Congress has done nothing. It has allowed its checks to lie fallow. If branches of government lack the spine to exercise even their regular constitutional checks, how can Schaeffer imagine that they will exercise irregular extra-constitutional checks?

The Apologetical Response to Encroaching Humanism

The previous section touched on a paradox. *A Christian Manifesto* is an apologetic *about* the public square. It begins by showing how the secular humanist worldview has come to dominate law, politics, and education and then goes on to show the implacable hostility of this worldview to justice and ordinary decency as Christians understand them. The paradox is that so many crucial pieces are missing from Schaeffer's apologetic *for* the public square. His book is written for Christians to discuss in their churches. Although he often spoke in highly public and highly apologetical contexts, he has no suggestions about what to say in the courtroom, the legislative committee, or that seven-second sound bite on the nightly news.

Of course, Schaeffer has plenty to say in his other books about how to persuade nonbelievers, but this material is difficult to use in the political arena. Schaeffer's method is one-to-one conversation, and his goal is to persuade the other person to embrace the Christian worldview as a whole. For the Christian political activist, these are luxuries. He needs methods that can reach many people at once, and his immediate aim is merely to promote a Christian position on the matter of justice at hand. In the long run, of course, conversion is much more important, and if personal conversation is what it takes, well, that is what it takes. But in the short run, our very liberty to go on having such conversations may depend on our willingness to use other methods as well. Suppose public officials tried to regulate whom the church may ordain or what the church may teach. Of course, Christians should try to convert those officials, but the immediate need is to persuade them to act less like Pharaoh and more like Cyrus. For this, one needs arguments that make sense to the unconverted, even to those who stop listening at the mere mention of Scripture.

When people are closed to special revelation, the only possible appeal is to general revelation, to the things we can't *not* know. The difficulty is that the nonbeliever may be self-deceived; he may tell himself that he does not know what he really does know. This is where Schaeffer becomes interesting. He identifies with presuppositionalism, a school of apologetics notoriously suspicious of general revelation. Surprisingly, although Schaeffer has been influenced by this suspicion, he does not entirely share it.

Some presuppositionalists—call them type A—affirm general revelation in principle but deny it in practice.[162] They do not deny the obviousness of the moral facts, but they consider unregenerate humans incapable of admitting the obvious. Like postmodernists, they think that once we reach the deepest presuppositions of a person's interpretation of the world, we are stuck, because the person does not acknowledge any deeper considerations in the name of which these assumptions might be challenged. Presuppositionalists are convinced, however, that nonbiblical worldviews are always incoherent. If only the nonbeliever can be brought to recognize the incoherence of his worldview, he will enter a crisis, for he must either hold on to it even though he knows it makes no sense or embrace another one that will inevitably have the same problem. When each refuge in turn has been shown to be futile, he may finally be ready to embrace a sane view of moral reality.

Unfortunately, type A presuppositionalism is itself incoherent. There is no *logical* reason why a nonbiblical worldview may not be perfectly coherent even though false, but if fallen man really is incapable of admitting the obvious, then why should he care even if his worldview *is* incoherent? The principle of noncontradiction will merely be one of those obvious things that he denies. If so, then it should be impossible to make real contact with him. Each worldview should be sealed unto itself, with no door in and no door out.

Schaeffer might be called a type B presuppositionalist. Although he agrees that the worldviews of nonbelievers are always incoherent, he does not regard this as a *logical* necessity. Instead, he views it as a consequence of the inescapability of

162. The next few paragraphs are borrowed and adapted from Budziszewski, *What We Can't Not Know*, 205–7.

general revelation. As he puts it, "I personally believe this very inconsistency is a result of common grace. The sun shines on the just and on the unjust, and illogically the unsaved man accepts some of the world as it really is, just as the Christian Scientists own good restaurants and have funeral directors."[163] Why can't the nonbeliever accept *all* of the world as it really is? Because reality poses a constant problem for fallen man. He wants to acknowledge some of the truths that press in on him, but taken together they point too strongly to other truths that he resists with all his might. In the end, he must deny so many obvious things that the work is just too difficult. He is like a man in a bathtub, surrounded by dozens of corks, trying to hold all of them down at once; whenever he pushes one down, another pops up somewhere else. His worldview is incoherent because bits of truth get into it that he does not intend, clashing with the self-deceptions he does intend.

In most cases, one of these bits of truth is the principle of noncontradiction. That is why the incoherence of his worldview bothers him, and that, in turn, is why we may get somewhere by pointing out his incoherence to him. But suppose he does deny the principle of noncontradiction; suppose he retreats into "the blackness of irrationality." Even then he cannot escape from common grace, because he knows the goodness of life. Otherwise he would have killed himself. To make the point, says Schaeffer, we can ask him why he hasn't.

It follows from Schaeffer's analysis that when a presuppositional apologetic works at all, what enables it to work is the flotsam of general revelation—those corks of truth that cannot all be kept down at once. But calling attention to the corks is the keystone of the natural law apologetic. Surprisingly, then, Schaeffer provides a point of contact, a bridge, with the older, natural law–friendly tradition that his type A colleagues reject.

To make this bridge secure, one thing more is necessary. Schaeffer's followers must learn to call attention to *all* the corks. Using only the principle of noncontradiction makes his method too negative and risks driving nonbelievers to despair instead of

163. This statement comes from Schaeffer's brief and widely overlooked article "A Review of a Review," *The Bible Today,* October 1948, 7–9. The full text of the article is posted at http://www.pcanet.org/history/documents/schaeffer review.html.

to truth. Schaeffer is more than willing to tell someone, "Your case is hopeless, for you cannot affirm A and go on affirming B," but he is far too hesitant to tell that person, "Don't you see that A implies C?" or "Notice how much more sense A makes if D is true as well!" These things that he hesitates to say are especially crucial in the public square, where the only hope for persuading confused fellow citizens to embrace a Christian position on an issue such as, say, the definition of marriage is to get out of the straitjacket of "rights talk" and connect with matters of general revelation that they know already—such as the need of children for a permanent mother and father.

In his letter to the church at Corinth, Paul describes the apostolic apologetic in military terms, declaring that "we destroy arguments and every proud obstacle to the knowledge of God, and take every thought captive to obey Christ" (2 Cor. 10:5). Two different arts of war are mentioned in this sentence, and they are equally indispensable, whether one is evangelizing or making an argument about public justice. In the end, the problem with Schaeffer's apologetic is that it employs one of them but not the other. It is so eager to destroy proud obstacles that it forgets to capture thoughts.

John Howard Yoder: Student of the War of the Lamb

We come at last to the fourth great influence on contemporary evangelical political thought: John Howard Yoder, the prolific advocate of nonviolent nonresistance and theorist of revolutionary subordination. It is fitting to make him the counterweight to the other three thinkers, because while Henry, Kuyper, and Schaeffer draw from the Reformed tradition, Yoder's roots are Anabaptist, and unlike their influence, his has been felt almost exclusively on the evangelical left. For both of these reasons—and also because his work demands unusually close reading—I give him more attention than the others.

Yoder's popularity among evangelicals could hardly have been predicted. In fact, he is surprised by it himself. In an address twenty-five years after publication of his most influential book, *The Politics of Jesus,* Yoder said:

I have been called both "fundamentalist" and "pietist" by un-sympathetic readers, since they put me in an already-closed slot in their minds, to which they had relegated the use of the Bible. They did not read me carefully enough to be aware that my reading of the scriptural texts was post- and not pre-critical. I did not offer that reading as a validating appeal to particular scriptural propositions, but rather reflexively as a test of the position of others who had set the ethic of Jesus aside on the ground of his being "apolitical." It may be that the reason the book stayed in print, by staying on the reading lists of church college courses, was that some teachers saw its stance as "evangelical," but that was not the readership for whom the book was intended. The intended readership was ivy league seminarians, who by and large did not read it, because their teachers did not, because Niebuhr had already closed their minds.[164]

One of the reasons why evangelicals are drawn to Yoder is that he takes the story of Jesus seriously. But there is a difference. Most evangelicals interpret the story of Jesus in the light of the teachings of Jesus. Yoder turns this around: He interprets the teachings in the light of the story. In fact, part of his reason for taking the story seriously is that he doubts the accuracy of the teachings:

164. John Howard Yoder, "The Politics of Jesus Revisited" (lecture given at the Toronto Mennonite Studies Center, March 1997, available through the John Howard Yoder archive maintained by Notre Dame University at http://www.nd.edu/~theo/jhy/). Is Yoder an evangelical at all? This question need not detain us; even so, his doubts about the biblical reports of the resurrection and of the details of Jesus' teaching (to be discussed later in this essay) are hard to square with a view of Scripture as propositional revelation. It would also be good to know exactly what Yoder has in mind when he says, "The Powers have been defeated, not by some kind of cosmic hocus-pocus but by the concreteness of the cross; the impact of the cross upon them is not the working of magical words nor the fulfillment of a legal contract calling for the shedding of blood, but the sovereign presence, within the structures of creaturely orderliness, of Jesus the kingly claimant and of the church which is itself a structure and a power in society" (John Howard Yoder, *The Politics of Jesus*, 2nd ed. [Grand Rapids: Eerdmans, 1994], 158). Obviously, Yoder takes the cross seriously. But what does he mean by "cosmic hocus-pocus"? Is he mocking only the superstitious reliance on pious words devoid of substance? Or is his barb meant also for the doctrine of substitutionary atonement—of Christ as bloody ransom for our sins?

Every New Testament author had his own sources and his own readership. Even the same author could address different guidance to different readers in different settings. Any redactor could pass on differing traditions from more than one source. This observation would be damaging against the claims of fundamentalism, or of high Protestant scholasticism, in which the content of belief to which people seek to be faithful is not really the Bible but the seamlessly consistent system of propositions in which one believes all its revelatory "teachings" cohere. This same awareness of diversity, however, does nothing to undercut a postcritical or narrative understanding, for which the witness of a text consists in the direction in which it pointed, along the trajectory from earlier tradition to present challenge, within the actual life of the community for and to which it spoke.[165]

He puts the point even more radically here:

There is widespread debate about the sense in which the resurrection reports can be called "history," or about how much the sayings and parables have evolved when we find them in their Synoptic settings. The doubts have not the same depth or breadth when we turn to the narrative skeleton of the Gospels, according to which Jesus gathered disciples, proclaimed the imminence of the kingdom, and was executed accused of insurrection.[166]

Another oddity of Yoder's influence is that there seem to be two of him. The reasonable Yoder is penetrating, temperate, and earnest in dialogue and comes brilliantly to the fore in some of his lesser-known works. The polemical Yoder is a very different fellow and wants to pick fights. As we will see later, he attacks straw men, frames questions tendentiously, and blames his opponents for thinking things that he seems to think himself. None of this is a reason not to read Yoder seriously. Some smart people happen to be prickly, and one must read with charity (but also with caution).

Oddest of all, Yoder's most influential book, *The Politics of Jesus,* is also his most awkwardly organized and least accessible. When he wants to, Yoder can write like an angel of clarity; here he does not. As we will see, *The Politics of Jesus* is also one of the

165. Yoder, *Politics of Jesus,* 16.
166. Ibid., 102.

works in which the reasonable Yoder and the polemical Yoder are at odds, and sometimes the polemical one gets the upper hand. Even so, this book is the obvious place to begin, and not only because of its influence. One other reason is that Yoder, a Mennonite, wrote it with the special intention of representing his views to the non-Mennonite world,[167] and it is the most comprehensive. Another is that he revisited the book for a new edition twenty-two years after its original publication, adding epilogues to most of the original chapters. These two facts make *The Politics of Jesus* in its second edition the most representative statement of Yoder's considered views. Because of its complexity, this work requires close discussion. However, the core of Yoder's argument may be summarized succinctly.

Paul tells us that to those who are called, Christ crucified is the power of God and the wisdom of God. The one who suffered, conquered; the one who submitted, overcame. Yoder gives this a political meaning: Submission, not strength, is what "goes with the grain of the cosmos."[168] In the example of Jesus' death, the church is shown a new way of life, and in following that example, it is made into a new kind of *polis*—a genuine commonwealth, though distinct from the civil one. Its main task is to be itself, accepting the burden of nonconformity. To do this, however, it must refuse all complicity in coercing, threatening, or taking life. Needless to say, a follower of Jesus may not be a policeman, a soldier, or a judge. However, he may speak to the political world, and he may even hold legislative office if he views it purely as a platform for this speaking; as Yoder remarks in another work, "It would be quite possible from the position of New Testament nonresistance to use selectively these means of

167. As he explains in "The Politics of Jesus Revisited": "The 1972 book *Politics of Jesus* was written under assignment. The assignment came from the Institute of Mennonite Studies, the research arm of the Associated Mennonite Biblical Seminaries, under the impulsion of the Peace Section of the Mennonite Central Committee and the Showalter Foundation of Kansas. They assigned the Institute to get someone to produce a presentation of a 'peace witness' which Mennonites could recognize as their own, yet which would be aimed at non-Mennonite readers, would not be based upon a denominational identity appeal, and would make its way with a nondenominational publisher."

168. Yoder, *Politics of Jesus*, 246.

communication without any compromise being implied."[169] But the Christian cannot *govern*, because ruling cannot be separated from responsibility for violence; there is no such thing as a vocation to statecraft. To abstain from governing, says Yoder, is not withdrawal, sectarianism, or pietism but witness—a witness most conspicuous in the church's evangelism, service to those in need, and "refusal to use means unfitting to her ends."[170]

Jesus as Radical Politician

According to the biblical witness, says Yoder, "Jesus is . . . a model of radical political action."[171] To call Jesus a model is to say that we should imitate him. The "What would Jesus do?" theology supposes that we should imitate him in every respect, but Yoder denies this. "Only at one point, only on one subject—but then consistently, universally—is Jesus our example: in his cross."[172] This raises the question of exactly what it means to follow the example of Jesus at just this one point—what it means that the disciple must take up his cross and follow him. Christian piety has long taken it to mean that we should bear every sort of *affliction* with humility and longsuffering, but Yoder denies this too. The believer's cross means one thing and one thing only: "Representing as he did the divine order now at hand, accessible; renouncing as he did the legitimate use of violence and the accrediting of the existing authorities; renouncing as well the ritual purity of noninvolvement, his people will encounter in ways analogous to his own the hostility of the old order."[173]

Before considering just how this particular ethic of imitation emerges from the gospel story, Yoder explains that the idea of imitating Jesus is not popular in the Christian academy. Liberal Protestant ethicists offer numerous reasons for not taking the example of Jesus seriously.[174] Some say Jesus' ethic was intended only for a brief interim before his return; others say it was meant

169. John Howard Yoder, *The Christian Witness to the State* (1964; repr., Scottsdale, PA: Herald, 2002), 27.

170. Ibid., 24.

171. Yoder, *Politics of Jesus*, 2.

172. Ibid., 95.

173. Ibid., 96.

174. Ibid., 4–8, 15–19.

only for a simple rural life or for people who have no control over the world in which they live—obviously not us. Others say the message of Jesus concerned only spiritual, not social, matters; along similar lines are those who say that Jesus proclaimed a difference between God and humans so great that it "relativizes" human ethics or that he died not to show us how we should live but to atone for our failure to live that way. Still others maintain that the Gospels do not say enough about him to guide our moral life, or that what they do say about him is inconsistent, or that we should pay attention to what he taught, not how he acted. Finally, some Scripture scholars insist on interpretive methods that set aside his most distinctive teachings; they run what he said and did through a filter.

Unable to base their ethics on the imitation of Jesus, the objectors have to base it on something other than Jesus. This usually turns out to be "common sense and the nature of things," and Yoder directs his complaint against all views in which "the nature of things is held to be adequately perceived in their bare givenness; the right is that which respects or tends toward the realization of the essentially given." The idea is that people take social life as they find it, turning what they find into an ethics of "vocation," "station," or "situation." Yoder groups all these ethical theories together under the heading "the theology of the natural," a term vaguely suggestive of natural law, although homage to the "bare givenness" of things is hardly what the natural law tradition has had in mind.[175] This view of natural law—hostile, yet seemingly uninformed—marks Yoder's other works as well.[176]

To demonstrate his claim that Jesus is a model of radical political action, Yoder analyzes the narrative structure of the Gospel of Luke. His approach is to look "more at the events than at the teachings, more at the outlines than at the substance,"[177] because it is much less difficult to get an idea of what Jesus did than of what Jesus said. As Yoder sees it, the outline of the story

175. Ibid., 8; compare 9.
176. See especially the symposium by Yoder and Donald H. Miller, "Does Natural Law Provide a Basis for a Christian Witness to the State?" *Brethren Life and Thought* 7 (Spring 1962): 8–22. Compare Yoder, *Christian Witness to the State*, 33–35. It must be conceded that Miller's account of the natural law tradition leaves much to be desired.
177. Yoder, *Politics of Jesus*, 13.

does *not* include the resurrection; the crucial things are that Jesus "gathered disciples, proclaimed the imminence of the kingdom, and was executed accused of insurrection."[178]

Yoder's reading of Luke's narrative is lengthy, but a rapid summary may be enough to suggest its flavor. What interests Yoder in the annunciation is not how readily Mary yields to the will of God but how much she sounds like a Maccabean; she plainly expects that "the one whose birth is now being announced is to be an agent of radical social change."[179] Zechariah, and later John, has the same expectation. At Jesus' baptism, Yoder understands the divine voice saying "Thou art my Son" not as "a definition or accreditation of a metaphysically defined status of sonship" but as "the summons to a task"—to be, "in history, in Palestine, the messianic son and servant, the bearer of the goodwill and promise of God."[180]

Yoder puts great emphasis on the temptation in the wilderness, the structure of which he finds repeated in the overall structure of the narrative. But he gives little real argument for his assertions. According to his view, for example, the tempter's suggestion that Jesus in his hunger command the stones to become bread really means, "Feed the crowds and you shall be king,"[181] but although Yoder says that our interpretive "filter" keeps us from seeing this, there is really nothing in the text to suggest his view; it seems that he is setting aside the plain sense of the text in favor of his own interpretive filter. Yoder also suggests that the temptation that Jesus bow the knee to Satan really means the temptation of "power hunger and nationalism"[182] and that the temptation that he throw himself down from the pinnacle of the temple really means the temptation to present a miraculous apparition to his followers, "appearing unheralded from above to set things right"—"the kind of 'sign' which Jesus consistently refused to give to the curious and dubious."[183]

In proclaiming "the acceptable year of the Lord" in the synagogue at Nazareth, what Jesus is really doing, according to Yoder,

178. Ibid.
179. Ibid., 22.
180. Ibid., 24.
181. Ibid., 26.
182. Ibid.
183. Ibid., 27.

is proclaiming a jubilee year, "the time when the inequities accumulated through the years are to be crossed off and all God's people will begin again at the same point."[184] In saying that "this word is fulfilled," he is really making clear his expectation of "a visible socio-political, economic restructuring of relations among the people of God, achieved by divine intervention in the person of Jesus as the one Anointed and endued with the Spirit." The calling of the Twelve, along with other highly public acts, is the reaffirmation of this "platform," because it constitutes "the formal founding of a new social reality," which provokes backlash from the religious establishment.[185] "As in the jubilee, and in the Lord's Prayer, *debt* is seen as the paradigmatic social evil."[186]

A pivot of the narrative is the feeding of the crowd in the desert, because the crowd would have made Jesus king. As any orthodox Christian recognizes, we see already in his refusal of kingship the shadow of the cross. The way Yoder puts it, however, is that "the cross is beginning to loom not as a ritually prescribed instrument of propitiation but as the political alternative to both insurrection and quietism";[187] in other words, the point of the cross is not that Jesus bore our sins (he calls this "hocus-pocus") but that he offered an example of what Yoder is to call "revolutionary submission." It is at this time, as the political authorities come to view Jesus as a seditionist and begin to seek his death, that Jesus emphasizes that his followers must be willing to take the same hostility upon themselves. When he reprimands his closest followers for their desire for privilege in the coming kingdom, he is admonishing them not for "expecting him to establish some new social order" but for "having misunderstood the character of that new social order which he does intend to set up."

The polemical Yoder now comes to the fore, for he implausibly describes the cleansing of the temple as a *"nonviolent* seizure of the holy place."[188] This requires him to ignore the violent character of overturning tables and pouring out coins and to claim that Jesus used the whip only to drive out the animals. Even more astonishingly, in his discussion of the whip, Yoder

184. Ibid., 29.
185. Ibid., 33.
186. Ibid., 34.
187. Ibid., 36.
188. Ibid., 41, emphasis added.

switches from Luke's to John's account of the incident without mentioning that he is doing so. All three of the other Gospels make it clear that the buyers, sellers, and money-changers were driven out too,[189] and Yoder's translation of the critical verse, John 2:15, is highly contestable. The Revised Standard Version renders it, "And making a whip of cords, he drove them all, along with [*ta te*] the sheep and oxen, out of the temple; and he poured out the coins of the money-changers and overturned their tables." Contrary to Yoder's assertions, the antecedent of "them all" can hardly be anything but "those who were selling oxen and sheep and pigeons, and the money-changers at their business," mentioned in the previous verse.

Another pivot of the narrative is the prayer in the Garden of Gethsemane. Asking what it could have meant for Jesus to pray that "this cup may pass," Yoder argues, "The only imaginable real option in terms of historical seriousness, and the only one with even a slim basis in the text, is the hypothesis that Jesus was drawn, at this very last moment of temptation, to think once again of the messianic violence with which he had been tempted since the beginning."[190] This assumes that Jesus *was* tempted to messianic violence at the beginning; Yoder here alludes to his earlier interpretation of the temptation in the wilderness. He also discusses various other incidents suggestive of revolutionary subordination, such as Jesus' admonishment of Peter to sheathe his sword when Peter sought to protect him from arrest. At various points in the narrative, Yoder suggests that some of the best evidence of the real character of Jesus' mission is found in the way the authorities reacted to it. In speaking about the crucifixion, he repeats the point with force: "Jesus' public career had been such as to make it quite thinkable that he would pose to the Roman Empire an apparent threat serious enough to jus-

189. Matthew 21:12 reads, "And Jesus entered the temple of God and drove out all who sold and bought in the temple, and he overturned the tables of the money-changers and the seats of those who sold pigeons." Mark 11:15 reads, "And they came to Jerusalem. And he entered the temple and began to drive out those who sold and those who bought in the temple, and he overturned the tables of the money-changers and the seats of those who sold pigeons." Most tellingly, Luke 19:45 reads simply, "And he entered the temple and began to drive out those who sold."

190. Yoder, *Politics of Jesus*, 46.

tify his execution."[191] This is "a proof of the political relevance of nonviolent tactics, not a proof that Pilate and Caiaphas were exceptionally dull or dishonorable men."[192]

Given Yoder's doubts about the resurrection reports, we must assume that he is equally skeptical of the reports of the post-resurrection appearances. However, he is willing to draw on such things when he thinks they show the "direction" of the narra-tive—in this case, that Jesus' followers finally got the political point. "Jesus' rebuke to the unseeing pair on the road to Em-maus," for example, "was not that they had been looking for a kingdom, and should not have been, [but that] they were failing to see that the suffering of the Messiah *is* the inauguration of the kingdom." What the "glory" revealed to them really means is that "the cross itself"—that is, submission, not resurrection—"is seen as fulfilling the kingdom promise." As Yoder puts it:

> Here at the cross is the man who loves his enemies, the man whose righteousness is greater than that of the Pharisees, who being rich became poor, who gives his robe to those who took his cloak, who prays for those who despitefully use him. The cross is not a detour or a hurdle on the way to the kingdom, nor is it even the way to the kingdom; it is the kingdom come.[193]

He concludes:

> Jesus was not just a moralist whose teachings had some political implications; he was not primarily a teacher of spirituality whose public ministry unfortunately was seen in a political light; he was not just a sacrificial lamb preparing for his immolation, or a God-Man whose divine status calls us to disregard his humanity. Jesus was, in his divinely mandated (i.e., promised, anointed, messianic) prophethood, priesthood, and kingship, the bearer of a new pos-sibility of human, social, and therefore political relationships. His baptism is the inauguration and his cross is the culmination of a new regime in which his disciples are called to share.[194]

191. Ibid., 50.
192. Ibid., 49.
193. Ibid., 51.
194. Ibid., 52.

Practical Implications

In another work, Yoder proposes nine rules of thumb to bridge the gap between "the general principles of Christological ethics" and their implications for particular social circumstances:[195]

1. The state exists for the sake of the church and not vice versa.
2. The purpose of the state is to hold violence to an absolute minimum.
3. Actual states tend to adopt more ambitious purposes, which are dangerous.
4. Christians should always speak of available alternatives rather than ideal states.
5. A kind of "moral osmosis" operates to make Christian values effective not only among committed Christians but also among "sympathizers" and among children of Christians who do not share their parents' commitment.
6. Christians will usually be on the unpopular side of social issues.
7. Although Christians cannot expect the state to adopt Christian principles, they should demand that the state adopt the least violent ways to accomplish its ends.
8. Although concepts such as orderly succession and consent of the governed should not be taken as universally valid criteria of legitimacy, in some circumstances they are useful in speaking to the state.
9. Governments assume that their task is to pick the alternative with the best results. On the contrary, "results are not calculable."

Although Yoder calls these "middle axioms," they are not very "middle," for they remain at a very high level of generality. Let us return to *The Politics of Jesus* to see if he is more specific. The first conclusion Yoder draws about the practical implications of his doctrine concerns the alleged announcement of the jubilee at the synagogue in Nazareth. He says:

195. Yoder, *Christian Witness to the State*, 35–44. For brevity, I am summarizing.

It is really a jubilee, conformed to the sabbatical instructions of Moses, that Jesus proclaimed in A.D. 26: a jubilee able to resolve the social problem in Israel, by abolishing debts and liberating debtors whose insolvency had reduced them to slavery. The practice of such a jubilee was not optional.[196]

But the reason Yoder devotes an entire chapter to the subject is that it has social implications for us as well. The jubilee that Jesus announced "here and now, once, in A.D. 26" was intended to *prefigure* the "reestablishment of all things."[197] When Yoder speaks of the reestablishment of all things, he is speaking not primarily (if at all) of the eschaton but of the new economic order that is to prevail in the Christian community. At times he seems to mean that Christians too should observe regular jubilees along the lines of the Mosaic law: "The jubilee is precisely an *institution* whose functioning within history will have a precise, practicable, limited impact. It is not a perpetual moral earthquake rendering impossible any continuity of temporal effort, but a periodic revision permitting new beginnings."[198] In the second edition of *The Politics of Jesus,* however, he expresses surprise that some people have taken these words literally and says that periodic jubilees are *not* what he means: "The fundamental notion of periodic leveling would have been lifted . . . from the level of some practices implemented every seven years or every forty-nine years. It would have become in Jesus' teaching a permanently defining trait of the new order."[199]

This is no more clear, for the mere remission of debts does not "level" people; although it puts them on the same plane with respect to debt, it hardly gives them equal wealth. Moreover, if we did level people, we would also destroy individual incentive, so that leveling as a "permanently defining trait of the new order" would require more than jubilee; it would require some form of communal ownership and management. Yet Yoder rules this out too:

196. Yoder, *Politics of Jesus,* 68.
197. Ibid., 70.
198. Ibid., 104.
199. Ibid., 71.

Still it is not our belief that Jesus prescribed Christian commu-
nism. If he had done this he would have left to his disciples either
monastic rules comparable to those of the Essenes, or some kind
of constitution for a Jewish collective state. This he did not do.
Collectivism was contrary to the spirit of Moses.[200]

Considering that Yoder mistrusts the record of Jesus' teaching, it
is difficult to see why he should be *less* mistrustful of the record
of Jesus' silence, but we may let this pass.

A possible example of what it might mean to act in the spirit
of jubilee as a permanent institution is to continue the development in bankruptcy law that began with the passage of the
federal Bankruptcy Act of 1898. Early English bankruptcy laws
were designed exclusively for the benefit of the creditor. They
were invoked at the creditor's initiative, were involuntary for the
debtor, and merely provided a way to seize the debtor's property
in order to pay off his obligations. Contemporary bankruptcy
laws are designed to relieve debtors of impossible burdens. They
are invoked at the debtor's initiative, are involuntary for the
creditor, and may be viewed as a partial and imperfect adapta-
tion of the underlying principle of the jubilee to our kind of economic system. As Yoder recognizes, jubilee was also imperfect;
"it froze credit."[201] For this reason, there was only one way for
it to work; the rich man must be generous enough to take the
risk of nonrepayment and not harden his heart against the poor
(Deut. 15:7–11). Similarly, there is only one way for our own
debtor-friendly bankruptcy laws to work; the debtor must be
honest enough to pay what he can and not take advantage of his
creditors. Because it is too much to expect everyone to practice
such virtue in a fallen world, both institutions are limited. Jubilee was not continuous but periodic; bankruptcy provides not
just for the remission of debt but also for its reorganization. We
may note in passing that jubilee was not only about remission
of debts; it also provided for the redemption of family property,
for the liberation of bondservants, and for an extended sabbath
for the land (Lev. 25). Presumably, adaptations of the spirit of
these other provisions of jubilee could be worked out too.

200. Ibid., 70.
201. Ibid., 64.

The only problem is that this could not be what *Yoder* has in mind. Like jubilee among the Israelites, bankruptcy is a civil ordinance. Yoder rejects participation in coercion, viewing it as incompatible with the example of the cross. This includes legislative and judicial coercion. Therefore, although the church does witness to the state, and might indeed *prefer* debtor-friendly bankruptcy laws (in a relative sense, even while rejecting the justice of having laws at all), Yoder is thinking not of what the state can do but of what the church can do. In other words, the spirit of jubilee ought to be practiced *voluntarily* among the followers of Jesus. Moreover, Yoder gives the impression that he has in mind something the church is not currently doing, something greater than the familiar modes of mercy to those in need. In the end, just what it would mean for us to practice continually the spirit of jubilee remains unclear.

The implications of Yoder's renunciation of coercion are more plain in the area of war. He does concede the *relative* legitimacy (though not the justice) of the state's police function.[202] As he recognizes, just war theory tries to extend the logic of policing to the international realm, proposing criteria for both when a state may have recourse to war and how a just war must be fought. Yoder grudgingly admits that a limited war that fully satisfied just war criteria would achieve the same relative legitimacy of policing.[203] However, he considers it obvious that these criteria could never be satisfied by a real war and thinks just war theorists are naive not to see this.[204]

Unfortunately, in the case of a regime like our own, Yoder's contrast between the military and the policing functions is misleading at every point, and he vastly underrates the changes in military practice that have come about through the influence of just war theory itself. First, "in the police function, the violence

202. Yoder is a bit more expansive about the relative legitimacy of the police function in *Christian Witness to the State.*

203. "At the very most the only relevance of Romans 13 to war would be to a very precise operation carried on within the very clear limitations of all the classic criteria that define the 'justifiable war'" (Yoder, *Politics of Jesus,* 204).

204. "The more we would attempt honestly to define and to respect such criteria, the more clearly we would see that as far as any real or conceivable war is concerned, in the name of any real or thinkable government, it is not honestly possible to include that function under the authorization given government by Romans 13" (ibid., 204–5).

or threat thereof is applied only to the offending party," but U.S. military doctrine forbids the deliberate targeting of innocents, and *unintended* harm to bystanders sometimes occurs in police work too. Second, "the use of violence by the agent of the police is subject to review by higher authorities," but the U.S. military is also subject to civilian control. Third, "the police officer applies power within the limits of a state whose legislation even the criminal knows to be applicable to him," but although it is true that there is no international government, the international conventions of war are known even to the rogue states that violate them. Fourth, "in any orderly police system there are serious safeguards to keep the violence of the police from being applied in a wholesale way against the innocent," but our officers are schooled in the concept of just war, our soldiers are given strict rules of engagement, military lawyers are brought into targeting decisions to make sure the laws of war are not violated, and members of the military who are found to have committed atrocities are severely punished. Finally, "the police power generally is great enough to overwhelm that of the individual offender so that any resistance on the offender's part is pointless," but an overwhelming preponderance of force is precisely what U.S. military doctrine demands.[205]

Even if war could satisfy just war criteria, however, Yoder denies that it would be really *just*. Even the domestic police function has only a relative sort of legitimacy. Christians may participate neither in war nor in domestic policing, he thinks, nor may they have responsibility for such violence. This argument puts Yoder in an odd position. He recognizes the necessity of suppressing wrongdoers and agrees that God uses the state to suppress them. Even so, he insists, this does not make the police function *good*; in using it, God is merely pitting evil against evil, one sinful force against another:

> However able an infinite God may be to work at the same time through the sufferings of his believing disciples who return good for evil and through the wrathful violence of the authorities who punish evil with evil, such behavior is for humans not complementary but in disjunction. Divine providence can in its own

205. For the preceding series of quotations, see Yoder, *Politics of Jesus,* 204–5.

sovereign permissive way "use" an idolatrous Assyria (Isa. 10) or Rome. This takes place, however, without declaring that the destructive action by pagan powers which God thus "uses" is morally good or that participation in it is incumbent upon the covenant people.[206]

For governments that intend justice and observe the rule of law, this is a hard analogy. It is as though God were to say to the police, "Through your efforts I suppress wrongdoers, commend rightdoers, and uphold order so that my people can live a quiet and peaceable life.[207] Now go to perdition."

What about the Rest of the Bible?

Yoder holds that his position is compatible with the witness of Scripture in both Testaments. However, he reads Scripture differently than evangelicals do. If we ask, "Can a Christian who rejects all war reconcile his position with the Old Testament?" then the answer, Yoder admits, is no. However, he holds that this is the wrong question. An ancient Israelite would not have asked it; what would have impressed an Israelite in the stories of wars approved by God was not that God approves some wars but that "Israel was saved by the mighty deeds of God on their behalf."[208]

Presumably, this is an example of what Yoder means by a "post-critical" reading of Scripture, but there are two problems with it. In the first place, although the stories do make clear that Israel owed its miraculous preservation to God alone, they make equally clear that at certain times God chose war as his means. Yoder rightly places emphasis where the text does: "Even when Israel uses the sword . . . the victory is credited not to the prowess of the swordsmen or the wisdom of the generals, but to the help of YHWH."[209] But it would have been equally true had he written that "even though the victory is credited not to the prowess of the swordsman or to the wisdom of the generals but to the help of YHWH, at times YHWH requires that Israel

---

206. Ibid., 198.
207. See 1 Tim. 2:1–2; 1 Pet. 2:13–14.
208. Yoder, *Politics of Jesus*, 76.
209. Ibid., 77–78.

use the sword." In the second place, the decisive question is whether the Old Testament record is true. If it is false, then Yoder is right; it cannot tell us anything about the will of God but can only recount what ancient Israelites believed. But if the Old Testament is true, then even if it were conceded that the ancient Israelites did not draw all of its logical implications, nothing in this prevents *us* from drawing them. If God did in fact approve certain Old Testament wars, then the generalization that "war is always contrary to the will of God" is in fact destroyed. One might rescue Yoder's doctrine of obligatory renunciation of violence by arguing a difference in dispensation, whereby what God approved in the old covenant he rejected in the new. But this argument is not available to Yoder, because he is trying to make the case for the essential continuity of the biblical witness against recourse to force.

The most problematic New Testament text for Yoder's view about the renunciation of force is Romans 13:1–7. Paul here urges the followers of Christ to be subject to the higher powers because they are ordained by God; the ruler "does not bear the sword in vain," for "he is the servant of God to execute his wrath on the wrongdoer." Christian exegesis has long recognized that Paul cannot mean every sort of subjection, because in a fallen world, rulers may make unconscionable demands. For example, when Peter and the apostles were commanded to stop preaching about Christ, their reply to the authorities was, "We must obey God rather than men." Even so, Romans 13 seems to suppose a rather high view of the state. Yoder rejects this view. First, he examines the New Testament view of higher powers in general; then he proposes a sweeping reinterpretation of Romans 13 itself.

Drawing heavily on the work of Hendrikus Berkhof,[210] Yoder observes that the term *Powers* (*exousiai*) has a wide range, including moral, religious, intellectual, cosmological, and political structures and agents.[211] Yoder's attitude toward the Powers is strikingly ambivalent. On the one hand, he emphasizes that they "are not simply something limitlessly evil"; in fact, they are "part

---

210. Hendrikus Berkhof, *Christ and the Powers* (Scottdale, PA: Herald, 1962).
211. Yoder, *Politics of Jesus*, 137, 142–43.

of the good creation of God." On the other hand, he makes the extravagant claim that in a fallen world "we have no access to the good creation of God."[212] Taken at face value, this would mean either that we no longer experience creational structures such as marriage, family, conscience, knowledge, and so on or that even though we continue to experience these creational structures, we no longer have any experience whatsoever of the good in them. Both alternatives seem equally impossible.

To recover from this incredible overstatement, Yoder is forced to acknowledge that "the Powers, despite their fallenness, continue to exercise an ordering function." If they do, then it would seem that even under the conditions of the fall we do have some access to the good creation of God, however impaired this access may be. Yoder seems to approach this conclusion when he admits that the Powers remain "necessary to life and society." The problem is that they have "claimed the status of idols and have succeeded in making us serve them as if they were of absolute value," which seems to mean that the root problem lies not in the creational structures themselves but in their absolutization.[213]

That is certainly true. Unfortunately, no sooner does Yoder make this more reasonable statement than he veers back into extravagance. He speaks of the Powers as though they are now *essentially* manipulative. If their *effects* are not limitlessly evil, the reason lies solely in God's overriding providence, in his sovereign ability to turn all things to his purposes, even rebellion.[214] The possibility that provisions for the punishment of rebellion may *themselves* be built partly into the design of creation, through the discipline of natural consequences—"whatever a man sows, that he will also reap"—does not occur to Yoder. Nor does it occur to him that this might be acknowledged by the doctrine of natural law, which he too routinely associates with the absolutization of the Powers in their present rebellious condition. The underlying problem is that for Yoder the order of providence does not seem to include the continuation of God's providence for us in creation.

212. Ibid., 141.
213. Ibid., 141–42.
214. Ibid.

The meaning of the cross in all of this, Yoder says, is that "if then God is going to save his creatures in their humanity, the Powers cannot simply be destroyed or set aside or ignored. Their sovereignty must be broken. This is what Jesus did." On the cross, he "disarmed" the Powers.[215] But what does this mean? In particular, what does it means for the participation of Christians in statecraft? As Richard J. Mouw has pointed out, it was precisely the disarming of the Powers that led Yoder's source, Berkhof, to consider the possibility of a Christianization of the fallen creational structures, whereby "the Powers, instead of being ideological centers, are what God meant them to be: helps, instruments, giving shape and direction to the genuine life of man as child of God and as neighbor." In particular, "The state no longer serves its own interest and no longer enslaves man to the world view it propagates; it becomes simply a means of staving off chaos and ordering human relations in such a way that we can lead a quiet and stable life and follow God's call, unhampered by external hindrances."[216] I note in passing that the idea of redeemed creational structures as "helps" recalls the doctrine of subsidiarity discussed earlier, according to which the state should regard itself as a help to the *other* creational structures—a help to the helps, a servant to the servants of the children of God.

Yoder reverses Berkhof's emphasis. However God may make use of the Powers, for Yoder they remain essentially outside the order of redemption. At least at this point, it does not seem to enter his reasoning that redemption means the redemption *of creation.*

> For the creation waits with eager longing for the revealing of the sons of God; for the creation was subjected to futility, not of its own will but by the will of him who subjected it in hope; because the creation itself will be set free from its bondage to decay and obtain the glorious liberty of the children of God. We know that the whole creation has been groaning in travail together until now; and not only the creation, but we ourselves, who have the first fruits of the Spirit, groan inwardly as we wait for adoption

215. Ibid., 145–46.
216. Berkhof, *Christ and the Powers,* 49–50, quoted in Richard J. Mouw, *Politics and the Biblical Drama* (Grand Rapids: Eerdmans, 1976), 97–98.

as sons, the redemption of our bodies. For in this hope we were
saved.

                                                    Romans 8:19–24

The way Yoder frames the issue in Romans 13 itself is somewhat puzzling. As Yoder knows, most Christians today acknowledge the propriety of conscientious objection to military service
for those who believe they are called to it by God. Indeed, the
precedent for such exemptions is very old. For example, Thomas
Aquinas argues that bishops and clerics may not bear arms, not
because doing so is intrinsically wrong but because the duties
of the two pursuits cannot fittingly be combined in the same
person.[217] Yet rather than discussing the point that is actually
at issue—whether Christians *may* participate in state functions
such as policing and soldiering—Yoder takes as his thesis a point
that does not seem to be in dispute: whether they are *required*
to participate in those functions.[218]

Another diversion concerns the translation of Romans 13:1.
The verse reads as follows in the King James Version: "Let every
soul be subject unto the higher powers. For there is no power
but of God: the powers that be are *ordained* of God" (emphasis
added). Some other translations say "instituted by God." Yoder
complains, "God is not said to *create* or *institute* or *ordain* the
powers that be, but only to *order* them, to put them in order, sov-
ereignly to tell them where they belong, what is their place."[219] It
is true that God is not said to *create* the Powers in the particular
verse at hand, but if Yoder wishes to deny that God created them,
then he must contradict what he said earlier: "These structures
were created by God."[220] Once again we see his deep ambivalence
about the created order. As for the other two words, *institute* and

217. Thomas Aquinas, *Summa Theologica* I–II, Q. 40, Art. 2.
218. "Let me then put most precisely the challengeable claim of the tradition I
intend to challenge; it is that by virtue of the divine institution of government as
a part of God's good creation, its mandate to wield the sword and the Christian's
duty to obey the state combine to place upon the Christian a moral obligation to
support and participate in the state's legal killing (death penalty, war), despite
contrary duties which otherwise would seem to follow from Jesus' teaching or
example" (Yoder, *Politics of Jesus*, 194).
219. Ibid., 201.
220. Ibid., 142.

ordain, the distinction he is trying to make does not exist; as a glance at the OED confirms, to ordain or to institute *means* to put in order.[221] To say that the Powers are ordained or instituted by God is to say that God thinks it fit for humans to have government and has so arranged matters that they do.

If we pass by straw men and distractions, we do reach arguments bearing on whether Christians may participate in government. One such argument arises from Yoder's conviction that Romans 12 and 13 form a single literary unit and must be read together. Romans 12:19 contains the exhortation, "Beloved, never avenge yourselves, but leave it to the wrath of God; for it is written, 'Vengeance is mine, I will repay, says the Lord.'" However, 13:4 declares, "But if you do wrong, be afraid, for he [the ruler] does not bear the sword in vain; he is the servant of God to execute his wrath on the wrongdoer." This is where Yoder finds the plainest proof that the Christian cannot "bear the sword," for the ruler must do the same thing that the followers of Jesus are commanded to leave to God;[222] it seems that government rebels not incidentally but in the very act of carrying out the functions that define it. To be sure, the almighty One can turn even rebellion to his good purposes, but mere humans should not pretend to his prerogatives.

Surely this argument misses the point. What Christians are forbidden to do in 12:19 is to give place to *their own* wrath. Rulers, of course, often do sin in that way. Yet insofar as the ruler really does behave as "the servant of God," he acts not on his own but as a delegate; he expresses not his own wrath but the just wrath of God. That is the plain sense of the passage. Yoder, however, will have none of it. Turning his attention to 13:6, "For the same reason you also pay taxes, for the authorities are ministers of

221. The OED gives the first meaning of the English word *ordain* as "to put in order, arrange, make ready, prepare," and the first meaning of the English word *institute* as "to set up, establish, found, ordain; to introduce, bring into use or practice." Compare Strong's definition for the Greek word in question: "to arrange in an orderly manner, i.e., assign or dispose (to a certain position or lot)." In short, the same idea of putting in order is at the bottom of all three words.

222. "The authorities are recognized . . . as executing the particular function which the Christian was to leave to God. It is inconceivable that these two verses, using such similar language, should be meant to be read independently of one another. This makes it clear that the function exercised by government is not the function to be exercised by Christians" (Yoder, *Politics of Jesus,* 198).

God, attending to this very thing," he argues that the standard translations are wrong. In the Greek, the verse does not actually say "the authorities are" but "they are." The referent of "they" cannot be "the authorities," he says, because this requires the antecedent to be in verse 3—"For rulers are not a terror to good conduct, but to bad. Would you have no fear of him who is in authority? Then do what is good, and you will receive his approval." "That is rather far back to reach," Yoder says. For this and other reasons, he concludes that verse 6 does *not* say that the authorities are "ministers of God." The ministers of God are in fact Christians themselves, and what the verse really means is that "Christians pay taxes because Christians also, as ministers of God, devote themselves to the end that the good be approved and evil reprimanded."[223] This seems an enormous stretch, but because I am not a scholar of Koine Greek, I am willing to let it pass; Yoder may have his interpretation of verse 6. It does not matter. The fact remains that the one who holds authority is called a minister of God in verse 3, and the whole discussion of verse 6 is therefore useless to establish his point.

Christians and Revolution

Yoder points out that a certain strain in Reformed thinking has tended to regard the exhortation of Romans 13:1, "Let every soul be subject," as applying only to governments that fulfill the purposes for which government is ordained: "As long as a given government lives up to a certain minimum set of requirements, then that government may properly claim the sanction of divine institution. If, however, a government fails adequately to fulfill the functions divinely assigned to it, it loses its authority."[224] Yoder's main objection to this view is that "the conception of a 'state properly so called,' in the name of which one would reject and seek to overthrow the state which exists empirically, is totally absent in the passage. In the social context of the Jewish Christians in Rome, the whole point of the passage was to take out of their minds any concept of rebellion against or even

223. Ibid., 207.
224. Ibid., 199.

emotional rejection of this corrupt pagan government."[225] Yoder has raised a cogent point here, one to which Reformed thinkers do not pay sufficient attention. Francis Schaeffer, for example, certainly does not.

We may elaborate the point as follows. In earlier Christian thinking, Christians may certainly seek to depose particular unjust rulers, but they must do so through regular constitutional channels.[226] Suppose that the king has become a tyrant. (By the way, the logic is essentially the same if, instead of a king, we think of a president or a parliament or a supreme court.) If the king is normally appointed by the senate, then the senate may depose him; if he is appointed by the assembly of the people, then the assembly may depose him. But suppose that the king protects his power by preventing the relevant body from convening. In this case, recourse may be had to the higher authority of the empire. (If it helps us to say "federal union" rather than "empire," we may do that too.)[227] But suppose the empire does not help. Then Christians must appeal to the highest authority, God himself, through prayer; no other means of deposing unjust rulers respects the *principle* of respect for legitimate authority affirmed by Romans 13. Another way to frame the argument is to ask whether revolution can be justified in the same way as just war. The answer seems to be no, for one of the criteria of just war theory is that war may be initiated only by competent public authority. Insofar as a revolution is against the authority itself, the criterion cannot be satisfied.

The Reformers *radicalized* the concept of competent public authority by pointing out that lower magistrates too belong to the government. Hence, *they* may initiate revolution. This move was deeply questionable. Romans 13 commands that every soul be subject to the *higher* powers; it offers no basis for the argument that the higher powers may be subjected to the lower. At best, one can argue that in a constitutionally divided government, like

225. Ibid., 200.

226. Though Yoder would be loath to acknowledge him as an ally, this is the view of Thomas Aquinas in his treatise *On Kingship*.

227. Our own federal union recognizes the principle of appeal to a superior authority against a tyrant in Art. IV, Sec. 4 of the federal Constitution: "The United States shall guarantee to every State in this Union a Republican Form of Government."

ours, powers can oppose powers of equal rank. Once we allow lower magistrates to initiate revolution, further radicalization of the concept of competent public authority swiftly follows. In a republic, can't the citizens be considered magistrates? Indeed, why should we restrict this principle to republics? John Locke held that the authentic higher power in *every* state is the majority of the citizens themselves—so *they* may initiate a revolution. As Locke himself observed, the majority is normally reluctant to revolt, but it did not take long to find a way around this obstacle either. Thomas Paine held that revolutionaries must sometimes *anticipate* the consent of the majority—toppling the government on the assumption that once the deed is done, the majority will surely approve.[228] By this reasoning, revolution becomes all but self-justifying, and any pretense of Christian discipleship has long since been left behind.

However, Yoder's second objection to the Reformers' doctrine of legitimacy is far less cogent. "Who is to judge," he asks, "how bad a government can be and still be good? How much deviation from the norm is justifiable on the grounds of human frailty? At what point is a government disqualified?"[229] Seemingly regarding such questions as unanswerable, he concludes that Christians must stop making distinctions among governments: They must "challenge the integral distinction between good governments, which Christians should bless, and bad ones against which they should rebel. They should rather rebel against all and be subordinate to all, for 'subordination' is itself the Christian form of rebellion. It is the way we share in God's patience with a system we basically reject."[230]

The astonishing thing about this objection is that Yoder makes distinctions himself—if not among governments themselves, then certainly among the things that governments do and the

228. "It is also certain that in the commencement of a revolution, the revolutionary party permit to themselves a discretionary exercise of power regulated more by circumstances than by principle, which, were the practice to continue, liberty would never be established, or if established would soon be overthrown. It is never to be expected in a revolution that every man is to change his opinion at the same moment" (Thomas Paine, *Dissertations on the First Principles of Government* [1795]).

229. Yoder, *Politics of Jesus*, 200.

230. Ibid., 200n10.

demands that governments make. The same kinds of difficult questions can be asked about his own doctrine of revolutionary subordination. "The Christian who accepts subjection to government retains his moral independence and judgment," he says, for "the authority of government is not self-justifying. Whatever government exists is ordered by God; but the text does not say that whatever the government does or asks of its citizens is good."[231] Yes, but who is to say what the *standards* for this independent judgment should be? How bad can the government's demands become before a citizen must refuse? At what point is compliance ruled out?

In another place he says, "Neither should we be understood as stating here an extreme application of some particularly radical ethical commitment, such as the argument that everything having to do with the structure of this world is impure or unworthy for the Christian because of the coercion or violence that governs society. There may well be certain circumstances in which the Christian, in order to be morally faithful, would refuse certain functions within society. Every ethical system draws some kinds of lines."[232] Yes, but who is to judge where the line should be drawn? How impure or unworthy can a social function be and yet be tolerable? At what point must a Christian withdraw?

In still another place, Yoder complains that "the doctrine of the 'just war' is an effort to extend into the realm of war the logic of the limited violence of police authority—but not a very successful one. There is some logic to the 'just war' pattern of thought but very little realism."[233] But who is to say *when* an effort to extend the logic of one thing to another is unsuccessful? How unsuccessful can it be and still be a relative success? At what point are we entitled to declare the theory a total loss?

I have commented on the Jekyll and Hyde character of Yoder's prose, and in the passages just quoted, we are dealing with the polemical Yoder. But the reasonable Yoder must be given his say. The reasonable Yoder admits that a theory does

231. Ibid., 205.
232. Ibid., 154.
233. Ibid., 204.

not become wrong just because it faces hard questions, and he concedes that his own theory faces hard questions too. One of Yoder's shorter works provides a luminous and penetrating example by showing that the competing theories of just war and nonviolent action are more closely related than readers of *The Politics of Jesus* might expect—and even that they can learn from each other.

> The fact that NV [nonviolent] conflict seeks to shed no blood does not exempt its combatants from needing to think about restraint, in ways that bear some analogy to JW [just war] criteria. The rupture of the normal social flow by a boycott or by a mass gathering, a strike or a march, should be subject to considerations of last resort. . . . To work through decisions of these kinds there needs to be some kind of "legitimate authority," qualified to lead and whose leadership is accepted. That qualification cannot have the shape of the "legitimacy" of government in states; therefore some other mode of validation is needed. Merely claiming ideological correctness (i.e., being on the side of the "people" or the "poor" or "the future") is not enough. . . . For such a decision about [nonviolent] "war aims" and last resort by some "authority" to be accountable, there needs to be as well some definition of the "people" in whose name the conflict proceeds. It cannot be, as is the case for war, the entire nation-state. . . . The use of nonviolence in settings of great conflict runs (knowingly, accountably) the risk of provoking counter-violence. . . . Thereby the classical JW considerations of proportion must arise.[234]

The reasonable Yoder points out in this passage that nonviolent action requires exacting discernment of much the same kind that just war requires. We might add that just war requires heroic restraint of much the same kind that nonviolent action does. The verdict between the two theories cannot be rendered by a simple gesturing toward the cross.

234. John Howard Yoder, "'Just War' and 'Non-Violence': Disjunction or Dialogue?" (paper presented at the World Conference on Violence and Coexistence, Montreal, July 1992). Published in Venant Cauchy, ed., *Proceedings of the International Association for Scientific Exchange on Violence and Human Co-existence, Second World Conference, 13–17 July 1992*, vol. 2 (Montreal: Editions Montmorency, 1995), 171–78.

Revolutionary Subordination and the Natural Law

At several points I have alluded to Yoder's views of creational ordinances, or natural law. The question of natural law comes to a head in his discussion of the New Testament "household codes," sometimes called *Haustafeln* after the term used by German scholars. A good example is provided by Ephesians 5:21–6:9. Beginning with the exhortation to "be subject to one another out of reverence for Christ," the passage goes on to urge wives to be subject to their husbands as to the Lord, husbands to love their wives as Christ loved the church and gave himself up for her, children to obey their parents, fathers to use proper discipline without provoking their children to anger, slaves to render service to their masters with a good will, and masters to "do the same to them" without threatening, because Christ, the master of all, has no partiality.

Liberal biblical scholars see in these household codes an onerous ratification of the oppressive status quo, taken over whole hog from late Stoicism. The burden of Yoder's argument is that they neither borrow from Stoicism nor endorse the status quo. Their literary antecedent is actually Old Testament apodictic law (the broad "Thou shalts" and "Thou shalt nots"), and what they really express is revolutionary subordination. This is where he provides the most careful explanation of the idea—along the way firing blasts against natural law tradition, which he considers the real inheritor of oppressive Stoic conventionalism.[235]

235. Oddly, in other places, Yoder makes the opposite complaint: not that natural law is conventionalist but that it "supposes that we can know clearly a pattern of ideal order which it is our assignment to impose on our society" (Yoder, *Christian Witness to the State*, 33). This is a common (but serious) misunderstanding, for the mainstream of Christian natural law thinking has demanded a number of qualifications to the efforts of the state to "make men good." First, the state should not try to use law as an instrument for making people right with God; government should be friendly and cooperative toward the church but should not try to take its place. Second, lawmakers should forbear from passing laws about the invisible movements of the heart; for example, the state may command an act, but it should not command an attitude or a belief. Third, the state should not try to forbid every act of vice; judgment must be exercised. One reason is that excessively strict laws tend to wipe out good things as well as bad ones. Another is that they provoke some people to break out into even greater crimes. Finally, neither should the state attempt to command every act

The differences between Stoic ethical codes and the household codes are profound. While Stoic codes merely *mention* persons of lower rank, the household codes actually address them. Moreover, the household codes always list social roles in pairs—husband and wife, parent and child, master and slave. Although the duties of the two persons in each pair are not identical, nevertheless they are reciprocal, based on love or respect of each for the other. Nothing like this appears in Stoic teaching, where the main concern is not that I make myself a servant, as Christ did, but that I maintain my dignity. In all these points and in others, Yoder is quite right.

Nonetheless, there is a problem. The way he thinks of the difference is that the Stoics are concerned with living up to their nature, while the New Testament writers are concerned with living up to the relationship. While this is a reasonable way to put it in the context of Stoic thinking about nature, in the context of *Christian* thinking about nature, it is profoundly misleading. A Christian recognizes that *certain* relationships—for example, the marital and the parental—are themselves part of the order of creation, part of "nature." They were devised for us, and we were designed for them. So while the New Testament emphasis on living up to these relationships is foreign to Stoicism, it is quite at home in Christian natural law thinking. The reason Yoder takes natural law thinking *as such* to be conventionalist is that he is not aware of this distinction.

There is a deeper problem. A Christian natural law thinker distinguishes the institutions of marriage and family from the institution of slavery. Marriage and family *as such* belong to the order of creation; by contrast, in an unfallen world, slavery would not have existed. The anomalousness of slavery is clear throughout the Bible, from the affirmation of the *imago Dei*, to the jubilee provisions for periodic liberation, to Paul's tender letter to Philemon about Philemon's runaway slave Onesimus, whom Paul has been sheltering and has adopted as his son. It follows from this fact that if the New Testament writers urge mutual (though asymmetrical)[236] submission in all three of the

---

of virtue, because the business of law is the common good, not the private good. See Aquinas, *Summa Theologica* I–II, Q. 91, Art. 4; Q. 96, Arts. 2–3.

236. "It should be noted that the point of Gal. 3:28 is not *sameness*, in the sense of overruling all variety of roles and rights, but unity. . . . Equality of *worth*

relationships just mentioned, the reasons for urging it cannot be entirely the same in all three cases. In marriage and family, we are obeying the ordinance of Christ, through whom and for whom all things were created[237]—*and* we are following the example of Christ, who, though he was in the form of God, did not count equality with God a thing to be grasped, but emptied himself, taking the form of a servant.[238] In slavery, we are still following Christ's example, but there is no specific creational ordinance to follow; slavery was not created.[239]

Yoder does not make this distinction. He treats marriage, family, and slavery alike, as conventions of the particular society to which first-century Christians belonged. Consequently, he understands Christians as subordinating themselves in exactly the same spirit within all three of these institutions. To be sure, this is a revolutionary and liberating spirit, because in all three cases, they are following the example of Christ. But the idea of marriage and family as creation ordinances is just not there—at least not at this point in Yoder's thought.

This leads to yet another problem. In the case of marriage and family, the way Yoder conceives the spirit of this subordination is a little *too* revolutionary. His overbroad language about "the liberation of the Christian from 'the way things are'" lumps together the aspects of "the way things are" that result from creation and the aspects of "the way things are" that result from the fall. By doing so, it *improperly* relativizes institutions such as marriage and family in the same way that it *properly* relativizes slavery. To be sure, some aspects of marriage and family deserve to be relativized. No matter which society's conventions we have in mind, not every conventional feature of these institutions belongs to the order of creation. That is why the household codes admonish *mutual* (though asymmetrical) submission between husbands and wives rather than the one-sided Tarzan and Jane

---

is not identity of *role*. To make of Gal. 3:28 a 'modern' statement on women's liberation, from which one can then look down on the rest of Paul's thoughts, not only misplaces this text logically . . . ; it also misreads the text itself" (Yoder, *Politics of Jesus*, 174n26).

237. See Col. 1:16–17 (compare John 1:3, 10; 1 Cor. 8:6).

238. See Phil. 2:5–8.

239. There is of course the *general* creational ordinance of love for the neighbor.

submission demanded in most of the ancient world. But to imply that marriage and family *as such* deserve to be relativized goes too far. Perhaps Yoder does not mean to relativize the creational structures, but he certainly gives that impression.

This impression is strengthened by certain overbroad remarks about "maximizing freedom."[240] Yoder observes that, according to the New Testament, a slave who can become free should do so, a forsaken woman whose husband dies is free to remarry, and a freed man must not become a slave again. From these instances he concludes, "Thus the Christian is called to view social status from the perspective of maximizing freedom." But this very up-to-date conclusion does not follow, for the cases are sharply different. Freed men are *forbidden* to take on the status of slaves, and slaves are encouraged to become free. By contrast, men and women are *permitted* to enter the status of spouses, and spouses are forbidden to divorce. Here again Yoder fails to recognize the scriptural distinction between marriage as an aspect of creation and slavery as a consequence of the fall.[241] Ironically, this error mirrors the mistake of liberal Protestant ethicists whom Yoder criticizes elsewhere: They insulate themselves from the force of Christ's example, he says, but he insulates himself from the force of Christ's creation.[242] These two must not be separated, for the incarnate exemplar is also the Lord of creation.

240. It is also strengthened by the undiscriminating praise he offers for the sundry liberation theologies in some of his other works. "The biblical appeal of the contemporary theologies of liberation has once more given occasion to fulfill the promise of John Robinson that 'the Lord has yet much more light and truth to break forth from his holy word.' It is an affirmation and not, as many conservative evangelicals have reflexively assumed, a questioning of biblical authority when the language of liberation and empowerment prove fruitful in understanding further dimensions of what salvation always meant according to the scriptural witness, even though we had not previously been pushed to see it that clearly" (John Howard Yoder, in Robert K. Johnston, ed., *The Use of the Bible in Theology: Evangelical Options* [Atlanta: John Knox, 1984], chap. 6, http://www .religion-online.org/cgi-bin/relsearchd.dll/showarticle?item_id=12).

241. Yoder, *Politics of Jesus*, 182.

242. Liberal theologians posit a "radical discontinuity between God and humanity, between the world of God and human values," the impact of which is to "relativize all human values" (ibid., 7). Other thinkers "relativize Jesus in the name of 'revelation.'" Astonishingly, Yoder includes in the latter category all ethicists who appeal to the order of creation: "This source of ethical substance . . . may well be spoken of in terms of the order created by God the Father" (ibid.,

Interestingly, although Yoder fails to distinguish the relationships of husband and wife and of parent and child from the relationship of master and slave, he makes a point of distinguishing all three from the relationship of ruler to subject. This brings us back to politics.

> After the invitation to wives we saw that the *Haustafeln* addressed a similar and immensely more novel call to husbands to love their wives; after calling slaves to be subject, the early Christian moralists called upon the masters to be equally respectful; after calling children to remain subordinate to parents, the admonition was turned about and addressed to parents as well.[243] When, however, the call to subordination is addressed to the Christian in his status as a political subject, then in these texts the exhortation is not reversed. There is no invitation to the king to conceive of himself as a public servant.[244]

Yoder dismisses the simplest explanation for this difference—that "as a matter of course, the apostolic preachers and authors recognized that there were no kings in their audiences." Instead, he suggests another: "Or was it that . . . Jesus had instructed his disciples specifically to reject governmental domination over others as unworthy of the disciple's calling of servanthood?" The reader of this passage cannot help feeling that once again Yoder is slighting certain facts in order to pass others more easily through his interpretive filter. In the first place, we have no record

---

8n13). Probably the reason Yoder refers to the Father rather than to the Son is that he is thinking of the "distributive" understanding of the Trinity proposed by H. Richard Niebuhr, to which he refers later: "One should not make Jesus too important for ethics, Niebuhr argued, since God the Father would call for a different (perhaps more institutionally conservative) social ethic, based on an understanding of creation or providence whose content is derived otherwise than from Jesus. God the Spirit might guide us toward another, also different ethic, based on the further revelations received since Pentecost, during the history of the Church" (ibid., 17). Unfortunately, Niebuhr is anything but the exemplar of Christian natural law thinking that Yoder makes him.

243. The last statement is misleading in its implication that the reciprocity between parents and children is symmetrical. In fact, the mode of submission on each side is quite different. In Eph. 6:1–4, for example, children are commanded to obey their parents; fathers are given the negative command not to provoke their children to wrath and the positive command to bring them up in the discipline and instruction of the Lord. (Compare Col. 3:20–21.)

244. Yoder, *Politics of Jesus*, 183.

that Jesus declared public office inconsistent with discipleship. In the second, although the household codes do not mention reciprocity between rulers and subjects, *Jesus does*:

> But Jesus called them to him and said, "You know that the rulers of the Gentiles lord it over them, and their great men exercise authority over them. It shall not be so among you; but whoever would be great among you must be your servant, and whoever would be first among you must be your slave; even as the Son of man came not to be served but to serve, and to give his life as a ransom for many."
>
> Matthew 20:25–28

The commonsense way to understand Christ's admonition is like this: (1) Just as ordinary people must submit to those who hold authority, so, in another sense, authorities should regard themselves as servants of those over whom they are placed. (2) Gentile rulers violate this norm. Christians must take care not to follow their example.

But remember that Yoder's view of Jesus' meaning is derived "post-critically," not so much from what Jesus *said* as from the way Yoder views the narrative outline of what Jesus *did*. Much less straightforward, Yoder's view of Christ's admonition seems to be more like this: (1) *Within the community of faith*, just as ordinary believers must submit to those who hold spiritual authority, so, in another sense, these authorities should regard themselves as servants of those over whom they are placed. (2) Although Gentile rulers do not observe this norm, they cannot be said to violate it, because *it is simply not intended for them*.

The commonsense interpretation does not forbid Christian participation in civic authority. Yoder's does.

This Yoderian view might be more compelling if at any place in Scripture the people of God were prohibited from holding high office in the state. What we find is quite different. Joseph was prime minister under Pharaoh; Daniel held high office under both Nebuchadnezzar and Darius. Rather than condemning them, Scripture holds them up as models of how to behave under pressure.[245] It does not follow from this that believers may conscientiously participate in *all* governments, but it certainly follows

245. See Gen. 41:39–44; Dan. 2:48–49; 6.

that they may participate in some. The mark of purity was not that Joseph and Daniel held themselves apart from the stain of government but that they held themselves apart from the stain of sin. Even in exile from our true Commonwealth, we may participate in the commonwealths of earth.

Concluding Observations

> Let us now praise famous men, and our fathers in their generations. The Lord apportioned to them great glory, His majesty from the beginning. There were those who ruled in their kingdoms, and were men renowned for their power, giving counsel by their understanding, and proclaiming prophecies; leaders of the people in their deliberations and in understanding of learning for the people, wise in their words of instruction. . . . All these were honored in their generations, and were the glory of their times. There are some of them who have left a name, so that men declare their praise. And there are some who have no memorial, who have perished as though they had not lived; they have become as though they had not been born, and so have their children after them. But these were men of mercy, whose righteous deeds have not been forgotten.[246]

We may be grateful to the evangelical political thinkers who have gone before us, grateful because they have given eloquent voice to profound concerns that have no place at all in secular political theory. Secularism knows nothing of grace or redemption; it has difficulty speaking of evil; it denies the reality of sin. The heights and the depths are alike unknown to it, and so man is unknown to it. However imperfect evangelical thought may be, it always remembers both the definition of man and his situation: the image of God, now fallen, but ever sought by his Maker.

May it not seem thankless to observe that, amid all these graces, serious problems appear in the political reflection of each of the four pioneers just studied. Moreover, these problems bear a certain similarity, despite the great differences among Carl F. H. Henry, Abraham Kuyper, and Francis Schaeffer, and despite the even greater ones between these three and John Howard Yoder.

246. Sirach 44:1–4, 7–10. Sirach is one of the books called by most Protestants "Apocrypha" and by Roman Catholics "Deuterocanonical."

All four thinkers are ambivalent about the enduring structures of creation and about the reality of general revelation. Although Henry vigorously affirms general revelation, he undermines it just as vigorously. Although Kuyper unfolds his theory mainly from the order observable in creation, he insists on hiding this fact from himself, regarding his theory of creational spheres as a direct inference from Scripture. Although Schaeffer acknowledges the importance of general revelation, he makes little use of any part of it except the principle of noncontradiction. No sooner does Yoder affirm God's good creation than he declares that we have no access to it.

All four thinkers are ambivalent about the ordained work of the state. Although Henry thinks he is proposing an approach to political activism, he just as often sounds as though he is proposing an alternative to it: Just convert everyone. Kuyper calls man a political animal, but at the same time he insists that the state is "something unnatural." Schaeffer recognizes the necessity for political authority yet regards it primarily as a response to human sin. Although Yoder acknowledges that the state is one of God's good creations, he views it as *essentially* unjust, an evil to be pitted by God's overriding providence against other evils.

I have presented abundant evidence that all four slip into projective accommodation, using inflationary strategies to read into Scripture more than what it contains. And it should by now be overwhelmingly clear that none of the four presents an adequate orienting doctrine, an adequate practical doctrine, or an adequate cultural apologetic.

These conclusions may seem harsh, and to many evangelicals, they will be unwelcome. In a fallen world, however, Christian minds cannot afford the luxury of lax reflection. This becomes more and more clear in our own secular culture, which seems increasingly determined not to drift into shadow but to accelerate into the abyss. We must understand the world and our responsibilities toward it, but we must understand these things precisely. Whatever genuine insight can be found in the words of the four thinkers just discussed should be cherished, but we must also be honest about their weaknesses.

If we mend our careless ways, perhaps we will become more sure-footed and sensible in our engagement with the public square. At least we may learn to speak to the people we find in it.

God willing, we may learn to bring up from beneath those truths of general revelation that they cannot fail to know but can all too easily push down. We may even learn to whet that inexplicable longing that can ultimately be satisfied only by Christ himself.

But if we *fail* to mend our carelessness, let us not be deceived: We will not remain where we are now. As we bludgeon our non-believing neighbors with proof-texts that they cannot comprehend, they will find us less and less intelligible. All that the centuries of faith have gained for our culture will be lost. Not only will the culture lose its memory of Christian truth, but it will even lose its grip on the sub-Christian verities.

I do not think God would desert us in such straits, but he chastens those whom he loves. At last, perhaps, from adversity itself, we would learn how important it is to think clearly and to use every bit of revelation vouchsafed to us, general as well as special. As G. K. Chesterton writes of that possible future:

> The great march of mental destruction will go on. Everything will be denied. Everything will become a creed. It is a reasonable position to deny the stones in the street; it will be a religious dogma to assert them. It is a rational thesis that we are all in a dream; it will be a mystical sanity to say that we are all awake. Fires will be kindled to testify that two and two make four. Swords will be drawn to prove that leaves are green in summer. We shall be left defending, not only the incredible virtues and sanities of mental life, but something more incredible still, this huge impossible universe which stares us in the face. We shall fight for visible prodigies as if they were invisible. We shall look on the impossible grass and the skies with a strange courage. We shall be of those who have seen and yet have believed.[247]

Still, it would be better to learn wisdom by a discipline other than adversity. In the words of Thomas Aquinas, may the God of lights give us grace "to desire ardently the things that please him, to investigate them prudently, to understand them truly, and to fulfill them perfectly, for the praise and glory of his name."[248]

---

247. G. K. Chesterton, *Heretics* (New York: John Lane, 1905), 304–5 (chap. 20).

248. "Ante Studium," the prayer of Thomas Aquinas before study.

3

Carl F. H. Henry on Civic Life

David L. Weeks

The contention made by J. Budziszewski in chapter 1 that evangelicals "have never developed a clear, cohesive, and Christian view of what politics is all about" may seem an affront to the late Carl F. H. Henry, given his lifelong attention to the topic. It is not. My assignment is to ensure that the contention does not preclude Henry from receiving his due, for few evangelicals have addressed political life with his depth, persistence, and passion.

While it is fair to say that Carl Henry's political thought has not been comprehensive, I dare say that the same is true of everyone who broaches the topic. It is true in Henry's case in part because, like the other three figures Budziszewski discusses (Kuyper, Schaeffer, and Yoder), Henry is a theologian with a theological outlook on a theological agenda. None of the four is a political philosopher, and, with the exception of Kuyper, they were not politicians. This is yet another reminder that the evangelical community is a religious community that looks to religious authorities for guidance on many matters, even those that are not expressly religious. Henry's lifelong theological agenda was the defense of propositional revelation, an agenda that affected all he wrote, even his political thought.

Budziszewski characterizes Henry as one of the "uncles" of the evangelical movement; I grant him a more direct genealogical designation in regard to social ethics: grandfather. Identifying the progenitor of a movement as multifaceted as modern evangelicalism is a dicey endeavor, but I believe an argument can be made that Henry's writings provide the theological and philosophical framework that shapes much of current evangelical political thought.

The Uneasy Conscience

Henry's leadership began when, as a young theologian, he published *The Uneasy Conscience of Modern Fundamentalism* in 1947.[1] In it, Henry argues that fundamentalists had forsaken the biblical mandate to be the salt and light of the world and that their "uneasy conscience" would be salved only by a rebirth of "apostolic passion."[2] Although initially the book did not attract much attention, its long-term impact was great.[3] The book launched a sustained debate and a profound change of heart within evangelical circles, particularly among the leaders of the movement. The late James Montgomery Boice, popular evangeli-

1. After being out of print for decades, this important work has been re-released. Carl F. H. Henry, *The Uneasy Conscience of Modern Fundamentalism* (1947; repr., Grand Rapids: Eerdmans, 2003).

2. "A Christianity without a passion to turn the world upside down is not reflective of apostolic Christianity" (ibid., 17). Introductions to Henry's early work include Augustus Cerillo Jr. and Murray W. Dempster, "Carl F. H. Henry's Early Apologetic for an Evangelical Social Ethic, 1942–1956," *Journal of the Evangelical Theological Society* 34, no. 3 (September 1991): 365–79; and Robert Booth Fowler, "Carl Henry: Pioneering Moderate," in *A New Engagement: Evangelical Political Thought, 1966–1976* (Grand Rapids: Eerdmans, 1982), 77–93.

3. See George Marsden, "The Way We Were and Are," *Books and Culture*, November/December 1997, 19; and Robert Linder, "The Resurgence of Evangelical Social Concern," in *The Evangelicals: What They Believe, Who They Are, Where They Are Changing*, ed. David Wells and John Woodbridge (Nashville: Abingdon, 1975), 221.

cal author and longtime pastor at Philadelphia's Tenth Presbyterian Church, wrote, "When I went to work at *Christianity Today* eighteen years after the publication of *The Uneasy Conscience* we still talked about it a lot. . . . [It] expressed what many of us were sensing at that time: that evangelicals had been avoiding the great social issues of the day."[4] Henry's little book became the "manifesto" of the burgeoning evangelical movement.[5]

The impact of *Uneasy Conscience* might have been much less had it not been for the timely launch of *Christianity Today* in the mid-1950s. When Billy Graham tapped Henry for the editorship of this nascent publication, he provided Henry with a platform that would greatly extend his influence. The two men had high hopes for *Christianity Today*; they aspired to dethrone the *Christian Century* as the most significant voice of American Christianity. Targeting clergymen, educators, and seminarians, Henry and Graham compiled an impressive cast of contributors, making the magazine "the prime agent in demarcating, informing, and providing morale" for the evangelical movement.[6] In those early days, *Christianity Today* was a window frame, delineating an entire movement, whereas today the magazine is more like a windowpane through which we see what is happening in the movement.

The first issue of *Christianity Today,* sent to 285,000 potential subscribers, notified America that evangelicals would no longer ignore intellectual or public life. Henry succeeded admirably in making civic engagement a persistent theme; during his twelve-year tenure, nearly 40 percent of the editorials were political.[7] Quite simply, in the words of Robert Linder, Henry "made *Christianity Today* the most formative influence on social ethics in the evangelical world."[8]

4. James Montgomery Boice, "On My Mind: Our All-Too-Easy Conscience," *Modern Reformation* 7 (September/October 1998): 44.

5. The oft-repeated designation "manifesto" was initially used in Dirk Jellema, "Ethics," in *Contemporary Evangelical Thought*, ed. Carl F. H. Henry (Great Neck, NY: Channel Press, 1957), 130.

6. Martin E. Marty, "The Marks and Misses of a Magazine," *Christianity Today*, July 17, 1981, 48–51, 58.

7. J. David Fairbanks, "The Politics of *Christianity Today*: 1956–1986," in *Contemporary Evangelical Political Involvement: An Analysis and Assessment*, ed. Corwin E. Smidt (Washington, DC: University Press of America, 1989), 32.

8. Linder, "Resurgence of Evangelical Social Concern," 221.

The next generation of evangelicals, convinced that political engagement was essential, embraced the challenge of returning to the public arena. The most visible indicator that Henry's work bore fruit is the Religious Right, although evangelical activists cover the entire political spectrum. Henry's "radical" call for political engagement has been answered.

Despite this achievement, Henry never claimed to have constructed a comprehensive political philosophy, though he wanted to do so. After publishing *Christian Personal Ethics* in 1957, he intended to write a volume on social ethics, but his editorial responsibilities at *Christianity Today* were too demanding. Instead, he issued a compilation of lectures delivered at Fuller Theological Seminary, *Aspects of Christian Social Ethics,* in which he says that "a fundamental analysis of politics from a Christian point of view lies outside the scope of this study, but it remains one of the urgent tasks of our age."[9] In the ensuing years, Henry continued to address political life in essays and speeches, many of which are reprinted in his books.[10] Because no one produced the systematic treatment he had hoped to write, evangelicals, he believed, remain "devoid of a comprehensive political philosophy"; their political thought remains simplistic, fragmentary, and reactionary.[11]

Nonetheless, Henry's political thought may be his most lasting contribution to evangelicalism. At many seminaries, the contemporary passion for narrative theology has superceded interest in Henry's more traditional theological approach. In the political

9. Carl F. H. Henry, *Aspects of Christian Social Ethics,* Payton Lectures at Fuller Theological Seminary (1964; repr., Grand Rapids: Baker, 1980), 77. As late as the 1970s, Henry was hoping to write a major work on Christian social ethics. However, in a personal letter dated June 1, 1988, he noted regretfully that he had given up his intention to write such a book.

10. For example, see *The God Who Shows Himself* (Waco: Word, 1966); *Evangelicals at the Brink of Crisis* (Waco: Word, 1967); *Faith at the Frontiers* (Chicago: Moody, 1969); *A Plea for Evangelical Demonstration* (Grand Rapids: Baker, 1971); *The Christian Mindset in a Secular Society* (Portland, OR: Multnomah, 1984); *Christian Countermoves in a Decadent Culture* (Portland, OR: Multnomah, 1986); *Twilight of a Great Civilization* (Westchester, IL: Crossway, 1988); and *Has Democracy Had Its Day?* (Nashville: ERLC Publications, 1996). One should also read relevant portions of Henry's magnum opus, *God, Revelation, and Authority,* 6 vols. (Waco: Word, 1976–82).

11. See Henry, *God, Revelation, and Authority,* 6:440; and idem, "The Uneasy Conscience Revisited," *Theology, News, and Notes,* December 1987, 6.

realm, however, we are still talking about Henry's contributions, and in some respects, only now are we addressing the implications of his work. Perhaps this brief summary of Henry's political thought, following the contours of Budziszewski's essay, will aid that process.

Henry's "Orienting Doctrine"

Budziszewski provides a threefold heuristic device for assessing evangelical political thought. An adequate political theory, he says, consists of (1) "an *orienting doctrine,* or guide to thought, explaining the place of government in the world"; (2) "a *practical doctrine,* or guide to action, explaining . . . how Christians should conduct themselves in the civic realm"; and (3) "a *cultural apologetic,* or guide to persuasion, explaining how to go about making the specific proposals of those who share the other two elements plausible to those who don't."[12] In the end, Budziszewski judges evangelicals deficient on all three accounts. Is this a fair assessment of Henry? Yes and no.

Like most other Christian political thinkers, Henry brackets his thoughtful orienting doctrine ("explaining the place of government in the world") with a reminder of God's sovereignty. With that sovereignty as his most basic political principle, Henry insists that all earthly authority, including that of the state, is derivative.[13] Nonetheless, he holds a high view of civil author-

12. My only reservation about this useful threefold formulation is that it might be misinterpreted to mean that these are the only important questions of political philosophy. Helpful introductory books used in college classrooms offer alternative formulations of the basic questions in the field: See Glenn Tinder, *Political Thinking: The Perennial Questions,* 6th ed. (Reading, MA: Addison-Wesley, 1997); Judith Best, *The Mainstream of Western Political Thought* (Lanham, MD: Rowman & Littlefield, 1997); and Larry Arnhart, *Political Questions: Political Philosophy from Plato to Rawls,* 3rd ed. (Long Grove, IL: Waveland, 2002).

13. "The implications of divine sovereignty . . . are far reaching. Take, for example, the political realm. . . . According to the Bible the state exists within God's providential will and has limited authority. When totalitarian states presume to define human rights and duties at will they illicitly claim divine prerogatives. The state's biblically stated role is to maintain God-ordained justice, not to devise or manipulate it" (Carl F. H. Henry, "The God of Bible and Moral Foundations," in *The Christian Vision: Man and Morality,* ed. Thomas J. Burke [Hillsdale, MI: Hillsdale College Press, 1986], 10).

ity: It is a providential gift from God, serving to promote justice and to preserve order.[14] Its most difficult and important task is to particularize the general principles of justice in formulating statutory law. When this is done properly, governments preserve justice without defining it.

What is this justice that civil authorities promote? Henry's understanding is clarified by Aristotle's distinction in the *Nicomachean Ethics* between universal justice and partial justice. Universal justice, Aristotle says, means "complete virtue or excellence," which extends beyond any legal requirement to include conduct in every realm of life. Partial justice, on the other hand, is twofold. First, it demands that the honor and wealth a city bestows upon its citizens should be distributed in relation to their contribution to the welfare of the whole: Partial justice demands proportionality. Second, partial justice demands exact equality in exchanges between individual citizens: Partial justice also requires parity.[15]

Henry uses a similar distinction in explaining the role of civil authority. Governments are neither able nor authorized to promote *universal* justice, in the sense of complete virtue or righteousness, a designation Henry applies only to those persons who have experienced "forgiveness of sins and new life in Christ." Rather, governments are to promote "relative" or "social" justice, meaning those standards that regulate conduct among individuals.[16] Justice in this sense requires fairness and impartiality, proportionality and parity.

Henry derives his twofold understanding of justice from Scripture. He points to biblical passages in which justice means different things: "Scripture nonetheless applies the term 'just' (*dikaios*) not only to the Messiah and to the meritorious faithfulness of devout believers (Matt. 1:19; Mark 6:20; Luke 1:17, 2:25, 23:50;

14. "God wills civil government as an institution for preserving justice and promoting peace and order in fallen society" (Henry, *Christian Mindset in a Secular Society*, 100).

15. The parallel between Henry's and Aristotle's understanding of justice is interesting, even if not exact. See Aristotle, *Nicomachean Ethics*, trans. with intro. and notes by Martin Ostwald (Indianapolis: Bobbs-Merrill Educational Publishing, 1962), 111–14; and Ernest Barker, *The Politics of Aristotle* (London: Oxford University Press, 1958), 362–69.

16. Henry, *God, Revelation, and Authority*, 6:414.

Rom. 1:17, etc.) but also to some who are not yet Christian believers (Acts 10:22)."[17] The Bible, Henry insists, does not mean that the unregenerate—men such as the Roman centurion Cornelius—are righteous; it means they are fair and impartial and conform to the dictates of law.

Justice in this limited or partial sense is the aim of civil authority.[18] Impartial and fair statutes that ensure proportionality and parity result when prudential judgments in the public arena are grounded on principle. For example, "the value of human life and property" is a constant principle, but its prudent application varies: "Britons may indeed drive to the left and Americans to the right, but what underlies each statute is not whim or happenstance, but the principle."[19] Prudential judgment, though fraught with difficulty, remains the task of civil authorities. It was the failure of conservative Christians to embrace this challenge that sparked Henry's lament in *The Uneasy Conscience*.[20]

Henry's "Practical Doctrine"

When evangelicals accepted the challenge and returned to the public arena, Henry, sensing that many believers were unschooled in the arts of governance, readily offered his counsel. He offered much in the way of what Budziszewski calls a "practical doctrine,

17. Ibid., 6:453–54.

18. "Scripture unequivocally declares that unregenerate man falls far short of God's righteousness. . . . But it also affirms that God has an eye for relative justice among men that avoids aggression and chaos and promotes peace and righteousness. God's establishment of civil government presupposes a fallen world in which God wills human civil authority for the preservation of justice and order. The fact that Jesus Christ is King of kings (Phil. 2:10) and will judge 'men and nations' at his return (Matt. 12:18) indicates both that in a fallen world civil government even at best achieves but broken justice, and that the rulers of this world are answerable to the justice of God. Throughout history God's transcendent righteousness not only points to the final judgment of mankind, but also, in anticipation of this, speaks of the present accountability of men and nations to the will and rule of the Creator and Lord of all" (ibid., 6:414).

19. Ibid., 6:442–43.

20. I address Henry's call for civic engagement using arguments based on the lordship of Christ, the stewardship of creation, and the servanthood of believers in David L. Weeks, "Carl F. H. Henry's Moral Arguments for Evangelical Political Activism," *Journal of Church and State* 40 (Winter 1998): 83–106.

or guide to action, explaining how Christians should conduct themselves in the civic realm." Much of Henry's practical counsel reflects his Baptist heritage, concerning itself with the separate roles of church and state.

Repeating the claims of Roger Williams, Henry views church and state as two distinct institutions created by God with separate purposes and powers.[21] The biblical basis for this claim is found in Mark 12:17: "Render to Caesar the things that are Caesar's, and to God the things that are God's."[22] The two institutions share responsibility for promoting justice and combating injustice yet have distinct missions: "While the state's primary concern is to preserve justice and maintain order, the church's role is to identify the true and living God and to proclaim the Good News."[23]

The church is concerned with universal justice, the righteousness that Christ imputes to the redeemed, which exerts a profoundly *transforming* effect on social order by *changing* individuals within it. The state focuses on particular justice, which exerts an essentially *preserving* effect on social order by *regulating* the conduct of individuals within it.[24] This emphasis on preserving the good in society contributes to a form of Burkean conservatism among evangelicals—a conservatism that endeavors to slow the pace of change and to preserve custom and tradition.

21. "The New Testament . . . declares both church and civil government to be divinely willed instrumentalities with distinct powers, spheres, and purposes under God" (Henry, *Christian Countermoves in a Decadent Culture*, 115).

22. "In view of Jesus' differentiation of the secular and the spiritual ('Render to Caesar the things that are Caesar's, and to God the things that are God's,' Mark 12:17), Christianity also has discriminated between the religious and political spheres, yet without fully disjoining them. Both are indispensable aspects of a faithful Christian calling, and each renders service to the other" (Carl F. H. Henry, "Church and State," in *Christian Thought and Action: The Christian as Citizen* [Carol Stream, IL: Christianity Today, 1985], 9).

23. Ibid.

24. "Although the Christian Church ought to rely on the spiritual regeneration of individuals to *transform* society, it must not on that account neglect the role of education and legislation in *preserving* what is valuable in the present social order. Christian social theory needs to distinguish between transforming and preserving, and to recognize that education and legislation can serve only the latter of these ends. But preserving the good in society is worth doing" (Henry, *Aspects of Christian Social Ethics*, 72).

Another factor contributing to evangelical conservatism is Henry's notion that the state's derivative authority requires limited government, an idea he believes originates in Christianity.[25] The state must govern the outward conduct of its citizens, but it should not be concerned with metaphysical or theological issues or with the epistemological basis for principles of justice or what motivates its people to obey. Furthermore, it should not "evangelize," "impose penalties for spiritual lethargy," or "decide between theological alternatives."[26] Henry also contends that the state is not to be an instrument of love, a "benevolence-dispensing agency." Justice, not charity, is the proper concern of the state.[27]

Henry also carefully circumscribes the role of the church. "The Church's mission in the world is spiritual. Its influence on the political order, therefore, must be registered indirectly, as a by-product of spiritual concerns."[28] It is clear to Henry that "preaching and discipling constitute the church's primary responsibility in the world."[29] The church must also pray for the state, model a just community, "encourage its individual members to fulfill their political duties as a spiritual responsibility," interpret the "revealed principles by which Christ the King of kings will ultimately judge nations and states," and "call upon rulers, even pagan rulers, to maintain order and justice [and] criticize those who violate, misapply, or refuse to enforce

25. Ibid., 89.

26. Carl F. H. Henry, "Biblical Authority and the Social Crisis," in *Authority and Interpretation,* ed. Duane A. Garrett and Richard R. Melick Jr. (Grand Rapids: Baker, 1987), 214.

27. Carl F. H. Henry, "Who Is My Brother's Keeper?" *Christian Herald* 85 (January 1962): 15. The best one can hope for is a society that impartially and fairly protects the rights of everyone. "In a fallen society justice best protects the civil and political rights of all because it is impartial; love is preferential" (Henry, *God, Revelation, and Authority,* 6:407).

28. Henry, *Aspects of Christian Social Ethics,* 105.

29. Henry, *God, Revelation, and Authority,* 1:27. He means proclaiming the "Good News of God's saving grace to a sinful and lost humanity" for the purpose of "persuading condemned and lost sinners to put their trust in God by receiving and accepting Christ as Savior through the power of the Holy Spirit, and to serve Christ as Lord in every calling of life and in the fellowship of His Church, looking toward the day of His coming in glory" (Henry, *Evangelicals at the Brink of Crisis,* 3–5).

the law."[30] The church is not to seek narrow self-interest, get involved directly in practical politics, or "use the mechanism of government to legally impose upon society at large her theological commitments."[31]

Henry also offers counsel to individual Christians. Their first duty is to obey the laws of their country. The only exceptions are "where civil law requires [one] to do what contravenes what God requires, or . . . to do what God prohibits."[32] In either instance, the consequences of civil disobedience should be freely accepted.[33] The second duty of individual Christians is to "work aggressively for the advancement of justice and human good to the limit of their individual competence and opportunity."[34] This necessitates working with non-Christians in pursuit of justice and compromising when necessary, recognizing that "in a tragic world of fallen men, government decisions often involve a choice between greater and lesser evils rather than between absolutes of good and evil."[35] He also discourages individuals from employing litmus tests, from promoting Christian political parties, from pursuing single-issue political campaigns, and from practicing "confrontational activism that promotes Christian legislation and a Christian state."[36]

It is, however, Henry's counsel on strategy that gives me pause. Having established the importance of Christian social involvement, he offers a particular strategic approach, the strategy of regeneration.[37] Henry describes this strategy as the "transforma-

30. See Henry, *Aspects of Christian Social Ethics*, 105; and idem, *Christian Countermoves in a Decadent Culture*, 118.

31. Henry, *Christian Countermoves in a Decadent Culture*, 118.

32. "When 'the powers' require what violates God's command, the Christian like the apostles will openly declare his or her supreme allegiance: 'We must obey God rather than men!' (Acts 5:29)" (Henry, *Christian Mindset in a Secular Society*, 122–23).

33. "The right of conscientious personal protest and disobedience is recognized, although the resister should be prepared to pay the legal penalties of civil disobedience" (ibid., 132).

34. Henry, *God, Revelation, and Authority*, 3:70.

35. Carl F. H. Henry, "Evangelicals in the Social Struggle," *Christianity Today*, October 8, 1965, 7.

36. Carl F. H. Henry, "The New Coalitions," *Christianity Today*, November 17, 1989, 27.

37. Henry emphasizes this strategy in several early works. See "Christianity and Social Reform," *Moravian Theological Seminary Bulletin* (1960): 17–33;

tion by supernatural impulse in individual lives whereby the social scene is renewed through a divine spiritual motivation."[38] He believes that, given humanity's fallen nature, we "must rely on spiritual regeneration for the *transformation* of society"; it is the only strategy providing any hope of satisfying the quest for justice.[39] "Unjust structures are, indeed, in need of change, but to expect utopian improvement is futile without a moral alteration of the character of humans who pervert the principles of justice."[40] Only regeneration sufficiently alters human character, providing a "spiritual renewal" that binds "man's will afresh to the purpose of the Creator and the Lord of life."[41] In other words, the redeemed, having experienced the imputed righteousness of Christ, have a vivified commitment to the underlying principles guiding partial justice in the earthly kingdom.

Henry's regeneration strategy holds out great promise for the future while maintaining tempered expectations for the present. The optimism is based on God's sovereignty and providence. God's promise will come into being when Christ returns to earth in all his glory. In the meantime, all utopian earthly schemes will fail. "Those who think altering existing institutions is the surest way to achieve a just society," Henry claims, "need to reread the biblical writings."[42] We can nevertheless remain soberly optimistic about earthly possibilities, for justice and peace can be achieved in particular times in particular places through the efforts of good people. But this achievement requires "a new race of men—men equipped . . . with new hearts."[43] The regenerate, equipped with "a mindset that prizes God's truth and stimulates wholehearted obedience to His will," can make a difference in the world.[44]

At this point, Henry's "biblical politics" emerges in full force, for the regenerational strategy insists that "the Church derives

"Perspective for Social Action, Part II," *Christianity Today*, February 2, 1959, 13–16; and *Aspects of Christian Social Ethics*.

38. Henry, *Aspects of Christian Social Ethics*, 17.

39. Ibid., 16. "Individual regeneration is not only a chief but an indispensable means of social reform" (Henry, "Perspective for Social Action, Part II," 15).

40. Henry, "Biblical Authority and the Social Crisis," 213.

41. Henry, "Christianity and Social Reform," 22.

42. Henry, *God, Revelation, and Authority*, 3:123.

43. Henry, *Aspects of Christian Social Ethics*, 30.

44. Henry, *God, Revelation, and Authority*, 4:501.

her social message from divinely revealed principles."[45] Only
by understanding the insights regarding the human condition
that God has revealed to us, Henry maintains, can we begin to
grapple with social and political problems. He highlights several
key biblical principles:

1. Above all else, the sovereignty of God is the most basic
   political principle. "The sovereign God is . . . the source,
   stipulator, and sanction of the right and the good. He is the
   ultimate ground of law and morality. He defines human
   rights and responsibilities and the powers and limits of
   human institutions. In matters of law and morality there
   is therefore a higher referent than the will of the state or
   the will of the majority, namely, the will of God."[46]
2. Justice has a transcendent basis in that the will of God is
   the very definition of justice. "God is intrinsically moral
   and the sovereign source of all ethical distinctions."[47]
3. "The permanent and universal rule of justice and peace"
   will eventually prevail but only when Christ returns.[48]
4. Justice is "biblically revealed as obligatory on all human
   beings and nations." "*Social justice is a divine requirement
   for the whole human race. . . .* The revealed commandments
   and rules of behavior are universally valid."[49]
5. Civil authority curbs the effects of sin. "God wills civil government as a framework in fallen human history for preserving justice and restraining disorder (Rom. 13:1ff.)."[50]
6. "The Bible, on the basis of a divine-command morality, sets
   forth certain enduringly valid social principles."[51] These
   principles expressly include the social commandments of
   the Decalogue.

45. Henry, *Aspects of Christian Social Ethics,* 21.

46. Henry, *Christian Mindset in a Secular Society,* 99–100.

47. See Henry, *God, Revelation, and Authority,* 6:437; and idem, "God of
Bible and Moral Foundations," 1–2.

48. Henry, "Biblical Authority and the Social Crisis," 218.

49. Ibid.; and Henry, "Perspective for Social Action, Part II," 15.

50. Henry, *God, Revelation, and Authority,* 6:437.

51. Henry, *Christian Mindset in a Secular Society,* 112; and idem, *God, Revelation, and Authority,* 6:444.

7. "Christians stand in the tradition of the godly prophets who proclaimed the justice of God and deplored injustice even at great personal risk." They cannot neglect their "sacred duty to . . . extend God's purpose of justice and order through civil government."[52]

8. Social and political problems are the result of personal sin. "The evangelical recognizes that social disorders are in the last analysis a commentary on the disorder of private life."[53]

9. The message of regeneration is vital. "Evangelical social action *throbs with the evangelistic invitation to new life in Jesus Christ.* 'Ye must be born again' is the Church's unvarying message to the world. Evangelical Christianity . . . holds hope for the social order because it offers the prospect of personal redemption. Individual regeneration is not only a chief but an indispensable means of social reform."[54]

10. The church must proclaim God's will. "The pulpit is responsible for proclaiming divinely revealed principles of social justice as a part of the whole counsel of God."[55]

11. The church must model a just community. "The regenerate church as a new society is to exemplify in mind and will the standards by which Christ will judge humanity and the nations." "The mission of the Church is not simply to condemn social injustices; it is to exhibit what can be done to transcend them in a spiritual society of redeemed persons."[56]

52. See Henry, *God, Revelation, and Authority,* 6:437; and idem, "Evangelicals in the Social Struggle," 11. "A sensitive Christian conscience may and should be one of the most potent forces for social justice, not only when law requires transgression of divine commandment, but also when law promotes or preserves what is unjust; the spirit of prophetic indignation and protest is the Christian's holy heritage. . . . Christians should be among the first to indict blatant and intractable injustice that contravenes the transcendent will of God" (Henry, *God, Revelation, and Authority,* 6:453).

53. Henry, "Perspective for Social Action, Part II," 15.

54. Ibid.

55. Henry, "Evangelicals in the Social Struggle," 11.

56. See Henry, "Biblical Authority and the Social Crisis," 218; and idem, "Perspective for Social Action, Part II," 16.

12. Human rights have a divine source and a divine sanction. God has granted the basic rights to life, property,
and religious liberty to all humans, rights that impose
corresponding moral duties for all.[57]

Although their lists of biblical principles are quite similar,
Henry seems more sanguine than Budziszewski about the Bible's adequacy as a guide for political life. Nevertheless, Henry's
cultural apologetic, explaining how to apply biblical principles
in public life, recognizes the challenges of a wholly "biblical
politics."

Henry's Cultural Apologetic

It is important to note that Henry's later writings acknowledge the limitations of a biblical politics and the strategy of
regeneration: The Bible is not a complete road map to political
life, he says, and salvation alone does not solve social ills. Henry
concedes that believers remain fallen and fallible, that many in
this world will never convert or accept biblical guidance, and
that nonbelievers are sometimes better suited to lead because
they are politically astute. Given these realities, the real world
of politics demands prudential judgment, and prudence dictates
that believers avoid the separatist temptation to employ rhetoric
that divides and offends. Consequently, Henry's later writings are
peppered with admonitions to evangelicals to develop a *public*
philosophy, to employ *public* reason, and to appeal to the *public*
conscience.

At this point, it seems to me, Henry's work goes adrift. His
cultural apologetic encourages Christians to downplay the supernatural source of their guiding principles. In promoting good
laws, he says, an evangelical should identify "ethical imperatives
consistent with and reflective of the will of God" and promote
them on grounds "familiar to the general public—that is, on the
basis of the general good, of desirable facets of social consensus,

57. See Henry, *Aspects of Christian Social Ethics*, 92; idem, *Christian Mindset
in a Secular Society*, 63–80; and idem, "The Judeo-Christian Heritage and Human
Rights," in *Twilight of a Great Civilization*, 145–60.

and then of the best remnants of cultural heritage."[58] Henry's most promising notions, however, entail vague references to a common moral ground based on general revelation and a "creation ethic," but he does not fully develop these ideas.

Pursuing the ideas of general revelation and a creation ethic to their logical conclusion could lead evangelicals back to the natural law tradition, a rich, Christian tradition that could provide evangelicals with a framework, consistent with their core beliefs, within which they could contribute to contemporary American political discourse. However, Henry explicitly rejects natural law. His rejection is not based on the arguments proffered by positivists, utilitarians, or historicists, all of whom offer biting critiques of natural law. Rather, it is based on a particular understanding of human depravity and an insistence on understanding natural law in wholly modern terms.

Henry believes the effects of human depravity on the intellect and the will have invalidated any hope for natural law.[59] While he concedes that God manifests himself in many ways—in Scripture, in history, in nature, in the human conscience, and in Christ—Henry downplays the significance of some of these forms of revelation, especially that which is often referred to as general revelation. Although he vigorously defends the *existence* of general revelation, Henry turns around and weakens its utility. "Because of sinful alienation from God," he says, "fallen man culpably thwarts the ongoing general revelation of God in nature and history."[60] Depravity affects our entire being—"in volition, affection, and *intellection*," making "a right perception of the truth . . . impossible."[61] The only solution to this epistemic flaw is scriptural revelation, which pierces the sin-depraved intellect, revealing truth to fallen humanity. The perspicuity of Scripture spurs some evangelicals to turn a theological principle, sola scrip-

---

58. Henry, *Christian Mindset in a Secular Society*, 124; and idem, *Twilight of a Great Civilization*.

59. This section borrows from my essay "The Uneasy Politics of Modern Evangelicalism," *Christian Scholar's Review* 30, no. 4 (Summer 2001): 403–18.

60. Henry, *God, Revelation, and Authority*, 1:223. "It is not in question that humans are confronted in general divine revelation by the will of the Creator. . . . What is in question is the ability of sinful humanity to translate the moral revelation into a universally shared body of ethical truth" (Carl F. H. Henry, "Natural Law and a Nihilistic Culture," *First Things* 49 [January 1995]: 56).

61. Henry, *God, Revelation, and Authority*, 1:226, emphasis added; 1:329.

tura, into an epistemological claim—that truth is accessible only in Scripture. It is not surprising, then, to see the emergence of a biblical politics.

Henry also insists on understanding natural law solely as a "rationalistic" enterprise wholly "loosed from spiritual moorings."[62] He contends that natural law thinking elevates autonomous human reason, implying that God and divine revelation are irrelevant to moral knowledge. This implication became apparent to all when "the medieval view that reason discovers natural law . . . yielded to the Enlightenment inversion that reason expresses and constitutes natural law."[63] Henry apparently believed that once natural law theory has been stripped "of any necessary dependence upon God," it cannot be restored.[64]

Concluding Observations

One should not understate Henry's importance; his contributions to contemporary evangelicalism are monumental, especially in the arena of civic life. He offers wise counsel on practical political matters, thoughtful exposition about the purposes and limits of government, careful exegesis of biblical principles, and a vigorous defense of religious liberty. His theological anthropology is deeply grounded in biblical teaching, and his arguments for political engagement are powerful.

My principal concern about Henry's political thought coincides with Budziszewski's contention: Evangelicals have neglected the natural law tradition, and Henry is partially responsible. Without this rich resource to guide their political activism, evangelicals have tended to rely on the moral authority of the Bible, even to the point of making inflated claims about it, and on their intuition, which they purport is guided by the Holy Spirit.[65] Both tendencies spark suspicion and hinder success.

62. Ibid., 6:426.
63. Ibid., 6:423. Henry blames Hugo Grotius for breaching this watershed in "Natural Law and a Nihilistic Culture," 58–59.
64. Henry, *God, Revelation, and Authority,* 6:405.
65. I do not underestimate the power of the Holy Spirit to guide human judgment, but I caution against viewing the Spirit's leading in wholly intuitive, as opposed to rational, terms.

One final observation: Given that the authority of Scripture is the hallmark of evangelicalism, it may be both undesirable and unrealistic to expect evangelicals to craft a distinctive view of politics. If biblical politics entails the inflationary and accommodating strategies Budziszewski describes, then it is undesirable, because evangelicals are inconsistently building an edifice on a nonbiblical foundation. And if the Bible does not fully address political life, then a biblical politics is also unrealistic, because evangelicals are precariously building an edifice on an inadequate foundation. Perhaps this alters the discussion. The question might then be asked, What, if anything, do evangelicals have to contribute, more broadly, to Christian political theory? Given Budziszewski's depiction of these four evangelical leaders, it would be ironic if future generations were to say that that contribution was a revival of natural law theory.

4

Abraham Kuyper and the Search for an Evangelical Public Theology

John Bolt

My task as I understand it is to answer three questions: (1) Do I agree with J. Budziszewski's general analysis of the state of evangelical political thought in the United States? (2) More specifically, do I agree with his review of Abraham Kuyper's strengths and shortcomings as a contributor to American evangelical public theology? (3) Do I have anything new to add to the discussion that is not included in Budziszewski's paper? In decreasing levels of intensity, the answers are YES, Yes, and yes.

First, then, concerning the present state of evangelical political thought: Is it as anemic as Budziszewski presents it? Do American evangelicals lack and badly need a well-developed public theology? Here my YES is the loudest.[1] I quite agree

---

1. I made the same point in John Bolt, *A Free Church, a Holy Nation: Abraham Kuyper's American Public Theology* (Grand Rapids: Eerdmans, 2001), chap. 2.

with Budziszewski that "among evangelicals, systematic political reflection has not yet risen to its task" and that therefore "certainly it is not yet a match for the dominant political theories of the secularist establishment." He is not the first to make this observation; Mark Noll also highlighted the inadequacy of evangelical political reflection in his wonderful "scandal" book.[2] What is particularly helpful about Budziszewski's introductory comments is his question, What makes a political theory evangelical? His answer—"at minimum, then, one would expect an evangelical political theory to be a *biblically illuminated* political theory"—and his observations about the "projective accommodation" in which evangelicals engage as they use the Bible also seem to be on target. The summary of biblical principles and the observations about "inflationary strategies" are thoughtful and cautionary. Most importantly, with his focus on general revelation and natural law as the missing piece of the puzzle, Budziszewski has put his finger on the real problem.

To this I would add only two brief comments. The first has to do with the concern about a distinctively *evangelical* political theory. Apart from the simple fact that American evangelicals in large number rediscovered their political responsibilities in the last three decades and became a noticeable political force, why do we need the qualifier "evangelical" for the political arena? Wouldn't "Christian" political theory suffice?[3] Historically, "evangelical" is a primarily soteriological and ecclesiastical qualifier; in contrast to the assumptions of other forms of Christendom—state churches; sacramentalist churches; mainline, establishment Protestant churches—evangelical churches insisted on personal faith as the criterion for membership. J. I. Packer usefully summarizes the characteristics of evangelical piety as "centering upon conversion, Bible-reading, evangelism, fellowship with God in assurance and trust, and fellowship with

2. Mark Noll, *The Scandal of the Evangelical Mind* (Grand Rapids: Eerdmans, 1994).

3. On a personal note, I am not uncomfortable with being called an evangelical, though I would prefer to be identified by my confessional tradition, Reformed. At the same time, I also consider myself a catholic (small *c*) Christian. For a ringing affirmation of the Reformed tradition as both evangelical and catholic, see H. Bavinck, "The Catholicity of Christianity and the Church," trans. John Bolt, *Calvin Theological Journal* 27 (1992): 220–51.

other believers in the shared joy of born-again life."[4] In addition, the evangelical tradition is essentially reactive: against Roman Catholic sacramentalism, against state-church ascriptivism, against theological modernism.

How does this meaningfully translate into a *political* identification? Political life, by definition, cannot be a sectarian activity; it must be an inclusive, consensus-building, even compromising activity. It cannot be limited to the intramural efforts of the born again.[5] Even a basic etymological consideration seems problematic: *Evangel* is "good news"; it is gospel. Then isn't the term *evangelical politics* a thorough confusion of gospel and law? Finally, doesn't the search for a distinctively evangelical political theory fuel the very problem of ignoring the larger catholic Christian tradition and the role of general revelation/natural law as used by that tradition?

My second comment concerning Budziszewski's analysis of the state of evangelical political theory is this: It is not only the theonomists and the Christian reconstructionists who use the "inflationary strategy" of assuming a quick move from Old Testament Israel's laws to the present. The same inflationary strategy is used when the Old Testament laws of jubilee are used as a paradigm for wealth redistribution, as in the recent evangelical push toward forgiving third world debt. It remains a legitimate question, of course, whether there are *principles* in the Old Testament code that may have universal application.

Kuyper among the Prophets

On the accuracy of Budziszewski's portrait of Abraham Kuyper, my Yes remains firm, though slightly muted. He is quite correct in calling attention to the importance of sphere sovereignty for Kuyper and its affinity with both Tocqueville's observations about the associational character of American society and the

4. J. I. Packer, "A Stunted Ecclesiology? The Theory and Practice of Evangelical Churchliness," *Touchstone* 15 (2002): 42–43.

5. Contemporary evangelicals in the political arena have not always realized this. However, the name Christian Coalition does seem to capture some of the more inclusive, appropriately political dimensions of recent American evangelical activism.

Catholic notion of subsidiarity. I think he missteps a bit when he comments that "despite the importance of the idea, Kuyper says surprisingly little about it and never develops it in detail." That may be formally true in terms of explicit terminology, but it overlooks two important areas of Kuyper's work.

First, for Kuyper, sphere sovereignty was a defense of metaphysical *pluralism* in the social realm in fierce opposition to all uniformitarianism and social *monism*. Thus, Kuyper's entire social ontology, his tirades against pantheism and materialistic evolutionism,[6] his defense of the family and the labor union, his distinction between the church as institute and as organism—in short, all the passions to which he devoted his journalistic career—were shaped by sphere sovereignty. Second, Budziszewski's comment overlooks Kuyper's sociopolitical activism and his detailed exposition of program and strategy in such major works as *Ons Program (Our Program)*, the thirteen-hundred-page platform of the Anti-Revolutionary Party published in 1879, and *De Gemeene Gratie (Common Grace)*, a three-volume work published in the 1890s.

Let me give two examples of such detailed outworking of sphere sovereignty. First, the tenth article of the Anti-Revolutionary Party (ARP) platform of 1879 reads, "It is the desire [of the ARP] that local and municipal autonomy be restored by means of decentralization, insofar as this does not conflict with the requirements of national unity nor violate the rights of individual persons"—a striking echo of the same-numbered (tenth) article of the United States Bill of Rights.[7] A second example: Article 15 of the ARP platform deals with public health, specifically purity of foodstuffs sold at public market; pollution of air, land, and water; respectful treatment of and burial of the dead; and communicable diseases.[8] The government responsibility for public health in these areas, according to Kuyper, is still limited by the superior claims of a free conscience before God. He finds it scandalous that in times

6. See, for example, the following essays in James D. Bratt, ed., *Abraham Kuyper: A Centennial Reader* (Grand Rapids: Eerdmans, 1998): "Uniformity: The Curse of Modern Life (1869)," "The Blurring of the Boundaries (1892)," and "Evolution (1899)."

7. See the discussion in Bolt, *Free Church, a Holy Nation,* 285–86.

8. Abraham Kuyper, *Ons Program,* 5th ed. (Hilversum and Pretoria: Höveker & Wormser, 1907), 268–79.

of epidemics, for example, magistrates use public health reasons as an excuse to close church buildings for worship and to halt burials by making the "pagan" practice of cremation compulsory. Kuyper also opposes compulsory vaccination on the grounds that the government is not authorized to declare a particular medical practice orthodox and thus required. While he does not use the exact terminology here, it is the principle of sphere sovereignty that is the foundation of his analysis and policy. Similar examples abound in Kuyper's writings. He *did* apply sphere sovereignty in sometimes painfully exacting detail.

Aside from this instance—where Kuyper *does*, contra Budziszewski, "explore which decisions are immunized by conscience and which are not"—I find the analysis and critique of Kuyper's doctrine of sphere sovereignty fair, clear, and helpful. Budziszewski is also quite right that, at least in his formal statements on sphere sovereignty (for example, in the Stone Lectures), Kuyper is explaining not a judicial framework but a *vision*. Let me underscore that point in connection with the project to articulate an evangelical political philosophy. Like subsidiarity or the principle of devolving power down to states and local authorities, sphere sovereignty is an *orientation,* even a rhetorically useful reminder to Christians debating political strategy and policy. It is a general road map not to be used by surveyors or cartographers in political theory. It is not a finely tuned political calculus by which intricate policy decisions and legislative choices can be made. We make a mistake when we expect too much (or too little!) from the idea.

Other insightful aspects of Budziszewski's analysis should be highlighted: Kuyper's ambivalence about the state; the paucity of scriptural warrant for sphere sovereignty (aside from the foundation of God's sovereignty over all things, of course); a conceptual lack of clarity about what a sphere is (Budziszewski's summary of possible definitions is particularly helpful); and the problems with Kuyper's ecclesiology and the exact nature of *religious* liberty in relation to pluralism (this last point is major, and I will return to it later). All these areas need much more work by evangelical political thinkers if Kuyper's vision is to have a lasting impact. Finally, I heartily endorse the call for further dialogue between the neo-Calvinist tradition and the Roman Catholic papal encyclical tradition of social teaching from Leo XIII to John Paul II; in particular, I add my amen to the call for North American neo-Calvinists to get over their hang-up about natural law.[9]

Abraham Kuyper's "American" Public Theology

Third, do I have anything to add? My third yes—lower case, softer—is a fruit of my personal commitment to Calvinism, a commitment that instructs me to be modest about my own contribution, to give glory to one infinitely greater, and to be on constant guard against self-promotion. My excuse for quoting myself now is that, having recently qualified for AARP membership, I really do not have all that many new thoughts; I am forced to repackage old ones.

The heading of this section is the subtitle of my book on Abraham Kuyper, *A Free Church, a Holy Nation.* Underlying the thesis of that book is a certain view of Kuyper's 1898 trip to America to deliver the Stone Lectures at Princeton Seminary. By then, Kuyper had absorbed from Alexis de Tocqueville, Douglas Campbell, George Bancroft, and others an understanding of the United States he valued so highly that he wanted to use the success of the American experiment for his own religious-political purposes in the Netherlands. He saw in America a liberty based on a commitment to divine sovereignty, a separation of powers, and a rich, pluralistic associational life, and he wanted to hold America up before his compatriots as a model for what a great Christian nation could and ought to be. As he said to an audience of his fellow Dutch Calvinists in Grand Rapids, Michigan, in October 1898, indicating his delight about the U.S. Congress's practice of beginning each session with prayer, "O! Were it thus on the other side."[10] For Kuyper, America represented the future of liberty on our planet. America was providence's destiny.

This is heady but also risky stuff. The idolatry of civil religion beckons. Yet let me offer a few propositions here.

9. One of my doctoral students, Stephen Grabill, is currently finishing a thesis on the positive role of natural law in the Reformed tradition from Calvin to Kuyper, including Turretin, Zanchi, and Althusius, among others. For a sampler, see Grabill's introduction to D. Hieronymus Zanchi, "On the Law in General," *Journal of Markets and Morality* 6, no. 1 (Spring 2003): 305–98.

10. Bolt, *Free Church, a Holy Nation,* 472.

Proposition 1

The future success of an American evangelical political philosophy depends on whether it is willing to affirm the providentially blessed reality of the American experiment in ordered liberty while successfully navigating the treacherous land mines of civil religion.

On this point, I have some key disagreements with many fellow North American Kuyperian neo-Calvinists.[11] My hunch is that most of them are less enthusiastic than Kuyper was, and than I am, about the American experiment in ordered liberty. James Skillen, for example, judges that I am too sympathetic to Kuyper's high providential view of America's place in human history and wonders if I in fact "believe that an American public theology in line with Kuyper requires a poetic rhetoric that is civil religious in character." Though he acknowledges my warning against theocratic impulses and civil religion, Skillen contends that "Bolt does not adequately explain how Kuyper's poetic political rhetoric (or a corresponding American Christian political rhetoric) supports a call for pluralism rather than Christian nationalism."[12] That is a good question, and I shall attempt to answer it, since it is relevant to our concerns about an evangelical public philosophy.

I believe it is possible (even necessary) to affirm the providential character of the American experiment in ordered liberty without lapsing into idolatrous civil religion. As an example of such an affirmation, I would call attention to the statement "Christianity and Democracy" written by Richard John Neuhaus, adopted by the Institute on Religion and Democracy in October 1981, and reprinted in *First Things* fifteen years later. The statement honors democratic government as pluralist (non-monist) and free and observes that "the United States of America is the primary bearer of the democratic possibility in the world today,"[13] an assertion even more true two decades later. The claim that "America has a singular responsibility in this world historical moment," the

11. In part, what follows is a response to an excellent review of my book by a Kuyperian whose person and work I respect highly, James Skillen. The review appeared in the *Calvin Theological Journal* 37, no. 1 (2002): 135–38.

12. Ibid., 137.

13. *First Things* 66 (October 1996): 34.

statement says, "does not mean that America is God's chosen nation, as for instance, Israel was chosen by God. God has made no special covenant with America as such. God's covenant is with his creation, with Israel, and with his church."

At the same time, this does not mean repudiating all providential purpose for America:

> However, because America is a large and influential part of his creation, because America is the home of most of the heirs of Israel of old, and because this is a land in which his Church is vibrantly free to live and proclaim the Gospel to the world, we believe that America has a peculiar place in God's promises and purposes. This is not a statement of nationalistic hubris but an acknowledgment that we bear a particular and grave responsibility. Beyond this, we are also mindful that this is the nation for which we are most immediately accountable.[14]

Finally, the fundamental conflict in the world today is not first of all military or political but spiritual and moral; it "is the conflict over the dignity and destiny of the human person, and the societal order appropriate to that dignity and that destiny." And then the conclusion, one I gladly endorse: "In this conflict, we believe that the United States of America is, on balance and considering the alternatives, a force for good in the world."[15] An American evangelical public theology that is biblically illumined should, minimally, meet the criteria of this affirmation and distance itself from the chorus of anti-Americanism so prevalent in the academy and among America's cultured elites, including the evangelical left.

This would mean, I believe, also distancing itself from the neo-Kuyperian criticism of America that almost turns religious pluralism into a dogma. Kuyper not only argued for social pluralism on the basis of sphere sovereignty but also firmly advocated a confessional pluralism and distinctly Calvinist social organizations, Calvinist day schools, and a Calvinist political party, thus helping to create the characteristic twentieth-century Dutch social phenomenon known as pillarization.[16] North American

14. Ibid., 34–35.
15. Ibid., 35.
16. See the discussion of pillarization in Peter S. Heslam, *Creating a Christian Worldview: Abraham Kuyper's Lectures on Calvinism* (Grand Rapids: Eerdmans, 1998), 2–4.

Kuyperians have appropriated not only Kuyper's doctrine of sphere sovereignty as a defense of structural pluralism but also Kuyper's insistence on religious or confessional pluralism.[17] Picking up this emphasis from Kuyper, James Skillen wonders if my approving discussion of the joint 1994 evangelical-Catholic statement "Evangelicals and Catholics Together" does not overlook the real "sectarian" character of Dutch political life with its distinctive Calvinist and Roman Catholic political parties. If I understand this correctly, the argument is that public policy should encourage religious pluralism as an advance for liberty. I wonder if this is truly Kuyper's vision; I think it ought not to be that of American evangelicals in search of a public philosophy.

Kuyper's emphasis on confessional pluralism was indeed a matter of liberty, but—and this is the crucial point—he did not see religious pluralism as a normative principle for Dutch national life. For Kuyper, the goal of his program was the *rechristianization* of Dutch national life. Of course, this was not to be at the expense of religious liberty; if it could be called *theocratic* in any sense, it was a theocracy to be established by testimony and persuasion rather than by coercion. In a February 1874 letter to the political theorist Groen van Prinsterer, Kuyper formulated his convictions in this way:

> Our foundational principle [*beginsel*] must not be [based on] an effort to [re]impose Christendom by means of direct or indirect coercion. Rather, if Christianity is to regain its free and unfettered territory, it must begin in faith; a faith that appeals to and thus emancipates the conscience of the nation and of individuals. . . . [Only in this way] can the Christian faith rule our social and civic life.[18]

Kuyper's political vision clearly repudiated theocracy, insisted on freedom of religion and noncoercion, and used a persuasive appeal to conscience, to the *national* conscience. Kuyper's ap-

17. See, for example, Rockne McCarthy et al., *Society, State, and Schools: A Case for Structural and Confessional Pluralism* (Grand Rapids: Eerdmans, 1981).

18. Adriaan Goslinga, *Briefwisseling van Mr. G. Groen van Prinsterer met Dr. A. Kuyper* (Kampen: Kok, 1937), 279.

plication of this strategy borrowed from Alexis de Tocqueville's insights about America.

Tocqueville's argument in *Democracy in America* is that religious faith is essential for the self-governing moral disposition and habits required by a democratic society. Furthermore, the health of religion in America depends on the vitality of its *voluntary associational* character; in Ernst Troeltsch's terms, the sort of religion that is needed to sustain democracy must be *sectarian*.[19] Tocqueville's remarkable insight into the genius of the American experiment was that its liberalism was reducible not to individualism but to what might be called "associationalism."[20] Conditions of equality, however, do tend to foster individualism, which then threatens liberty itself. Tocqueville salutes the wisdom of the American founders, who "thought it also right to give each part of the land its own political life so that there should be an infinite number of occasions for the citizens to act together and so that every day they should feel that they depended on one another." Tocqueville concludes, "Local liberties, then, which induce a great number of citizens to value the affection of their kindred and their neighbors, bring men constantly into contact, despite the instincts which separate them, and force them to help one another."[21] Formulating this into a social "law," Tocqueville regards the following as "more precise and clearer" than any other: "If men are to remain civilized or to become civilized, the art of association must develop among them at the same speed as equality of conditions spread."[22]

Kuyper understood well this Tocquevillian insight. We have already taken note of his own insistence, formulated in Article 10 of the Anti-Revolutionary Party's platform, on the desirability of

19. Alexis de Tocqueville, *Democracy in America*, trans. George Lawrence, ed. J. P. Mayer (New York: Harper & Row, 1966), 240–45, 287–301, 442–49, 509–24; and Ernst Troeltsch, *The Social Teaching of the Christian Churches*, trans. Olive Wyon, 2 vols. (1931; repr., Louisville: Westminster John Knox, 1992), 2:993–94.

20. This insight has been "rediscovered" in Barry Alan Shain, *The Myth of American Individualism: The Protestant Origins of American Political Thought* (Princeton: Princeton University Press, 1994).

21. Tocqueville, *Democracy in America*, 510–11.

22. Ibid., 517.

shifting political power away from federal to local jurisdictions.[23] The same *associational* bias can be seen in Kuyper's ecclesiology. In keeping with his anti-theocratic, anti–state-church perspective, Kuyper pleaded for ecclesial communities characterized by what he called "a free multiformity."[24] Church reform, he insisted, was not to be achieved by repristinating a past ideal national church unity, an approach that was nothing more than an effort "to restore an ecclesiastical form that has already proven unfit. Any new church formation, no matter what, should first of all completely purge away the curse of uniformity, which is the mother of lies."[25] Then follows Kuyper's twofold plea for freedom of conscience and freedom of association. Genuine liberty tolerates no coercion, he says:

> Nothing should be forced and nothing united which is not organically one. If there are people of good will who are one in mind and spirit, let them join together and courageously confess the faith of their hearts, but let them not claim any greater unity than that which is really their common possession. Thus, with complete autonomy let groups and circles unite who know what they want, know what they confess, and possess an actual, not merely a nominal, unity. If here and there such circles exist which share a common life-trait, let them become conscious of their unity and display it before the eyes of the world, but let it be only that feature and no other bond that unites them.[26]

Kuyper insists that what he is advocating is not congregationalism but rather the principle that "true connections between souls" can manifest themselves only "by a voluntary chosen kinship" and that "the life of a free church community can manifest itself only where that life finds its own form."[27] Kuyper continues in that same address with a ringing appeal for a recovery of the *national* Dutch soul, a recovery that is essential if the nation is

23. Earlier in this essay I called attention to the parallel with Article 10 of the U.S. Bill of Rights.

24. Abraham Kuyper, "Uniformity: The Curse of Modern Life," in *Abraham Kuyper: A Centennial Reader*, 39.

25. Ibid.

26. Ibid.

27. Ibid.

to regain and retain its liberty, a recovery that is dependent on strong religious faith:

> So then, people of the Netherlands, if you want to remain a people, let godliness be your primary weapon in the struggle for independence and only secondarily artillery and sidearms. If you love your country, know your calling to become ever more devout, more religious, and believe that the larger the number of children of God who inhabit the land of our fathers, the higher will be the wall which protects its liberty.[28]

Tocqueville would have understood.

Kuyper's appeal to conscience has parallels as well to the civil rights rhetoric of Martin Luther King Jr. Here it is instructive to consider King's rhetoric as paralleling Kuyper's strategy in appealing to *national conscience*. King's call to white America was always a call to the Christian, national American conscience. In addition to his use of the exodus metaphor and Old Testament prophetic passages such as Amos 5:24 ("But let justice roll down like waters, and righteousness like an ever-flowing stream"), King appealed to America's founding and its Constitution as moral grounds for the just treatment of his people. Here is a characteristic passage from his April 3, 1968, sermon to the Memphis sanitation workers:

> All we say to America is, "Be true to what you said on paper." If I lived in China or even Russia, or any totalitarian country, maybe I could understand the denial of certain basic First Amendment privileges, because they hadn't committed themselves to that over there. But somewhere I read of the freedom of assembly. Somewhere I read of the freedom of speech. Somewhere I read of the freedom of the press. Somewhere I read that the greatness of America is the right to protest for right. And so . . . we are going on.

King then joins American conscience with Christian content. "We need all of you. And you know what is beautiful to me is to see all of these ministers of the Gospel. It's a marvelous picture. Who is it that is supposed to articulate the longings and aspirations of the

28. Ibid., 43.

people more than the preacher?"[29] That combination articulated by King illustrates perfectly what Kuyper meant by a *Christian* and *national* conscience, something to which he consistently appealed throughout his journalistic and political career.

But this appeal, arising from and directed to the actual historical-religious life of a people, suggests limits to as well as freedom for conscience and expression. In Kuyper's understanding, the state is under divine obligation. Article 4 of the Anti-Revolutionary Party platform puts it this way:

> Civil authority, as God's servant, in a Christian (and thus non-atheistic) nation is obligated to honor God's name, implying the following:
>
> a. To govern and to pass laws that permit the free influence of the Gospel among our people;
> b. to restrict itself deliberately from any and all direct interference with the spiritual development of the nation;
> c. to treat all church fellowships or religious societies, and thus all citizens, with absolute equity, indifferent to what they may believe concerning eternal matters;
> d. to recognize the limits of its power with respect to human conscience, insofar as the presumption of respectability is not absent.[30]

The next article (5) sets forth corresponding positive obligations:

> Civil authority rules by the grace of God and derives its legitimacy from God. It thus has the right to ask [citizens] to swear an oath; to set aside the Lord's Day as a day of rest and to pass laws concerning Lord's Day observance that are beneficial to its citizens, to the extent possible refraining from its own activities on the rest day and by means of legal concessions encouraging all commercial enterprises to refrain from activity either partially or completely.[31]

29. In *American Sermons: The Pilgrims to Martin Luther King Jr.* (New York: Library of America, 1999), 879–80.

30. Kuyper, *Ons Program*, 71. I am indebted to my colleague Henry De Moor for his help in translating this syntactically complex legal article.

31. Ibid., 90.

Kuyper acknowledges up front that the Anti-Revolutionary platform at this point clearly distinguishes itself from the "liberal"
political vision. The key difference is that the liberal state is "godless," an "atheistic" state. Specifically, though religion is granted
a private, subjective place in the lives of individuals, the public
square must be secular, naked of all religious elements.[32]

What Kuyper is arguing for in his exposition of the Anti-Revolutionary Party platform is a position that is neither theocratic
nor radically secularist (liberal). With the tradition of classic
liberalism (Locke, Mill), Kuyper wants full freedom of religion;
he is opposed to all coercive violations of human conscience.
However, he wants full freedom of religious *expression*, also in
the public sphere. The difference between him and his liberal
opponents, he says later in *Ons Program*, comes down to this:
"Our opponents want religion kept out of public life; they believe
mixing religion [with politics] will corrupt government. We argue
for non-interference [in religious faith by government] to preserve the holiness of worship." In other words, "the liberal seeks
to restrict and enclose the life of faith within the most strictly
confined and private limits while we seek exactly the opposite,
the expansion of faith's power and influence as far as possible."[33]
Kuyper believes that this free *public* exercise is essential for the
nation's civic health; in Tocquevillian fashion, he insists that
failure to *publicly* recognize a higher authority than the state
itself will inevitably lead to state apotheosis and tyranny.

As the language in the previous paragraph has suggested,
we can understand Kuyper's position by considering the two
key clauses in the first article of America's Bill of Rights, the
nonestablishment clause and the free exercise clause. The full
article reads: "Congress shall make no law respecting an establishment of religion, or prohibiting the free exercise thereof."
The intense legal debate in American courts during the second
half of the twentieth century was usually framed in such a way
that the secularist advocates of "nonestablishment" were pitted
against religious proponents of "free exercise." As Jean Bethke
Elshtain and Nicholas Wolterstorff have argued recently, in separate essays, what might be called the "liberal strict separationist"

32. Ibid., 72.
33. Ibid., 76.

position seems to have gained the legal day in America.[34] This view holds that "it's just too dangerous to let religious people debate political issues outside their own confessional circles, and to act politically, on the basis of their religious views."[35] Elshtain describes this liberal view as "strong separationist," by which she means the view "seeks not only a properly secular [i.e., nontheocratic] state—which we have—but also a thoroughly secularized society, one stripped of any and all public markers and reminders of religion."[36] Not only are church and state to be separated, but religion must be similarly separated from all public life. Elshtain observes that implicit in this view is a reluctance to permit free exercise of religion and a deep hostility to religion. Religion must be privatized so that it will "become invisible to public life" and, it is hoped, eventually disappear.

> There is in this position a built-in animus against the determina-
> tion by religious denominations to sustain their own network
> of schools, welfare provision, political advocacy, and so on. It
> presupposes a harsh opposition between Enlightenment values
> and religious faith. Because there is a wall of separation between
> religion and society on the level of what holds a democratic society
> together—a unity that religion always threatens to disrupt—the
> secular state goes on a rampage and gobbles up society so that it,
> too, might be thoroughly secularized. That, at least, is the dream
> outcome for ardent separationists.[37]

In a phrase that Kuyper would heartily approve of, since he used a version of it himself, Elshtain refers to this view as "liberal monism," the "view that all institutions internal to a democratic society must conform to a single principle of authority, a single standard of what counts as reason and deliberation."[38]

34. Jean Bethke Elshtain, "The Bright Line: Liberalism and Religion," *New Criterion* 17 (March 1999): 4–13; and Nicholas Wolterstorff, "Why We Should Reject What Liberalism Teaches Us about Speaking and Acting in Public for Religious Reasons," in *Religion and Contemporary Liberalism*, ed. Paul J. Weithman (Notre Dame: University of Notre Dame Press, 1997), 162–81.
35. Wolterstorff, "Why We Should Reject What Liberalism Teaches," 167.
36. Elshtain, "Bright Line," 8.
37. Ibid.
38. Ibid., 9.

One of Elshtain's most provocative claims in this essay is that, precisely where the liberal monist view claims to celebrate pluralism and diversity, thanks to its drive toward privatization, it in fact "fosters a form of pluralism that requires uniformity and that winds up excluding religion."[39] By excluding public religion *in the name of diversity*, liberal monism not only marginalizes religion but also undercuts the very foundations on which genuine pluralism can rest. The proof of this important point can be seen clearly in the currently regnant ideology of multiculturalism.[40]

Multiculturalism is ostensibly and potentially a vehicle for enriching all citizens with the cultural treasures of people other than their own. However, in the hands of ideologically driven educators, it has become yet another tool to marginalize religion, at least the Christian religion held by most of the citizens of the United States. According to Peter Lawler, multiculturalism as practiced in many North American universities "really defends egalitarianism or permissive democracy against the claims of all cultures, even as it empties culture of its content by separating it from intense devotion to a particular country or religion."[41] In the hands of leftist ideologues, what is called multiculturalism is not so much an effort to enter empathetically into the culture of another people as it is a reason to be critical of Western culture and its Judeo-Christian roots. In Lawler's words, "Multiculturalism properly understood is a tool used to devalue one's own culture, meaning one's own religion, with the equal and incompatible claims of others."[42] One of the great ironies here, according to Lawler, and observed by others as well,[43] is

39. Ibid.
40. A distinction must be made between multicultural education, which "presents and examines the values and practices of other cultures objectively and critically in a nondoctrinaire manner," and the ideology of multiculturalism "that sees all cultures as essentially equal" except for "Euro-American culture with its Judeo-Christian underpinnings," a culture that is condemned for its "racism, sexism, and classism" (Alvin J. Schmidt, *The Menace of Multiculturalism: Trojan Horse in America* [Westport, CT: Praeger, 1997], 3).
41. Peter Augustine Lawler, "The Dissident Professor," *Intercollegiate Review* 34, no. 2 (Spring 1999): 14.
42. Ibid.
43. See Schmidt, *Menace of Multiculturalism*; and John J. Miller, *The Unmaking of Americans: How Multiculturalism Has Undermined America's Assimilation*

that this multicultural critique of Western and American culture and society is itself a thoroughly Western project, cannibalistically feeding off the very cultural capital it seems intent on destroying.[44]

Multiculturalism of the ideological sort that nurtures hostility toward America is socially destructive. David Brooks comments:

> It's simply unrealistic to expect a nation to embrace an ethos that prominently features guilt and self-flagellation. So it's no surprise that faith in public institutions has plummeted as the multicultural ethos has achieved hegemonic control over the schools and public discussion. If multiculturalism is the only public narrative on offer, then most people will cease to identify with public narratives and withdraw from public life.[45]

Since the religious dimension of America's national epic is central to most American conservative evangelicals, ideological multiculturalism marginalizes them from the deepest wellsprings of their patriotism and citizenship. They begin to experience life in their own country as something alien; it seems to them that hostile usurpers have captured the throne; a secular coup has taken place. Kuyper would have understood perfectly. It is exactly how he portrayed the secularizing liberal tendencies in his own country a hundred years ago.

What this all suggests is that the relationship between religion and public life, particularly political life, is a delicately balanced one. The ideal of religious liberty itself is threatened no less by an "atheistic" civic polity that deliberately excludes religion and thus encourages an apotheosis of the state than by a self-consciously articulated theocratic vision. Kuyper was as rigorous an opponent of theocracy as he was a proponent of self-consciously Christian involvement in political life. He believed that the liberal vision finally would be incapable of sustaining

---

Ethic (New York: Free Press, 1998).

44. Lawler, "Dissident Professor," 14; cf. John Ellis, *Literature Lost: Social Agendas and the Corruption of the Humanities* (New Haven: Yale University Press, 1997), 12.

45. David Brooks, "Politics and Patriotism from Teddy Roosevelt to John McCain," *Weekly Standard,* April 26, 1999, 20–21.

genuine liberty, and he pleaded simply for the legal right to free exercise, also in the public arena. The civil authorities must permit free exercise, he argued, and while they are therefore not to privilege any particular religion, they also must not, in their zeal to be secular, arm non-Christian citizens who promote a "contra-Gospel."[46] That, for Kuyper, was what the school struggle was finally all about. The state schools were promoting a religion of secular monism that threatened the conscience of Christian believers and their free exercise. As he put it in his "Maranatha" address of 1891, pleading for "freedom of conscience . . . to be completely restored":

> All [the gospel] asks is unlimited freedom to develop in accordance with its own genius in the heart of our national life. We do not want the government to hand over unbelief handcuffed and chained as though for a spiritual execution. We prefer that the power of the gospel overcome that demon in free combat with comparable weapons. Only *this* we do not want: that the government arm unbelief to force us, half-armed and handicapped by an assortment of laws, into an unequal struggle with so powerful an enemy. Yet that *has* happened and is happening *still*. It happens in all areas of popular education, on the higher as well as the lower levels, by means of the power of money, forced examinations, and official hierarchy. For this reason we may never desist from our protest or resistance until the gospel recover its freedom to circulate, until the performance of his Christian duty will again be possible for every Dutch citizen, whether rich or poor.[47]

This excursion into Tocqueville and multiculturalism is to illustrate an important Kuyperian point. Kuyper's appeal to the "conscience of the nation," to the Christian understanding of providential national purpose and destiny, has direct parallels with contemporary American conservative Christian political analysts and activists who insist that maintaining liberty and genuine diversity requires staying true to a national mythology. There are limits to the kind of pluralism that civil authority should encourage. Freedom of conscience requires that no one be coerced to act contrary to his or her convictions, and the very

46. Kuyper, *Ons Program,* 81–82.
47. Abraham Kuyper, "Maranatha," in *Abraham Kuyper: A Centennial Reader,* 224–25.

idea of a "thought police" is repugnant to any lover of liberty. But the government acts in a self-destructive manner when, in the name of diversity or pluralism or multiculturalism, it actively promotes religious beliefs or ideologies that insist on the denial of free, public religious exercise, particularly free exercise of the religions that are integral to that nation's very history and character. What is true of ideological multiculturalism is even more true of militant Islam. There seem to be limits to religious pluralism. This leads me to my second proposition.

Proposition 2

An evangelical public theology will be most effective if it appeals to the authentic voice of conscience to be found in the founding vision and documents of the American experiment in ordered liberty. It is counterproductive, in the name of an abstract liberty, to promote a religious pluralism that may be at odds with that originating vision.

(Let me add a postscript to this proposition: It would be a worthwhile project to examine the notions of confessional pluralism and multiculturalism from the perspective of Madison's counsel about "factions" in *Federalist* 9 and 10.)

One of the problems North American Kuyperians have encountered is the accusation that Kuyper's public theology is literally *foreign* to the American experiment and experience. Kuyperians give unnecessary credibility to that charge when they fail to appreciate how remarkably American Kuyper's public theology in fact was.[48] Kuyperians fail to show Kuyper's remarkable relevance for evangelical public theology today when they do not recognize natural allies in social thinkers and political philosophers who, using somewhat different language and terminology, make similar points. This is true, for example, in the case of Alexis de Tocqueville, whose insights remained unknown to this Kuyperian until the last decade.

Let me call attention to two other instances of sphere sovereignty thinking by two people who may never have heard of Abraham Kuyper: Peter Berger and Neil Postman. It seems to me

---

48. Or so I have tried to demonstrate in *Free Church, a Holy Nation*.

indisputable that Peter Berger and Richard John Neuhaus's little gem titled *To Empower People: The Role of Mediating Structures in Society* utilized sphere sovereignty thinking, yet I discovered significant neo-Kuyperian resistance when I made the claim to colleagues at Redeemer College in the 1980s. And Neil Postman in his *Teaching as a Conserving Activity* uses a sphere sovereignty argument in defense of a more restrictive role for the school. Postman contends (rightly, I believe) that a major problem facing American schools today is that they have, with noblest intentions, usurped the roles and tasks of other social spheres such as the family and the church. Teachers are called on to serve as priests, psychologists and therapists, political reformers, social workers, sex advisors, and parents, while the school feeds children hot lunches as well as trains their minds. Postman points to the limited competence and resources of teachers to fulfill all these roles and contends that "schools should not, except under the most extreme provocation, try to accomplish goals which other social institutions traditionally serve." Not only does this expansion of tasks go beyond the competence of the school, but there is a destructive social consequence as well, according to Postman. "The more one social institution encroaches upon the functions of another, the more it weakens it. This idea . . . comes from the field of ecology, where it is understood that as one system begins to preempt the purposes of another, the functional capacity of both is undermined." Postman concludes, "As the school blurs the lines of authority between itself and other institutions, it tends to weaken not only its own capability but the capabilities of other institutions as well."[49] Kuyper could hardly have said it better himself. That brings me to my next proposition.

Propositions 3 and 4

Proposition 3: For evangelical public theology in America to make effective use of Kuyper's insights, it will have to appropriate those ideas that have the greatest affinity to the American experience itself and make strategic intellectual and political alliances with indigenous American thought that shares its values.

49. Neil Postman, *Teaching as a Conserving Activity* (New York: Dell, 1979), 106–8.

If we agree with Budziszewski that an evangelical public theology or political philosophy ought to be, minimally, a biblically illumined one, on what do we focus the light of biblical revelation? I wonder if evangelicals have made a major mistake by attempting to create a biblical sociology, a biblical theory of social institutions, such as the state. Let me propose a different focus with my fourth and final proposition:

> *Proposition 4*: An evangelical public theology that is rooted in biblical revelation will focus its attention on a biblical anthropology, a biblical understanding of the dignity and worth of the human person.

It is here that one can note the most significant overlap with the American founding vision. If we are to find affinities with the Christian message in the Declaration of Independence, the Bill of Rights, or the Federalist Papers, it is in the view of the human person as created in God's image. This is the need of the hour, the area of greatest and gravest crisis in our culture and society. Here evangelical public theology can work with and build on the great tradition of Christian personalism developed in the social teaching of John Paul II.

5

Francis Schaeffer
and the Public Square

William Edgar

My assignment is to respond to what J. Budziszewski says about
Francis Schaeffer's approach. In addition, I would like to add two
other comments: first about the paper as a whole, with a question attached, and then, after focusing on the views of Schaeffer,
about natural law and general revelation.

Not the least of the virtues of Budziszewski's fine paper is the
care with which he has studied and characterized both the issues
and the major thinkers in his purview. Whatever else they might
say in answer to him, they would have to agree that they were
on the whole fairly represented. As most of us can testify, this is
not a given. Second, this study is timely, in a number of ways.
His conclusions, though they might profit from a bit of fine-tun-

ing, are right on target. To engage in statecraft properly, at the level these four thinkers require, we must heed Budziszewski's call to take the norms of creation more seriously and to begin not with the fall but with the criteria of God's revelation. The absence of such a starting point, manifested in different ways and in different degrees for these thinkers, is surely representative of much contemporary evangelicalism, especially as it contemplates statecraft.

Budziszewski points out that many evangelicals who have a concern for cultural engagement lack not only an "orienting doctrine" that makes a case for the proper place of government but also a "practical doctrine" and a "cultural apologetic" that would actually involve them in the trenches of public policy. In the first case, he remarks, evangelicals tend to read their preset political views back into the biblical text rather than asking the hard theological questions of Scripture that may yield uncomfortable answers. In the latter two cases, he makes the point that often what is lacking (in some more than others) are the actual platforms, as well as a way to persuade others about the virtues of those platforms. Here he has put his finger on one of the abiding problems of being *in* the world of politics but not *of* it. What is the Christian view of farm subsidies or the power of labor unions, not to mention the more loaded issues in such areas as civil disobedience and same-sex partnerships? And then, assuming one develops a particular legislative or judicial conviction, how does one argue for it with those who do not share one's starting point?

Origins of Evangelicalism

Let me ask a parenthetical question at the outset. Budziszewski explains evangelicalism in a way many historians would accept, beginning with the Great Awakening. He follows Mark Noll and many others, as he states at the beginning. But I wonder if this is quite adequate. My concern is that it may leave out people from the past and the present who qualify as evangelicals simply on a confessional basis but are not the kinds of "pietists" (using the word in the good sense) generally meant by the standard historiography. Darryl Hart, for example, agrees with defining evangelicalism from the Great Awakening, but that allows him to lodge a criticism of the movement that might not apply if it were defined differently. In his fascinating book *That Old-Time Religion in Modern America,* Hart argues that conversion, scriptural authority, and populism characterize evangelicalism more than any particular theology or worldview.[1] He traces the rise and fall of the cultural impact of evangelicalism, including the significant though limited renewals of thought and engagement in the twentieth century that have included some of the thinkers under consideration here. It leads Hart to the conclusion that at bottom an evangelical is not so much a conservative Protestant (many are not) as a low-church or even parachurch pietist.

Crucial to evangelical prominence is the pietist notion (as Hart understands it) that no real barriers ought to exist between the practice of faith and its implications for every area of life. Yet he makes the point that, while pietism allowed evangelical faith to penetrate into every area, it masked the profoundly secular character of the nation that these evangelicals had supported. Evangelicals were thus unprepared for the restrictions put on religion in the twentieth century and for the relegation of faith to the private sphere.[2] They simply could not understand the diminished role of faith and the fact that government did not seem to have a soul.[3]

Hart makes a strong point here, one that lends support to Budziszewski's broad affirmation that evangelicals lack a comprehensive doctrine of politics and thus to his view that they tend to react by what he calls "inflationary strategies." Yet I think Hart may be leaving out a number of significant groups who still ought to be characterized as evangelical, simply because they believe the gospel: more traditional Reformed believers, conservative Lutherans, and various ethnic minorities. Actually, certain minority churches might fit the label "evangelical" according to the criteria Hart suggests, but he does not include them in his study. My concern is not for diversity, certainly not for political correctness, but for defining the movement properly. The category of "evangelical" ought not to leave out nonwhites

1. Darryl Hart, *That Old-Time Religion in Modern America* (Chicago: Ivan R. Dee, 2002), 6–12.

2. Ibid., 206–7.

3. Ibid., 215.

or mainline believers who, while they may not be direct heirs of the Great Awakening, espouse evangelical tenets.

The point should not be lost that the strong populist character of much evangelicalism was its great strength until recent times, when the movement has not known how to face some of the challenges of modernity. As Mark Noll argues in *America's God: From Jonathan Edwards to Abraham Lincoln,* the new American republic saw a parallel rise between democratization and evangelicalism, followed by a gradual secularization and toning down of Protestant religion.[4] Republicanism so informs evangelical religion that in the twentieth century the fear of elitism pervaded the cultural critique made by believers who looked to save a godly republic. After the Civil War, Protestants tried to civilize (and Christianize) the United States and succeeded in damaging the commonsense approach to religion. Surely the Scopes Trial was really all about the conflict between populists and the more domesticated views of education and the Bible.

Understanding Francis Schaeffer

Now on to J. Budziszewski's views of Francis Schaeffer. Allow me to begin with a personal remark. I began my own Christian journey at L'Abri back in 1964. My long search for truth (as it turned out, it was actually a search for me!) ended in the magical mountain village of Huémoz-sur-Ollon. Everything came together for me in an extended conversation with Francis Schaeffer. I spent many months at L'Abri and developed a close friendship with both Francis and Edith Schaeffer, and in some ways, the work I am doing today is rooted in the vision I embraced in those days. Several other leaders at L'Abri influenced me, especially Hans Rookmaaker and later Os Guinness.

Budziszewski has pointed out certain weaknesses in Schaeffer's thought, some of which are certainly there. But I think he may have missed the forest for the trees. He praises Schaeffer in a number of ways; for example, he spoke out to alert Christians to

4. Mark Noll, *America's God: From Jonathan Edwards to Abraham Lincoln* (New York: Oxford University Press, 2003). Noll refines and builds on the work of Nathan Hatch, Gordon Wood, and others.

the deeper issues in the surrounding culture. And Budziszewski recognizes many other virtues in the popular apologist. Yet it seems he does not place the *Christian Manifesto* within the larger setting of Schaeffer's oeuvre and therefore misses the broader sweep for which L'Abri stood. Let me comment on his analysis under three headings: "Schaeffer the Conservative," "Schaeffer the Culture Warrior," and "Schaeffer the Resistance Worker."

Schaeffer the Conservative

Understandably, given the topic, Budziszewski culls almost all of his remarks about Schaeffer's politics from one book, *A Christian Manifesto*. Is he right to do so? Some have argued plausibly that this book comes from the "second" Schaeffer, the one who developed in the late 1970s and early 1980s, when he moved away from the open and free cultural comments of the 1960s and developed more specifically right-wing values. It may be true that in his later years Schaeffer was more explicit about his sympathies with political conservatives and groups such as the Moral Majority. It is no doubt the case that the realm of politics and law became predominant in his speaking and writing during those years, to the profound disappointment of many who knew the earlier Schaeffer. But the basic convictions were there all along. In making this choice, then, Budziszewski is not altogether unfair.

I can remember some early lectures based on the work of Rousas Rushdoony, the pioneer of theonomy, in which Schaeffer explained his sympathies with a little book just published called *This Independent Republic: Studies in the Nature and Meaning of American History*.[5] The chapter that intrigued Schaeffer was on the difference between the American Revolution and the French Revolution. Drawing on scholars such as Peter Drucker and James C. Malin, Rushdoony challenged the propriety of calling America's defensive war against Great Britain a true revolution. According to him, it was instead a "conservative counter-revolution," whose purpose was to preserve American liberties from their usurpation by the British Parliament. It owed nothing to

5. Rousas Rushdoony, *This Independent Republic: Studies in the Nature and Meaning of American History* (Nutley, NJ: Craig Press, 1964).

the Enlightenment. By contrast, the French Revolution was the direct result of the Enlightenment ideology, along with the organizational strategies fostered by various secret and illuminist societies. In addition, he claimed, 1789 was the beginning of the modern welfare state, itself a radicalization of the monarchy, and the death knell of private charity and individual responsibility.

Though at the time I was too much a novice in history to judge the accuracy of Rushdoony's thesis, I now realize that he was giving us something like a "Christian America" point of view, along with elements of theonomy, the view that Old Testament law remains authoritative unless specifically qualified in the New Testament. Rushdoony's approach affirmed that the U.S. Constitution, with its loud silence on the Christian faith, only *appears* to be a secular document. In fact, its genius is as a minimalist document whose purpose is to ensure the vitality of local government. Here Rushdoony added a distinctive view, one that would become a leitmotif throughout his long career and would have a wide impact on various players in his sphere of influence: The reason the Constitution did not need to include a Christian confession in its text is that the states were already a Christian establishment or settlement. The First Amendment prohibits laws respecting the establishment of religion because religion was already established at the local level. There were sabbath rules, religious tests for citizenship, laws regarding heterosexual fidelity, and blasphemy laws, all of which were strongly connected to biblical law. The First Amendment protected the states from interference by the federal government.

Indeed, central to nearly all of Rushdoony's writings was the preservation of freedom at the local level, so that all people can faithfully obey God's law without interference from the outside. America holds a special place in world history for Rushdoony because it began as a Christian civic structure, though it is now in desperate need of regaining its original vision. What is needed, then, more than anything else is "pressing the crown rights of Jesus Christ in all spheres of life," as the Chalcedon slogan has it. Francis Schaeffer was clearly in sympathy with this entire line of argument. His conservative leanings did not begin in the late 1970s. Indeed, his own much earlier background involved collaboration (and then a rift) with Carl MacIntire, the anticommunist separatist who founded the Bible Presbyterian Church.

The arguments made in *A Christian Manifesto* often echo this point of view, adding some of the larger cultural material Schaeffer developed at L'Abri and also adding a good deal of specific data from contemporary legal battles. As Budziszewski reminds us, Schaeffer regarded the ascendancy of political conservatism (connected with the Ford and Reagan administrations) as a window of opportunity. To his credit, Schaeffer warns his readers against simply mimicking conservatism and against the temptation to look to conservatism simply for personal peace and affluence. At the same time, on the whole he does side with conservatism, even when it is not founded on particularly Christian principles. He applauds what he calls the "minority of the Silent Majority" for standing on principle and entertaining "at least a memory of Christianity."[6] He is favorable to Jerry Falwell and his Moral Majority, although with some reservations.[7]

I can remember conversations in the late 1970s in which I challenged him about his alliance with Falwell. I tried to see if he was willing to accept the difference between a pro-America fundamentalism and a more Kuyperian Reformed outlook. He was fairly defensive about being Falwell's friend, and he said that after many years of reflection he had chosen to call himself a fundamentalist, despite the caricatures the term might invite. Although his ministerial credentials were in a Presbyterian church, he was rather suspicious of some aspects of the Reformed mentality, as he understood it. He did not talk about the cultural mandate, or common grace, or even the sovereignty of God in a traditionally Reformed manner. And, of course, he and Cornelius Van Til, though they had many things in common, got into serious tangles about apologetics.

On politics, and also on economics and other public issues, then, Schaeffer was generally an American conservative. Thus, the Supreme Court gets much of the blame for the culture's caving in to a humanist worldview. Danger signs in society include the gagging of Christian expression in the public schools, the impending tyranny of government, and bias in the media. Here I think Budziszewski makes a controversial point. Schaeffer is

6. Francis Schaeffer, *A Christian Manifesto,* rev. ed. (Wheaton: Crossway, 1982), 77.
7. Ibid., 56.

impatient with ordinary politics, he says. Accordingly, Schaeffer has "almost nothing to say about the everyday work of reversing them [injustices] by trying to get better laws, better judicial decisions, and better public officials." In addition, Schaeffer gives us little or no guidance about persuasion, about confronting hostile judges, about judging whether peaceful protests at abortion clinics are counterproductive, and the like. Budziszewski suggests that the main reason for this is that Schaeffer was not a political activist but an apologist, and an impatient one at that. Thus, his job was to make broad-stroked judgments about culture, not to devise plans for the trench warfare of daily politics.

I cannot bring myself to agree with this. Whatever else may be said about him, Schaeffer was an extraordinary persuader. He had plenty to say about reversing injustices and obtaining better laws. For example, together with C. Everett Koop, President Reagan's surgeon general, Schaeffer was quite articulate about such matters as protection of the unborn and the dangers of euthanasia. Another example would be his strong promotion of the arts. Furthermore, he was ahead of his time as an evangelical who was actively concerned for the environment. He railed against both the pantheist nature-mysticism and the mindless violations of God's creation in the name of progress.[8] To be sure, Schaeffer was not always a man of details. He could even annoy careful scholars with his from-the-hip generalizations. But I think Budziszewski has put his criticism far too strongly.

I do concede that Schaeffer occasionally displays a deficiency in his own worldview that precipitates his tendency to let apologetics play a more prominent role than politics. It has something to do with Budziszewski's finest point, about the lack of a creation perspective in all these thinkers. Somehow the original call to subdue the earth and have proper dominion over it under God's blessing has been downplayed. When it comes to discussing the cultural mandate in his book on Genesis, Schaeffer says very little about culture, making it quite subordinate to "the first call," which is to align with Abel's descendants.[9] In Schaeffer's conservative vision, politics is almost a necessary evil, where at

8. See Francis Schaeffer, *Pollution and the Death of Man: The Christian View of Ecology* (Wheaton: Tyndale, 1970).

9. Francis Schaeffer, *Genesis in Space and Time* (Downers Grove, IL: InterVarsity, 1972), 35, 82–84.

best the government is a sort of referee to allow generally fair play. This is for the purpose of keeping absolutes alive but especially to allow the Christian faith a chance to permeate. When things go wrong, to use Richard John Neuhaus's phrase, Schaeffer posits a naked public square that gets occupied by the wrong people. From a biblical perspective, however, there should be not a naked public square but a good, though fallen, one. Statecraft may be a limited calling, but it is a legitimate calling, one that has an important part to play in the ordering of God's world. We are still called to subdue and have dominion over all things.

The framework of creation/fall/redemption is not as clearly expressed in Schaeffer's view of culture as we would like. For example, following, as he believes, Henry de Bracton, he wants to put justice first over against power.[10] But is he right to do so? Is power the real problem? Is justice *better* than power? Power can corrupt and can *be* corrupt, but power in government is a good thing in itself. There ought to be a creation/fall/redemption framework within which we can understand power. Still, I think Budziszewski states matters too strongly. Schaeffer's position is far more thought-out and applicable than first meets the eye.

Schaeffer the Culture Warrior

Schaeffer's understanding of culture is much too big a topic to be tackled here. I will just touch on a couple things. To be personal again, it was Schaeffer's diagnosis of cultural trends in the world that first awakened me to the great significance of Christian faith for all of life. It was so exciting to be around L'Abri in the 1960s and to find that someone could make sense of much of the chaos surrounding us. Furthermore, the endorsement of the arts in the vision of L'Abri meant a great deal to me. Being a jazz lover, I was amazed to encounter Hans Rookmaaker, who had a Christian approach to African American music. I believe he and Schaeffer were mutually influential in all kinds of fruitful ways. In general, Schaeffer was not entirely comfortable with a Kuyperian outlook, but he was enormously influenced by Rookmaaker, who came to the field of aesthetics from the

10. Schaeffer, *Christian Manifesto,* 28.

Amsterdam philosophy. Schaeffer is notoriously hard to label, which is a good thing!

So how does Schaeffer understand the dynamics of culture? Perhaps the best way to put it is to say that his strength was his weakness. His strength was to see everything as interrelated, and this really does go back to his strong view of the creation. However inconsistently he applied it, he certainly started with a robust view of the original order of things. Throughout his work, he rails against dichotomies, such as the pietism of Christians who separate their spiritual life from the rest of life. He understands that everything holds together, that "what we face is a totality and not just bits and pieces."[11] In this way, he even joins company with all those who speak of a *zeitgeist*, or a spirit of the age.

Why is this also a weakness? Because it tends toward the monolithic or, perhaps, toward the Manichean. Schaeffer's basic time line for Western culture rises from a corrupt Middle Ages to a high point in the Protestant Reformation, both in Europe and then in America, and then gradually declines to the present time. This approach is not without some nuances. For example, Schaeffer does praise some of the art in medieval times. He recognizes that there were blind spots in the Reformation. He believes some windows of opportunity exist even today. *A Christian Manifesto* is in this way no different from many of his other books. But it is especially hard-hitting against those who cannot see the great clash of worldviews in the present culture. On one side, we have a worldview that is Christian (or, in the case of the West, at least incorporates a vague memory of Christian faith). On the other side, we have humanism (that is, "destructive humanism," not to be confused with Renaissance humanism). The heart of humanism is to believe that "the final reality is impersonal matter or energy shaped into its present form by impersonal chance."[12]

Two factors come into play in Schaeffer's argument. First, the forces of destructive humanism are seeking to dominate the social consensus. Words such as *control, takeover,* and *authoritarianism* permeate the book. Government and law are especially

11. Ibid., 115.
12. Ibid., 18.

responsible for the movement toward a full humanistic control. Although our country was "born out of the Judeo-Christian base," it is now threatened by the tyranny of humanistic elites. We are in a culture war (not his term) between a Judeo-Christian and a humanistic worldview. Here is where some of his allies are used for support. "The Moral Majority," Schaeffer says, "has drawn a line between the one total view of reality and the other total view of reality and the results this brings forth in government and law."[13] Second, he blames various leaders, particularly lawyers, liberal ministers, and educators, for letting this happen. There is a good deal of guilt attribution in this little volume; several times I wrote in the margins such comments as "not much grace here" or "why blame only them?" To be sure, the book is prophetic and informal. But even the bleakest of the Old Testament prophets utters significant words of light and hope as well.

I suppose that certain cultural traits can predominate in a country and that government and gatekeepers have a significant part in establishing them. But reality is far more complex; indeed, it is messy. To put a more positive spin on it, God's creation ordinances herald a rich fabric of human history, where forces and counterforces are at work. Government and law are important parts of the fabric of culture, but so are many other forces and institutions: geographical location, economics, families, schools, denominations, the arts, health care, cybernetics, astrophysics, agriculture, and so forth. Philosophies of life rarely come to a consensus, even in one country. Schaeffer often refers to the Iron Curtain countries as a foil. But oppressive as they were, not everything within them could be defined in terms of the subjugation. Further, there are many types of non-Christian views, not just the raw atheism that reduces all to matter, energy, and chance, as he suggests. Many of them are quite religious. Some are legalistic. Some are mystical. And while no doubt the greater center of vitality in the church can now be found in the Southern Hemisphere, there is perhaps far more Christian faith—as well as common grace—present in the North than Schaeffer implies. The wheat and the tares are growing up together. Lots of decadence, to be sure. Sometimes the courts act

13. Ibid., 60–61.

like lawmakers and usurp power, to be sure.[14] But there is still a good deal of justice, progress in racial equality, more benefits for more people, and the like. According to our Lord's teaching, the last days will be characterized not only by a coldness of heart with persecutions but also by the proclamation of the gospel, and even normal things such as people "marrying and giving in marriage" (Matt. 24:12, 38).

The problem with Schaeffer's historiography is not only theological. Culture studies have for thirty years or more recognized the great complexity of trends as well as the rich matrix of indicators in human life, more so than did earlier anthropology. The work of Clifford Geertz, Arjun Appadurai, Terry Eagleton, and many others has helped us to see the rich layering as well as the multiple expressions of cultural trends. Culture is not a single, fixed entity but a dynamic matrix, centering not only on ideas but on problems like meaning, suffering, and mystery. To describe culture rightly thus requires what Geertz called "thick description."[15] History informs culture but not always in a trickle down from ideas. Decolonization, globalization, consumption, and so many other forces are at work, both to shape our ideas and to give them expression.[16] Many Christian scholars are recognizing the development of the very concept of worldview from its distant origins in Kant, through James Orr and Abraham Kuyper, and down through the social sciences.[17]

I do not want to overstate this critique. Francis Schaeffer was an evangelist. We cannot blame him for not knowing the work of Geertz and others. There are times when sweeping accounts of human culture are needed. There are times when it is right

14. The increasing number of decisions based on "the right of privacy" is a good example. This so-called right is not stated in any founding document; it appears to have emerged in connection with decisions such as *Roe v. Wade* and made its way into the mythology.

15. Clifford Geertz: *The Interpretation of Cultures* (New York: Basic Books, 1973), 90ff. See also Sherry B. Ortner, ed., *The Fate of "Culture": Geertz and Beyond* (Berkeley: University of California Press, 1999).

16. See, for example, Arjun Appadurai, *Modernity at Large: Cultural Dimensions of Globalization* (Minneapolis: University of Minnesota Press, 1996).

17. Paul Marshall, Sander Griffioen, and Richard J. Mouw, eds., *Stained Glass: Worldviews and Social Science* (Lanham, MD: University Press of America, 1989); and David K. Naugle, *Worldview: The History of a Concept* (Grand Rapids: Eerdmans, 2002).

to adopt the style the apostle Paul shows in Romans 1–3, where a part may be legitimately taken as representative of the whole, rather than his approach in Acts 17, where he is specifically responding to a question about the resurrection, using local philosophies as a witness to the truth.[18] Schaeffer's purpose was to open our eyes. He concludes the *Manifesto* with the words of Revelation 3:2: "Wake up! Strengthen the things that remain, that are about to die." There are times when this sort of appeal is the right "jolt" in preparation for the truth. Budziszewski says it well, noting that Schaeffer treats all differences among unbelieving worldviews as unimportant. But perhaps for Schaeffer's purposes they *are*!

I want to be very careful here to strike the right balance. Schaeffer was one of the great persuaders of his era. He often did use the method of Acts 17, as he jousted with unbelievers who could not successfully live out their positions. Freud, he taught us, was a rationalist who yet asked his fiancée to love him "irrationally." John Cage was a believer in randomness and pure chance who nevertheless collected his mushrooms in a taxonomy of strict order. Bernard Berenson famously lived in promiscuous relations, which he justified by calling attention to our animal natures, yet he could not abide some of the weirder modern artists because they were "bestial." These are brilliant rhetorical moves on Schaeffer's part. They work because of the way things are in God's world. I am not quite sure Budziszewski has caught the genius of it.

Still, I concede that there is something awfully alarmist about Schaeffer's presentation. Maybe it is rooted in a premillenarian eschatology. I can remember coming down the mountain from L'Abri and expecting the stock market to cave in, a priestly elite to take over American government, and enemies to poison the drinking water. I was almost disappointed when these things did not happen. Later, I began to see two things that I did not learn at L'Abri, or at least do not remember hearing there. The first is that God furthers his kingdom in a sinful world far beyond the work of missions and that he lavishes his gifts on the just

---

18. Ultimately, the two approaches overlap and accomplish the same things. Romans 1–3 certainly uses the world's decadence to testify to the truth of God's wrath, and Acts 17 certainly accuses unbelief of being "ignorant" in a culpable manner.

and the unjust. Instead of seeing every work of music and art, every law passed in Congress, as a sign of the impending final catastrophe, I began to notice God's patience and love at work in myriad places. I am quite certain that Schaeffer believed in common grace, but the impression was often given that the downward spiral of culture was a far more prevalent trend.

Second, I began to realize that evil, when it is manifest, is actually deeper and thus more pernicious than the impression given at L'Abri. It is certainly more than a government conspiracy. There is corruption at every level of culture. It is not quite as easy to identify the "good guys" as it might appear in the *Manifesto*. They may be good in some ways and bad in others. As I see it, the mistake made by the culture war model is to settle for a winner-takes-all approach that overlooks the many layers and spheres of society. Again, this was more of an unspoken feeling than a carefully argued point of view.

Paul Weyrich has taken a good deal of grief for his famous call to rethink our position on social and political involvement. When he saw no real moral majority out there, he declared, "I believe we probably have lost the culture war"; he then called evangelicals to question their involvement in public institutions and instead to practice "holiness."[19] Weyrich later protested that he never spoke of withdrawing from society. But he still does not seem comfortable with a view of holiness that can and must be practiced in a variety of callings, including politics and moving on to homemaking, education, science, the arts, and so much else. Deep-rooted cultural transformation is measured not by winning a war but by the less visible means of engaging in multiple battles. Schaeffer was always far more involved in practice than the likes of Paul Weyrich, but at times he sounded like him.

Schaeffer the Resistance Worker

Finally, because it is such an important part of his argument, I need to say a few words about Schaeffer's view of civil disobedience. Budziszewski has done a great job here of walking

19. Paul M. Weyrich: "A Moral Minority?" *Free Congress Foundation*, February 16, 1999, 1.

us through Schaeffer's basic approach to graduated resistance, based on his interpretation of Samuel Rutherford's *Lex Rex*. Schaeffer is careful to warn against vigilante justice. Indeed, in my judgment, he is fairly close to Rutherford's view, which has great strengths but also significant problems. Basing his arguments not only on Scripture but also on natural law and various parts of Roman law, Rutherford came to the conclusion that tyrants may be resisted under certain circumstances. But it is not entirely clear what those circumstances are.

Like Calvin, and unlike John Locke, Rutherford believed one must vest any power to resist in lower magistrates, such as states and inferior judges. This was supported by his understanding that tyranny could not dissolve the constitution, but lawmakers, using the constitution, could "make kings, make laws, and raise armies."[20] Theorists in the Covenanter tradition after the Restoration were far more extreme, having given up hope in the lower magistrates. But unlike some of them, Rutherford would want an individual to be passive unto death before killing the king. So when and how may we resist?

John Coffey, Rutherford's modern biographer, sees two forms of discourse in *Lex Rex*, the one being natural law constitutionalism and the other a religious covenantalism similar to the theocracy ideal of the Old Testament. The first, which is more like Locke, makes Rutherford look like an advocate of popular sovereignty, the rule of law, and resistance to tyranny. The second looks to impose the first table of the law on the country and purge it of heresy and unbelief, harking back to the ideals of Christendom.[21] I find elements of both views in Schaeffer's application of Rutherford. He holds to a certain constitutionalism, which promotes freedom from tyranny because God is the lawgiver, and not the people. At the same time, there appears to be a very close connection between American history and Christian faith. He certainly does not want to be a Covenanter, nor does he think we should "wrap Christianity in our national flag."[22] Yet with his particular way of connecting the founding of America with

20. Samuel Rutherford, *Lex Rex* (1644; repr., Harrisburg, VA: Sprinkle, 1982), 377.

21. John Coffey, *Politics, Religion, and the British Revolutions: The Mind of Samuel Rutherford* (Cambridge: Cambridge University Press, 1997), 187.

22. Schaeffer, *Christian Manifesto*, 121.

Judeo-Christian principles, then showing the utter decline into materialistic humanism, Schaeffer may exhibit some theonomic tendencies. He warns that, because of the "immense power of the modern state," we, unlike the Pilgrims (and thus the epoch of Rutherford), may have no place to flee.[23] But flee from what? How bad does it have to be before we resist?

Budziszewski rightly chides Schaeffer for his lack of specifics, and behind that his lack of trust in general revelation to help us decide what to do and when. I would add (unless I am saying the same thing) that, because he lacked both a positive view of the state and statecraft and a complex view of culture, Schaeffer is necessarily vague, just as Rutherford was in his own way. Of course, one might legitimately ask, should not a Christian approach to civil disobedience be properly vague? There never is one clear scenario where we can apply the law, going from point A to points B and C, regardless of the particulars. It was surely Schaeffer's purpose to present not a program for a particular date and time but a mentality, a philosophy that would have to be applied differently according to an assessment of a particular predicament. There are times when it is all right to be vague! Still, we need more help than Schaeffer was able to give.

Back to Creation

The paradox in Schaeffer's thought, says Budziszewski, is that the book is *about* the public square, because it gives us a dire analysis of the spirit that occupies it, but that it lacks an apologetic *for* the public square. The point in itself is excellent. But I want to quarrel with Budziszewski's view of the basis for this paradox. To give it a name, he says Schaeffer is unable to explain the public square because he is a presuppositionalist. The connection is that presuppositionalists either deny or do not practice a salient reliance on general revelation. In Budziszewski's words, they are "notoriously suspicious of general revelation." As a presuppositionalist myself, I must say that this one really made me scratch my head. Not only do we believe in general

23. Ibid., 107.

revelation, but for most of us there is no more important component in our worldview.

The critique holds that presuppositionalists have a view of unbelief that makes it impervious—or at least not fully accessible—to general revelation. Since unbelievers are closed to *special* revelation, they must be resistant to *general* revelation as well. If this is so, then how can any bridges be built to reach them, particularly in matters of civil life? Here, says Budziszewski, is the reason for Schaeffer's inability to get down to specifics. Budziszewski classifies presuppositionalists into two types: One denies that unbelief can be logically coherent, and the other admits that unbelief cannot be logically coherent because of the pressure of general revelation. In the first case (type A, as he calls them), there is a fundamental problem: Unbelievers *can* be logically coherent, and even when they are not, it does not matter, because they do not care about consistency. So there is no way to make contact with this person. In the second case (type B, which includes Schaeffer), general revelation serves to make unbelief impossible, not so much logically but at every level. This allows for some strength in negative critiques but not for building a public square. The presumed remedy to this deficiency would be a commitment to natural law.

Several issues are involved here. Perhaps it is well to say at the outset that certain presuppositionalists can and do sound uneasy with general revelation. They may sound more like Barth than Calvin, which is not their intention. Looking around for thinkers exhibiting this problem, I did find a few who so abhor the concept of natural law that they come across as uncomfortable with general revelation as well. Gary North, in a polemical book titled *Westminster's Confession,* claims that John Calvin was so confused about the relation of the Bible to the classical heritage from the past that he defended a scholastic notion of civil law.[24] We had to wait for Rushdoony—the author Schaeffer loved in the early days of L'Abri—in the 1950s for a view that thoroughly broke with natural law tradition in the civil realm. Even though Rushdoony based his purging on Cornelius Van Til, North feels Van Til himself was not consistent, because he did

24. Gary North, *Westminster's Confession: The Abandonment of Van Til's Legacy* (Tyler, TX: Institute for Christian Economics, 1991), 50–52.

not apply his presuppositionalist principles to the civil realm. According to North, Van Til skirted the problem and let Calvin off the hook.

North then proceeds to defend theonomy, which we have already mentioned. Among other things, it is the view that God's law, including the Mosaic law, has a direct bearing on legislation in the post-Pentecost era. Of course, North's point is not at all to deny general revelation; unlike Barth, he has a robust view of its role. But he does despise the idea that general revelation should govern decisions made in cultural or political matters, because that should come from special revelation. North does not accept the Westminster Confession of Faith when it says that the judicial laws of the Old Testament had expired, "not obliging any other now, further than the general equity thereof may require."[25] General equity is far too vague for him.

North's view is quite extreme. There are no doubt other presuppositionalists who act as though they did not believe in general revelation. As Budziszewski says, they "consider unregenerate man incapable of admitting the obvious." But this is really not the case for the mainstream. If Cornelius Van Til may be used to represent presuppositionalism (I am not sure whether he would be type A or type B), then one finds something quite different in his construction. In his work on epistemology, not only does knowledge *allow for* general revelation, but that revelation is its foundation. For both unbelievers and believers, Van Til states that knowing anything at all is possible only because of knowing God. This is so because we are God's image bearers. In an unfallen world, that would mean a perfect, though finite, operation of the thought process, because we would receive and reinterpret God's revelation, both general and special, without sin. We would base our interpretation of reality on his interpretation of reality. But in a fallen world, the "non-regenerate consciousness" tries to build a counterfeit system, or "to create its own interpretation without reference to God." This means not that God can be no part of an unbeliever's construction but that God is not there as self-sufficient or self-complete.[26]

25. Westminster Confession of Faith XIX.4.
26. Cornelius Van Til, *The Defense of the Faith* (Philadelphia: Presbyterian & Reformed, 1976), 47–49.

Thus, a presuppositionalist apologetic has a different concern about logic than what Budziszewski suggests. What matters most is whether a philosophy lives up to God's logic or not. For example, Hume may be quite "logical" in his skepticism. If God is good and powerful, there could not be evil, he claimed. But it is the wrong logic. The premise of what goodness means, and how it coordinates with power, must be a biblical one if the logic is to be true logic. Similarly, Aristotle's laws are quite "logical." But are they self-evident criteria for truth? To transgress them may or may not be a good move, depending on what you are trying to achieve. For example, to hold that God is both one and three violates a surface interpretation of Aristotle's law of contradiction. If you changed the law to include such a paradox, then you would be biblical but not Aristotelian about logic. To fault presuppositionalists for looking for logical inconsistencies in unbelief does not accomplish anything, unless one establishes what sort of logic we are discussing. What this school is trying to establish is that when an unbeliever's views are faulty, it is because they are illogical on their own terms.

The point is that we live in God's world, which is revelation intensive. Everything in this world reveals God, not just certain aspects of it such as the beauty of nature or the moral conscience. For the type B presuppositionalist, it is not so much that an unbeliever's world is "incoherent because bits of truth get into it that he does not intend," as Budziszewski suggests. It is rather that an unbeliever's view is systematically and organically opposed to God's law. To use technical language, presuppositionalism wants to argue *transcendentally*, not just look for certain types of contradictions. Because of the rebelliousness of unbelief, it seeks, unsuccessfully, to deny revelation. To try to persuade an unbeliever, then, an apologist must look for ways in which that attempted denial will not work. Sometimes that way will be through some flaw in the philosophy itself. More often it will be in a disconnect between the claims and the way of life. Thus, arguments from natural law or from various theistic proofs do not penetrate nearly deep enough into the fabric of a world-and-life view.[27]

27. Paradoxically, because of the transcendental approach, Schaeffer was delighted to work as cobelligerent with unbelievers on various issues. For example,

To be sure, it does often appear as though Schaeffer was not fully transcendental in his arguments, which is perhaps what Budziszewski has struggled with. This would make Budziszewski right to identify the problem of noncontradiction and irrationality as one of the keystones of Schaeffer's critique of unbelief, because it has made him *sound* as though the main concern was over logical fallacies. After all, Schaeffer uncritically borrowed from both coherency and correspondence definitions of truth. Budziszewski is also right to see this limitation as a factor that keeps Schaeffer from being fully comfortable with the reality of common grace. But in this Schaeffer is less than fully a presuppositionalist.

At the same time, some of his arguments against unbelief are thoroughly presuppositional and marvelously on target. His frequent observation that certain unbelievers have a fairly coherent system but cannot themselves live with it is preeminently presuppositionalist. Many of us recall his insight into Jean-Paul Sartre's philosophy of authenticity: Sartre based it on the refusal of any "essence," but he always espoused leftist causes. We also remember Schaeffer's discussion of morals with an atheistic Jew who maintained that everything in ethics boiled down to social convention until Schaeffer broached the subject of the Holocaust with him. "Oh, no," he said forcefully; "*that* was evil." Although Schaeffer may have been less consistently presuppositional than Van Til, he certainly was amazingly effective as a hybrid-presuppositional evangelist.

On Natural Law

But now a critical distinction has to be made, one that is not always fully appreciated by the critics of presuppositionalism: Neither general revelation nor the sense of deity is equivalent to natural law. Of course, there are many versions of natural law, and this is not the place for a full discussion of the subject.[28]

---

while he opposed radical feminism, he could militate with radical feminists against abortion on the grounds that it turned women into objects.

28. It is true that Calvin used the expression "natural law," and so do many Reformed theologians after him. But in my opinion, he and they are a long way from the medievals, or even Augustine. That is a discussion for another time.

As both Schaeffer and Van Til understand natural law, it claims to provide a foundation to be built on, because even the natural man can see the obvious using unaided reason. Natural theology can be done because of the way things are. However, Van Til replies, the natural man is not qualified to judge these things without a measure of grace to open his eyes. Yes, revelation tells us at every point about the true story of the universe, creation/fall/redemption. But no, this is not a sure enough foundation for doing common work. Our ability to interpret the data has been skewed because of sin. Thus, we cannot judge correctly whether marriage should be monogamous, whether private property is good, and the like by the light of reason alone.[29]

So how can we do anything in common with unbelievers? Not because of natural law but because of common grace. We can work with unbelievers and make sense of problems with them because God has given all of us gifts of undeserved wisdom. Our reason itself must be reformed. And we may do apologetics despite the chasm between the fundamental commitments of belief and unbelief because the sense of deity in every person connects us. Because they have a conscience, says Van Til, unbelievers know deep down that the Christian story is true. "Whatever may happen, whatever sin may bring about, whatever havoc it may occasion, it cannot destroy man's knowledge of God and his sense of responsibility to God." Indeed, even sin cannot be what it is without the "ineradicable knowledge of God." Van Til is not reticent to call this *common* knowledge.[30] So much is this the case that to persuade men and women about the Christian position we must move over on to their ground, for argument's sake, to show both their system's incapacity to square with reality and also God's call to the prodigal to come back home. So much is this the case that not only can we live comfortably in a world that does not openly confess the truth, but we can take an active part in it, fulfilling various callings.

See, though, James W. Skillen and Rockne M. McCarthy, "Subsidiarity, Natural Law, and the Common Good," in *Political Order and the Plural Structure of Society,* ed. James W. Skillen and Rockne M. McCarthy (Atlanta: Scholars Press, 1991), 377–95.

29. Van Til, *Defense of the Faith,* 155ff.

30. Ibid., 153.

One of Van Til's more interesting insights concerns the unity of general revelation and special revelation. They presuppose and supplement each other because (1) they emanate from the same God, and (2) they are aspects of "one general philosophy of history."[31] As in much Reformed theology, Van Til affirms that the wrath of God is revealed in nature. But unlike some of it, he also affirms that the *goodness* of God is revealed in nature, citing the covenant with Noah as an example. Van Til furthermore labels *both* special and general revelation with the traditional attributes: necessary, authoritative, sufficient, and perspicuous. He does this not by collapsing the one into the other, in a Barthian manner, but by assigning each a specific purpose within the whole of history. For example, natural revelation is sufficient not because it can stand alone when supernatural revelation is not available but in the sense that it was always meant to be the concomitant of supernatural revelation. Presuppositionalists are not deists, simply hoping that out there somewhere there is an ultimate starting point. They are biblical theists, who believe nothing makes sense without a Creator God who is actively revealing himself to our fallen creation.

Furthermore, and this was not fully developed in Schaeffer's thought, we have in the presuppositionalist position an eschatological account of creation/fall/redemption. Even if sin had not entered the world, the era before the fall was not meant to exist forever unchanged. The creation mandates announced a future for the human race, one that would explore the riches of the world, and one that would need political organization. To put it perhaps anachronistically, statecraft was envisaged from the beginning. It is not a concession to the fall. This understanding allows us to work with people who do not share our deepest convictions. This world is being redeemed, and God is showing his patience and benevolence as we await the consummation.

This is what allows us to live in the world of politics and persuade unbelievers. Budziszewski has a nice phrase in which he says of public officials, "Of course, Christians should try to convert [them], but the immediate need is to persuade them to

31. Van Til writes about this relationship in a number of places. Perhaps the most cogent is "Nature and Scripture," in *The Infallible Word,* ed. Paul Woolley (Philadelphia: Presbyterian & Reformed, 1946), 263–301.

act less like Pharaoh and more like Cyrus." But then he adds, thinking to disagree with presuppositionalists, "For this, one needs arguments that make sense to the unconverted, even to those who stop listening at the mere mention of Scripture." But in one way, no arguments make sense to the unconverted, at least in a persuasive way. Unbelief does not reject Scripture while accepting general revelation. The characteristic of unbelief is just that: to rebel against the truth, however it may come. Persuasion to act less like Pharaoh and more like Cyrus will be more likely to occur when arguments remain faithful to the Christian view of history. One does not accomplish that by choosing one sort of revelation over another but by being faithful to whatever is true. To do that in politics is surely not easy. But the task is no easier in the arts, in the schools, or in any other area of life.

Certainly, an appeal to Scripture in the public square is not always a wise strategy. But this is a strategic choice, not the preference of one kind of revelation over another. All of revelation is full of insights for us in public life. The basis of our hope is not that one kind of revelation will "work" better than another but our knowledge that this is Christ's world and that, whether magistrates like it or not, they are appointed by him to do his will. To walk into politics with this assumption does not mean awkwardly to draw the sword of the Bible at every point but to remind fellow politicians of what they know already, by virtue of general revelation, and to defend justice as it is biblically defined, with wisdom and grace, argued vigorously and honorably.

A few final thoughts. These issues are not easy to discuss. Despite the differences of interpretation set forth on these pages, we ought to go back to the fundamental thesis, which is that the creation matters deeply to our stance on public policy. Here we must admit that a number of our evangelical heroes have been deficient. So whether we defend natural law or general revelation, whether we are presuppositionalists or classical apologists, whether we think in terms of culture wars or a plurality of battles over sovereignty, we can at least agree that without a robust theology of the creation we will not get very far at all, whether in public philosophy or anywhere else.

6

John Howard Yoder and a Church-Centered Political Theory

Ashley Woodiwiss

While I am not a Yoderian, I am convinced that John Howard Yoder offers evangelicals an option we must take seriously, even if we ultimately part company with him. It is in this spirit that I come to J. Budziszewski's analysis. I find Budziszewski here, as in all his work, a serious and probing thinker; yet I do have some concerns about whether he gives us enough so that we really "have Yoder." My concerns are threefold: I find a conceptual problem, a problem of scope, and a problem of method.

First, and perhaps most obviously, Yoder was not and never claimed to be a political theorist. Thus, to develop a model of political theory, as Budziszewski did in his first section, and then to fault Yoder for not meeting his criteria is surely problematic. Yoder was not a political theorist, but neither was he a systematic theologian. Rather, he was a theological ethicist focused chiefly on particular *practices* that mark a specific Christian way of being in the world.

One catches the spirit of Yoder's unconventional orientation early on in *The Politics of Jesus* when he says, "Theologians have long been asking how Jerusalem can relate to Athens; here the claim is that Bethlehem has something to say about Rome—or Masada."[1] Here Yoder jettisons the typical conceptual approach that marked theology as essentially an academic project; in its place, he offers a reading that situates the Christian narrative in a particular (i.e., Anabaptist) understanding of the Christian faith as determined more by Christian *practice* than by theological systems.

Yoder fleshes this out when he states his purpose: "I propose to read the Gospel narrative with the constantly present question, 'Is there here a social ethic?'"[2] That this is not political theory is evident. But that Yoder's approach is *suggestive* to the development of Christian theory can be seen when he follows up the above statement with his hypothesis: "The ministry and the claims of Jesus are best understood as presenting to hearers and readers not the avoidance of political options, but one particular social-political-ethical option."[3] Therefore, we will encounter difficulty in considering Yoder's importance or significance for evangelical political thought if we ask of him that which he cannot provide.

My second concern has to do with scope. Certainly, no one can claim to offer a serious probing of Yoder's thought without giving close attention to *The Politics of Jesus.* But I think Budziszewski falls into an opposite problem: He limits his account almost exclusively to that work. In an analysis that includes eighty notes, Budziszewski cites Yoder works other than *Politics* just six times, with three references to articles and three to Yoder's (pre-*Politics*) 1964 volume, *The Christian Witness to the State.* Those of us fortunate enough to teach political theory are expected to offer our students some of the great texts in our field. For example, one cannot understand Marx without studying the *Communist Manifesto,* but none of us would rest our treatment of Marx solely

1. John Howard Yoder, *The Politics of Jesus* (Grand Rapids: Eerdmans, 1994), 3.
2. Ibid., 11.
3. Ibid.

on this slim volume. Pre-*Manifesto* works such as the *Economic and Philosophic Manuscripts* and *The German Ideology*, along with such post-*Manifesto* works as *Grundrisse* and *Das Kapital*, have to come into the conversation if we are to give a truly sufficient account of Marx's theory. Thus, the *Manifesto* is necessary but not sufficient for any comprehensive understanding of Marx.

This same condition applies to our understanding of Yoder. Mark Thiessen Nation's "Comprehensive Bibliography of the Writings of John Howard Yoder" catalogues several hundred works by Yoder.[4] We certainly cannot expect Budziszewski to take on the sum total of such a prodigious output; an editorial scalpel must be applied. But the instrument employed here is too blunt. An exclusive focus on *The Politics of Jesus* might misshape or distort our understanding of Yoder.

In *The Politics of the Cross: The Theology and Social Ethics of John Howard Yoder*, Craig Carter acknowledges the central importance of *Politics*.[5] However, he claims that the totality of Yoder's political vision lies in this classic plus four other books of essays dealing with theology and ethics, *The Original Revolution: Essays on Christian Pacifism* (1971) and three later collections: *The Priestly Kingdom: Social Ethics as Gospel* (1984), *The Royal Priesthood: Essays Ecclesiological and Ecumenical* (1994), and *For the Nations: Essays Public and Evangelical* (1997). About that early work *The Christian Witness to the State*, the only Yoder volume other than *Politics* that Budziszewski cites, Carter says that, while it demonstrates some of the themes that concern Yoder throughout his career, it "would not be as important to read" as the last three books of essays.[6] We are left to wonder: Even if Budziszewski gets Yoder in *The Politics of Jesus*, is his account sufficient for a full reckoning?

Serious Yoderians would say no. Yoder's later career was marked by changes in direction and elaborations beyond his 1972 classic. Yoder's work "would be much easier to dismiss," says Carter, "if he had not moved beyond the focus on individual discipleship to develop his ecclesiology in such significant ways

4. *Mennonite Quarterly Review* 71, no. 1 (January 1997): 93–145.

5. Craig Carter, *The Politics of the Cross: The Theology and Social Ethics of John Howard Yoder* (Grand Rapids: Brazos, 2001).

6. Ibid., 245.

during the last two decades of his career."[7] Particularly, in the 1994 volume, *Royal Priesthood,* Yoder develops his ecclesiological theme more deeply and richly than in his brief (five-page) comments in *Politics.* These later developments are absent from Budziszewski's treatment.

A third difficulty with Budziszewski's analysis of Yoder has to do with method. After inveighing (correctly!) against evangelicals' insufficient analytical rigor, Budziszewski himself employs just such an "evangelical" method in his reading of *The Politics of Jesus.* That is, he sticks exclusively to an individual (dare I say "intuitionist") reading of this lone text without recourse to a single secondary source, either among those referenced by Yoder himself in *Politics* or, perhaps more importantly, among the scholarly literature about Yoder. Yoder's text is elaborately situated in an ongoing theological discussion of text, interpretation, meaning, and method, but Budziszewski's account lacks all of this. It is simply the sound of one voice speaking. We may like and/or agree with what that one voice says. But I would submit that the kind of serious work that Budziszewski calls for in his conclusion would require, at a minimum, a more informed commentary on the text.

The partial picture of Yoder that Budziszewski gives us will be virtually unrecognizable to Yoderians. Let me suggest two points at which serious students of Yoder could challenge Budziszewski's overly narrow scope and method. One is an error of commission, the other of omission.

Yoder and the Resurrection

At several points, Budziszewski questions Yoder's confidence in the resurrection of Jesus. To be sure, in *The Politics of Jesus,* Yoder is relatively silent about this doctrine, and this has given cause for some of his critics to question (as Budziszewski does) whether Yoder is right on this central claim of the Christian faith. Yet there are at least three answers to this challenge: (1) *Politics* is almost exclusively limited to a consideration of the meaning of the cross as normative for Christian life in the

7. Ibid., 226.

world, and so the resurrection is not relevant for what Yoder is about *here*; (2) Yoder does offer a much more explicit account of his views of the resurrection in his *Preface to Theology: Christology and Theological Method*; and (3) Yoder was not, as mentioned previously, a systematic theologian but took up topics or conversations in a rather ad hoc manner. To be sure, Carter argues that the next generation of Yoderian scholarship must in fact fill in where Yoder was untidy, unclear, and unsystematic. But with respect to whether Yoder believed the historic doctrine of the resurrection, Carter concludes, "Yoder believed in the bodily resurrection of Jesus Christ as an event in history. It would be hard for any serious reader of his writings to conclude otherwise."[8]

Indeed, Yoder may not be as vague about it even in *Politics* as Budziszewski suggests. Budziszewski says Yoder is making a radical point when he compares the "historicity" of what Yoder calls the "narrative skeleton" of the Gospels with the more debated resurrection accounts. But Yoder is here only summarizing the current (at that time) theological debate and does not commit himself to one side or the other. Indeed, in his very next paragraph, Yoder argues that to get into *that* debate would change his focus from exegesis to dogmatics. Were he to make that move, he says, "I would seek simply to demonstrate that the view of Jesus being proposed here is more radically Nicene and Chalcedonian than other views. I do not here advocate an unheard-of modern understanding of Jesus."[9]

A too limited approach has led Budziszewski to a conclusion that a broader and more capacious reading of Yoder would not have maintained. In general, I do not find Budziszewski's account very faulty in terms of commission. However, I do think that an insufficient consideration of Yoder's later and more ecclesiologically developed thought leads him to omit what may in fact be most promising for the development of a distinctive evangelical political theory. I want to turn now in this more positive direction and ask, What would it mean for Christian theorists to take ecclesiology seriously?

8. Ibid., 236.
9. Yoder, *Politics of Jesus,* 102.

Returning Theory to the Church

In recent years, two distinctive lines of development of a "political theory from the church" have begun to emerge. One is explicitly Anabaptist and in a direct line with Yoder. The other draws more from some contemporary Continental philosophical impulses. (I omit here any mention of the work of Stanley Hauerwas, which of course is deeply Yoderian yet distinctive. Hauerwas must count as a third, though less developed, version of an ecclesiocentric political theory.) Both of these lines of inquiry claim that authentic Christian theorizing about the "political" must take its inspiration from the practices and historical situation of the church. Thomas Heilke and I coedited *The Re-Enchantment of Political Science*.[10] I would like to use Heilke's contribution to that volume as my first example. My own work will be illustrative of the second approach.

In his wonderful article "At the Table? Toward an 'Anabaptist' Political Science," Heilke (invoking Yoder throughout) begins the elaboration of an Anabaptist political theory by setting out the necessary distinctions of how Anabaptist theory would reread (or, following Alasdair MacIntyre, renarrate) the emergence of modern history; its chief institutional embodiment, the state; and the place of the church. This retelling situates the voice of the church as a "supportive resident alien," one that is neither "a manipulator of social forces nor an apologist for political necessity."[11] In other words, Anabaptist political theory avoids the pitfalls of both rightist and leftist liberationist theologies or ideologies, on the one hand, and secular and Christian versions of realism, on the other. It works as a "revisionism with a vision" by (1) opening up the political imagination to possibilities other than the standard statist accounts of what constitutes the nature and practice of "the political," (2) making these insights public by reflection on the practices of the church by use of Yoderian middle axioms, and (3) working in an ad hoc and context-dependent way. Just as feminist, queer, and postcolonial theory have forced a reconsideration of the self-understandings (and meth-

10. Thomas W. Heilke and Ashley Woodiwiss, eds., *The Re-Enchantment of Political Science* (Lanham, MD: Lexington Books, 2001).
11. Ibid., 57.

odological practices) of American political science, so Anabaptist theory "might suggest new directions for research based on the kinds of middle axioms we noted earlier that emerge from a pacifist, minority standpoint."[12] In this essay, then, Heilke respects the insights of Yoder while translating them into the idiom of an academic specialty. That is, Heilke is setting forth a Yoderian political theory.

A second approach for ecclesiocentric political theory relies less on such Anabaptist insights and more on certain secular philosophical currents in which the narrative of the church may be strategically situated. Specifically, I would argue that such a resituating fits our real, historical context better than the vestiges of Constantinian thought found in Reformed (common grace) and Catholic (natural law) thought. In our post-Christendom context, the Christian narrative—which earlier served and was served by these premodern theologies—no longer rules, but neither is it powerless. How can we develop an authentic Christian political theory both sensitive to the church's historical claims and situated in a time when those claims, while still potent in some ways, no longer possess the public-ordering authority they once had? We no longer live in Jerusalem, but neither do we live in Babylon.

It strikes me that an "agonistic Augustinianism" is needed. Following the recovery of the political exhibited by agonistic democratic theory (e.g., Mouffe, Laclau, Isaac), agonistic Augustinianism accepts the irreparably conflictual nature of politics while positing the church as the location of a truly "altera civitas," an "other" city, as John Milbank has expressed it. Here, then, is another expression of an ecclesiological political theory. The church, now defined by its sacramental practices rather than by Yoder's communal practices, constitutes its own polis and in doing so reads and critiques the self-understandings, practices, and institutions of the modern polis. But because of (1) its complicity in making and justifying the modern polis and (2) its present marginalization in public ordering, the church can neither rule (*pace* Constantinians) nor simply survive (*pace* Hauerwas). Rather, it must become more political; it must negotiate the concrete particulars of its narrative engagement with the modern polis site by site, issue by issue. With agonistic Au-

12. Ibid., 53.

gustinianism, the political is inescapable but also replete with possibility. This kind of ecclesiological theory arguably makes us more political because we must be more ad hoc and less systematic, more discerning (recovering the virtue of prudence) and less naive or suspicious, better readers of what is possible and what is not—ultimately, more pragmatic and less totalizing. And this method does recall Yoder's own.

Budziszewski is right to call us to the serious work of reflection. I would suggest that Yoder can help us see how to be political in a way that is both fully engaged with the world and authentically Christian, rooted in the message and practices of the church. The church exists in the United States as one of what Nancy Fraser calls "subaltern counterpublics."[13] In her account, which is concerned with feminist developments, the "subaltern counterpublic" serves a twofold project of identity and subversion. The former may be thought of as a moment of (Anabaptist?) separation in order to nurture, form, and strengthen one's primary identity. But this first moment is inextricably linked to the next: the re-insertion of the (now more fully formed) self back into the public "political" with the kind of service that is at the same time a form of subversion. It strikes me that Christians should understand themselves to be involved in just such a project, just as feminists, queers, and other marginalized voices have been.

As a good evangelical, let me conclude this response by going back to the Bible. Consider Daniel as an example of the kind of posture I have been describing. Daniel understood the logic of Babylon and was under no illusion that it would or could become Jerusalem. Still, when given the opportunity for high-level public service, he took it. But he did so in a way authentic to his primary community; in fact, he did so at great personal risk and for the sake of his community. Esther is a similar example. We need the kind of Christian political theory that can help our ecclesial communities understand the moment we dwell in and can equip our daughters and sons to go out and be Esthers and Daniels. Although John Howard Yoder will ultimately prove insufficient for our task, his voice and his vision are serious, strong, and necessary. We would be wise to "take up and read."

13. Nancy Fraser, "Rethinking the Public Sphere," in *Habermas and the Public Sphere,* ed. Craig Calhoun (Cambridge: MIT Press, 1991), 109–42.

Afterword

A Friendly Outsider's Reflections

Jean Bethke Elshtain

My billing as a "friendly outsider" is accurate. I did not have the experience that some of those who took part in this seminar had and have spoken about very movingly—a profound moment when I came to Christ, or discovered Christ, or was brought to Christ. For some, this moment came when they were in college. When I was in undergraduate school, I was busy moving in the other direction. I spent about fifteen minutes thinking I was a deist. Then I thought, well, maybe agnostic, but that seemed too uncertain. And atheism never worked. Eventually, I thought: I am either going to abandon this altogether or become a Roman Catholic. So while some of the seminar speakers were finding something, I was still looking at all sorts of alternatives, both with religion and with politics. I have been poised between Lutheranism and Catholicism for some years now.

Something else that struck me as very interesting was that the evangelical scholars under consideration made great contributions to the speakers' formation, in part because they gave evangelicals freedom to think about a range of issues. I had always believed this was a freedom I had as a birthright. I did not require some kind of permission to think freely; that was just a part of being an American. Despite our divergent trajectories,

195

however, we have similar concerns, especially about the future of our country. What I offer here are reflections on what others have said. Then, toward the end of these reflections, I talk a bit about political theory and religion.

As I began to read J. Budziszewski's challenging paper, I thought about how people's minds can be jolted to think about things in a different way. Pointing out logical contradictions or incoherencies often does very little to persuade or dissuade. So what works? How do we break through hardened hearts? One powerful way is through an illustrative story that invites people in and takes them on a journey toward a point. The parables of Jesus can do this, or the example of people who have led exemplary lives. I have long thought that one of the greatest strengths of Roman Catholicism is its saints. Some of the saints were rather peculiar; some did very strange things. There are a variety of ways to join that august company. Human beings have many different gifts, and we all bring something unique to the human story.

One way Dietrich Bonhoeffer tried to call the attention of his fellow Christians to the situation in Nazi Germany in the 1930s was to argue, as he does in *Letters and Papers from Prison,* that What is the moral or right thing to do? is not the question that should engage us. What should engage us is, rather, What is to come? If we stay on this course, what is the likely outcome? And what are we obliged to do? What is the nature of Christian responsibility? Another essay of his, part of the unfinished—or, rather, incomplete—*Ethics,* is on what it means to tell the truth. Bonhoeffer criticizes Kant severely. He talks about the cruelty of the kind of moralism that puts people in impossible situations with lofty standards they cannot possibly live up to, assuring them that if they simply subscribe to one categorical imperative or another, they can never be in conflict *within* themselves, because in principle these categorical imperatives cannot conflict. And yet the reality of the world is such that we find *goods* in conflict, not just a clear-cut good confronting a clear-cut wrong.

The portion of Kant that so agitated Bonhoeffer was in a discussion of lying, where Kant argues that one is obliged always to tell the truth. If someone who is seeking to harm a friend of yours knocks on your door asking for his whereabouts, and your friend is hidden on the premises, then you are obliged to turn your friend over. You are not permitted to lie; telling the truth is a categorical imperative. You cannot lie or try to deceive the person who means to harm your friend. But Bonhoeffer says that at that point the moralist turns into a tormenter of humanity. Better to lie and to spare your friend, to smudge yourself with the hard complexities of the world. Those are the kinds of moral dilemmas that interest me as a political thinker.

Bonhoeffer wrestles with the problem of "dirty hands." When we act in the world, we cannot control the consequences of our actions. People respond to our actions in ways that we can neither predict nor control. So, Bonhoeffer asks, do we remain in a position of purity, above the fray, where we can bask in our own virtuousness? Or do we enter the fray, knowing that it is likely to get us dirty? We cannot remain absolutely pure.

How do we think about political issues? Do we do it through a comprehensive political theory? Or are there other approaches that are not necessarily superior but are different?

Budziszewski charges his four thinkers with lacking a comprehensive political theory. I wonder just how big a problem this is for each of them. It strikes me that, in the case of theological ethicists and theologians, the first questions to ask are theological ones. How compelling is this person's theology? How do we understand that theology in light of the requirements of Scripture and the Christian tradition and its centuries of interpretation and action?

The truth of the matter is that biblical truths are compatible with many political systems, not just one. There are some political systems that we cannot in any way square with biblical truths—fascism, for instance, or Stalinism. But we can certainly see how biblical truths are compatible with some forms of monarchy, with constitutional democracy, with a variety of other political configurations. Scripture does not dictate one kind of regime.

That said, the direction of Christian political philosophy over the last half century is interesting. One of the key figures here is Pope John Paul II, who affirmed that the political form that most fully sustains the dignity of the human person and the possibility of human flourishing is democracy. Democracy speaks most clearly to the desire for both freedom and justice, and this is part of our human inheritance. Budziszewski's general-revelation claims would come in here.

Questions to ask of any religious thinker would include, What lessons do you draw from the fact that we are created in God's image? How much conceptual weight should that have? What is your understanding of worldly authority, of God's sovereignty in relationship to political sovereignty? What about individual moral autonomy: Are we sovereign selves? If we are not sovereign in the sense of wholly autonomous laws unto ourselves, then what is the purview of moral autonomy and free will? We are born into and for community, in some profound sense, yet at the same time we are sites of willing and autonomous individual action.

Without these central terms of discourse or categories of political thought, we do not have anything that would approach a political theory. We need some account of authority, power, legitimacy, freedom, and justice. Our theology need not delineate an account of justice, but we certainly have to be able to draw from it some implications for justice. Some accounts within the history of Christian thought say more than others specifically about justice. Catholic social thought is a key example here. So is Abraham Kuyper's thought, in which justice is one of the central themes and in which the implications for our understanding of justice are directly drawn both from Scripture and from the history of political thinking.

We must also consider the political implications of the powerful stories in the Old and New Testaments. I once held a conference on the political implications of Scripture, to which we invited a diverse group of thinkers to reflect on some particular scriptural passages, including Jesus' "render unto Caesar, render unto God" reply about the coin; his feeding of the five thousand; and the temptation in the wilderness, in which Jesus was offered a worldly kingdom and worldly power.

Let us think for a moment about the concept of Christian rule, that is, rule by Christian kings or emperors. Although many people thought the Holy Roman Emperor was neither holy nor Roman nor an emperor, this was a period of Christian rule. Oliver O'Donovan seeks to resurrect something like that in his challenging book *The Desire of the Nations*. But today, even if Christian rule were desirable, most people think it would be impossible in light of our current circumstances. Despite this, I would commend to you O'Donovan's book. He begins with a reflection on Hobbes's great work, *The Leviathan,* then goes back and rereads the Old Testament with an eye to notions of rule. The Old Testament is, of course, full of accounts of political rule, of kings and kingdoms and worldly authority. If you excise the Old Testament from your account of scriptural politics, you are going to miss the story of the people of Israel, the accounts of wars and justice, and other such things that politics, for better or for worse, has always been about.

In discussing Carl F. H. Henry, Budziszewski says that we cannot derive an entire political theory from the Bible. That seems to me correct. We can, however, derive ideas about political rule, governance, fairness, misuse of authority, cruelty and how to respond to it, the importance of forgiveness, and many other politically important topics. One of the great political theorists of the twentieth century, Hannah Arendt, called forgiveness the greatest political contribution of Jesus of Nazareth. For every wound there is counter-wounding, and we get into those cycles of what Nietzsche called "the eternal return of the same." But with forgiveness, the possibility of something new emerges. Arendt argued that the way we break through that eternal return of the same is by teasing out the political implications of forgiveness. So that would be another route into some of the questions about the Bible and politics.

I think that what Budziszewski is saying in his discussion of Henry is that, for many issues, clear biblical guidelines are not available, there are not ready-made answers for every situation. This is another way of describing political life, the role of prudential judgments made by political actors in situations where perfect knowledge is never available, where we have to anticipate the reactions to what we are planning to do but can never control them. We are always working in a kind of twilight. Clausewitz talked famously about the "fog of war." There is a fog of politics too. We just cannot know everything there is to know. The world of politics is the world of prudential judgments, compromises, and half measures. We can create elegant scenarios and make lots of things work on paper, but to slog through these scenarios in the real world is something else entirely. Augustine defined politics as "the attempt to reconcile conflicting human wills," and I think that is a reasonable way to put it.

The book to which Budziszewski devoted the bulk of his Henry analysis, *The Uneasy Conscience of Modern Fundamentalism*, launched a sustained debate in evangelical circles, in part because Henry made social engagement such a central theme without ever claiming to have written a comprehensive political epic. That raises a question about thinking about religious figures politically. Is it fair to criticize them for what they have *not* done, what they knowingly did not do? Whenever people offer reflections that put them into a political universe and encourage others to engage in politics, we can quite reasonably put to them certain political questions. But are they obliged to offer us some kind of comprehensive account of politics? Or should we be content with the political insights and possibilities that—in the case of these religious thinkers—they believe are scripturally derived?

Much of the seminar discussion of Henry centered on how we attempt to preserve what is good in society, preserve what is best in custom and tradition, those things we believe are central to any decent political culture, while at the same time thinking about salutary changes. Several times the question of inner transformation or regeneration came up. From what does such transformation proceed? Do we have to rely on the inner transformation of persons in order for something genuinely transformative to occur in society? Or do we assume that we have to change social structures and that somehow transformation of human beings will follow on the heels of that?

This is often posed as an either/or dilemma. I am not sure that is the best way to put it; my hunch is that these things always work in some complicated way in tandem. But those of us who do political thought have inherited this way of thinking, largely because of a famous point in Rousseau (who I must say is not my all-time favorite thinker). Rousseau says in *The Social Contract* that the very changes needed to generate the just republic are in fact the transformations in individuals that would *follow* on a just republic. He leaves the dilemma hanging there: To bring about the social contract, we need the kind of people whom the social contract will create. That is not very helpful. Certainly, much of what we do, much of what we think, even our understanding of who we are, depends on the contexts in which we find ourselves. But it is also possible for us to alter those contexts. To use an overused term—one I became allergic to in the 1960s and 1970s—there is a kind of "dialectical relationship" between the two points that are often cast as polarities. So I am suggesting that inner transformation and alterations in context work in tandem.

Another matter that came up a number of times in our conversation is the fall of man. How far have we fallen, and what effect does that have on political possibility? If we believe we fell all the way and are depraved creatures, that will affect our understanding of what our political possibilities are. Those of us familiar with Hobbes's *Leviathan* will know that he has a very low anthropology, to put it mildly. Life in the state of nature is "nasty, brutish, and short," as described in that famous phrase of his. Hobbes is a master of consistency, so he goes on to create an authoritarian structure, a Leviathan, because we need that to hold unruly, depraved creatures in check. It would be incoherent to move from Hobbes's anthropology to a benign utopia in which we all get along fine with one another. There is always a connection in one's understanding of the human creature and the political possibilities that such a creature can reasonably aspire to.

I was telling Budziszewski—somewhat jocularly, but not completely so—that the most convincing support for his thesis about general revelation may be some recent studies with capuchin monkeys. It turns out they have a rudimentary sense of fairness. These monkeys like grapes, and they do not particularly like cucumbers. When they were given grapes as rewards for performing tasks, they kept working hard to earn the rewards, but given cucumbers, they went on strike. The researchers put a couple of monkeys side by side and gave one a grape for performing a task and another a chunk of cucumber for doing an identical task. The monkey that got the cucumber was quite distressed and started to attack the one that got the grape. The researchers say, Well, if a sense of fairness exists in a capuchin monkey, it probably developed early in the primate line, and the genes that promote that behavior are likely to be present in people too. There you go—*general revelation.*

So perhaps morality is imbedded in the genes. There *is* something that can be appealed to in us, even though we are fallen creatures. That is a very powerful idea with a long history, and it has played a central role, certainly in Catholic thought.

In his *Ethics*, Dietrich Bonhoeffer appeals to that which is *natural*, a category that came to rest almost exclusively within the purview of Catholic ethics. Bonhoeffer argues that Protestants need to recapture this and to find a way of talking about nature and the natural. Then he lists some things that he believes are *against* nature—that is, against our standing as embodied creatures. Although he does not say "this is happening now in my country," we know that it was. He talks about the destruction of the lives that were considered not worth living. As you know, the first Nazi killing programs were aimed at persons with disabilities. Horrible programs that took place in hospitals had nurses and doctors killing retarded children. That is an assault against nature and the natural. The physically and mentally handicapped are people who appear among us from time to time, and we are obliged to love and cherish them as we do all other human beings. Bonhoeffer lists the killing of prisoners of war, people who have surrendered and therefore now have the status of noncombatants. He also lists abortion. He says that, if we start to think about nature and the natural, there are implications for justice, housing, penal systems, and a whole range of other things. All this is just *there*, as a task for Protestant theologians and ethicists to undertake.

A question that came up repeatedly in our discussions was how we who are both believers and citizens talk about these issues. *Citizen* is a word we might have used in our discussions more than we did. As believers and citizens, how do we talk when we enter the public arena?

I think someone mentioned that we need to be "bilingual." How do we speak inside the community of the church, and how do we address those who are out in the world? One of the most powerful and inescapable systematic political philosophies in the last quarter of a century is John Rawls's *Theory of Justice* and his subsequent works following up on that. Rawls insists that those who hold what he considers to be sectarian or particular commitments, especially religious belief, are obliged to leave those commitments behind when they enter the public arena. Religious believers cannot use religious terms directly; religiously derived political commitments have to be cast in the language of what

Rawls calls "deliberative reason." I, for one, have no idea exactly what that is, except something really abstract. But, according to Rawls, the language of deliberative reason is the language in and through which politics should take place.

That is now a pervasive theme in much of contemporary political thought, so that there is an allergic reaction whenever anyone uses a biblical term or religiously derived understanding in the political arena. One gets a lot of traction in the abortion debate and a number of other debates by saying, "Well, your private religious beliefs shouldn't have any impact on public policy." Part of the trajectory here is the need to privatize religion. Religion becomes like a hobby. It is just something one does, like being a beekeeper. One is a believer. One does not derive public policy from that; it is a private business. One can say things like what Governor Cuomo or Geraldine Ferraro did—i.e., "As a Catholic, I am personally opposed to abortion, but I support the right for the public"—and not be thought incoherent.

We have been on this trajectory for quite a while. In Western political thought, John Locke helped to inaugurate this tendency with his justly famous letter and essay on toleration. Locke argues that state-craft and soul-craft are separate enterprises, that what is acceptable in the realm of soul-craft cannot spill over into the world of what he called magistracy, and that this is the necessary precondition for religious toleration. Remember, toleration is what Locke, writing just after the religious wars, was worried about. So there is a long trajectory to the demand that the religious voice should be silent in the political arena. We may have our religious beliefs, but we must translate them into other arguments and concerns and not bring them directly into the public arena.

The second religious thinker Budziszewski looked at was Abraham Kuyper. I think it would be interesting to explore a bit further Kuyper's understanding of the state. I said in our discussion that I was not sure the umpire image was a fair characterization of Kuyper's view of the state. Certainly, in Catholic social thought, the state is not just an umpire; it is an active instrument of the common good. But what does it mean to be a citizen *and* a believer? What does it mean to be under God's authority in an arena in which we are also under Caesar's authority? What does it mean to render what is due both to Caesar and to God?

One thing in Budziszewski's section on Francis Schaeffer that we did not talk about much was the *Humanist Manifesto*. Secular humanism was not just a tendency; it was a systematic program. I recalled the metaphor Albert Camus uses in his brilliant novel *The Plague* about those he calls "the humanists." These are the people who are not prepared to deal with political evil because it is "unreasonable." It just does not fit with the world that they believe is rational, the world they can control. The humanists, as Camus describes them, can actually squish under foot a rat that has died from the plague and say, "There are no rats in Oran" (the city in North Africa that is the setting for the novel). How much more complicated is the task of dealing with political evil in our day and age, and not just because of a certain strand that tends to equate evil with a kind of irrationalism and atavism. It is also difficult because a highly therapeutic language is in vogue. We are comfortable talking about syndromes, but we had better not try to talk about sin.

Talking about evil is considered really rather crude. I mentioned in my most recent book that on the first Sunday after 9/11 we went to a Methodist church in Nashville. My husband is Jewish, I am Lutheran/Catholic, and our daughter and son-in-law attend a Methodist church with their children. The visiting Methodist minister said with a kind of frozen smile on his face, "I know it has been a terrible week." Then after a pause, he continued, "But that's no reason for us to give up our personal dreams." I thought, "Good grief! Shouldn't you say *something* about what happened and how Christians are to think about it?" If one has lost the term *evil* from his or her theological vocabulary, then it is not easy to talk about such a thing.

Robin Lovin is a theologian who wrote a wonderful book called *Reinhold Niebuhr and Christian Realism*. Some of the work Lovin is doing currently is an attempt to reverse the usual line of query, which is, How can we set up the political world in such a way that it can accommodate religion? That is the way it is usually put. Instead, Lovin says, Why don't we think about what kinds of politics we require in order that religion can play the public role it is called to play? He has argued that perhaps the problem is not in a threat from religion but in too narrow a construal of politics and political life. This is certainly something we all should keep in mind as we try to think of ways in which the state can be turned to purposes we consider salutary.

Let us move on to John Howard Yoder. I am concerned that there is a tendency among Yoderians to see all government as a bad thing, failing to make a distinction between different kinds of states. In his response to Budziszewski on Yoder, Ashley Woodiwiss noted a move that Yoder makes: Rather than think about the relationship between Athens and Jerusalem—What can Jerusalem learn from Athens? What can we take and turn to Christian purposes?—we should think about *Bethlehem* in relation to *Rome*. A couple of interesting things happen when we do that. One is that Jerusalem is out of the picture. That is, we all know that Jesus was a Jew, but the whole power of Jerusalem as an image of the central hopes and despair of the Jewish people goes away. The God of justice is in many ways sidelined. We see Bethlehem and a God of love.

Another thing that happens is that with Bethlehem/Rome we are working with a model of subjugation, of an empire and an occupied territory, a tiny spot in Roman-controlled Palestine. If that becomes our dominant imagery for the political world, then we are going to be stuck with a master/slave narrative. It is always the big powerful "them" and the little powerless "us"; God forbid that we should ever gain power, because with power comes responsibility, and perhaps we do not want that either. So I think that the Bethlehem/Rome configuration is *more* political, in many ways, than Athens/Jerusalem, where we find an image of two powerful centers of cultures and their relationship to each other. This may help to account for some of the problems with Yoder and Yoderianism.

I want to conclude with a couple of other points. First, worldly vocations and where we are in relation to them. I think there is a tendency to want to recapture some authentic moment that is invariably one of powerlessness. It is a tendency toward a kind of repristinization of the Christian tradition. Yet here we are in the world—people with various offices, vocations, and degrees of responsibility.

Luther, when he talked about people who were threatening him, said, "They sentence us to death; they would do better to sentence us to life." In a way, death is an easier prospect than life with the kinds of responsibilities it gives us for the here and now. There is something very attractive about the eschaton, which may be one reason some Yoderians like to talk about the possibility of martyrdom. I think that, as Augustine warned us, the sin of pride is often involved when we are actively seeking out the possibility of martyrdom.

That idea does something strange to our thinking about politics, because it always comes down to something *extreme* rather than politics as Max Weber defined it: "a strong and slow boring of hard boards." A lot of often rather dull public work has to be done; we have to sit on committees; we have to work on compromises. I do not think we sufficiently honor the people who do that. It takes a certain courage to enter public life, considering how brutal it can be, especially given the way the media operate today. It takes courage to stand before one's fellow citizens and offer oneself up for their judgment in that way. We do not sufficiently honor that.

When Vaclav Havel went from being a dissident to being president, many of his friends were stunned by this sudden transition from powerlessness to power and the difficulty of that transition. One of the very wise things Havel said was, "We have now entered the long tunnel at the end of the light." That tunnel is, of course, called politics.

It may be helpful for us to recall H. Richard Niebuhr's five-part Christ-and-culture typology as we think about these four figures in evangelical political thought. The first is Christ against culture; that would be more of the Yoderian position. The second is Christ of culture; that is probably Kuyper (though he might also fit into Christ the transformer of culture). Third is Christ above culture. I am not sure who if anyone would quite fit there. The other two categories are Christ and culture in paradox, which would be Luther's position, and Christ the transformer of culture. This typology might be a helpful framework for sorting out these thinkers.

In the last chapter of a book of mine called *Who Are We? Critical Reflections and Hopeful Possibilities,* I talk about the logic of cultural engagement for those who live in hope, namely, the Christian community. I suggest four rules, if you will, for what Christians as citizens ought to be about.

First, insist on naming things accurately and appropriately. Take the measure of what it is we are dealing with. If we are dealing with something like 9/11, it seems that using the term *evil* is entirely appropriate.

Second, be prepared to offer a reasoned defense of our position. Engage interlocutors from a stance of preparedness and openness, tethered to an insistence that there is some truth to be found, that it is not just a matter of endorsing things we like.

Third, display the incarnation as what being in the world is all about. We should always remember that when we are dealing with politics, we are dealing with human bodies, with soft-shelled, fragile creatures who can bleed. A mother in Argentina who had lost all three of her children, all of whom had been tortured and had "disappeared," said to me, "What we learned is that politics is about bodies and bones."

Fourth, ensure that our churches play a critical role as interpreters of the culture to the culture. How do we interpret the culture, and in a critical but generous way? I offer some examples in my book of using films as entry points into serious discussions of theological issues. For instance, Clint Eastwood's film *Unforgiven* powerfully poses questions about vengeance and violence and forgiveness and justice. A film called *Seven* raises the theodicy question in a big way: Two detectives (Morgan Freeman and Brad Pitt) discover that to understand what a serial killer is doing they need to go back to the resources of the Christian tradition and the definition of the seven deadly sins. Nothing within their detective kit of modern techniques helps them understand what message this killer is sending.

Let me conclude by returning to Budziszewski's assessment that none of the four thinkers considered has presented a complete orienting doctrine, a complete practical doctrine, or a complete cultural apologetic. I have a hunch that this may be too much to expect from these thinkers, or perhaps from *anyone*, not because in principle it cannot be done but because the consequences of sin are such that we should be rather humble about our political philosophies and what we can hope to accomplish through them. Such humility would befit our natures as fallen creatures who are nevertheless called to hope and to possibility.

Contributors

John Bolt is professor of systematic theology at Calvin Theological Seminary. He is the author of *A Free Church, a Holy Nation: Abraham Kuyper's American Public Theology*.

J. Budziszewski is professor of government and philosophy at the University of Texas. He is the author of *Written on the Heart: The Case for Natural Law, The Revenge of Conscience: Politics and the Fall of Man, What We Can't Not Know*, and *How to Stay Christian in College*.

William Edgar is professor of apologetics at Westminster Theological Seminary. He is the author of *Reasons of the Heart: Recovering Christian Persuasion*.

Jean Bethke Elshtain is the Laura Spelman Rockefeller Professor of Social and Political Ethics at the University of Chicago. Among her books are *Women and War, Democracy on Trial, Jane Addams and the Dream of American Democracy*, and *Just War against Terror*.

David L. Weeks is professor of political science at Azusa Pacific University. His Ph.D. dissertation was on the social ethics of Carl F. H. Henry.

Ashley Woodiwiss is associate professor of politics and international relations at Wheaton College. He is presently working on two separate volumes: *Neither Babylon nor Jerusalem* and *Political Theory after Liberalism*.

Index